THEORIZING GLOBAL STUDIES

D0219392

Theorizing Global Studies

Darren J. O'Byrne

and

Alexander Hensby

First published 2011 by
PALGRAVE MACMILLAN

Palgrave Macmillan in the UK is an imprint of Macmillan Publishers Limited,
registered in England, company number 785998, of Houndmills, Basingstoke,
Hampshire RG21 6XS.

Palgrave Macmillan in the US is a division of St Martin's Press LLC,
175 Fifth Avenue, New York, NY 10010.

Palgrave Macmillan is the global academic imprint of the above companies
and has companies and representatives throughout the world.

Palgrave® and Macmillan® are registered trademarks in the United States,
the United Kingdom, Europe and other countries.

ISBN 978–0–230–51731–8 hardback
ISBN 978–0–230–51732–5 paperback

This book is printed on paper suitable for recycling and made from fully
managed and sustained forest sources. Logging, pulping and manufacturing
processes are expected to conform to the environmental regulations of the
country of origin.

A catalogue record for this book is available from the British Library.

A catalog record for this book is available from the Library of Congress.

10 9 8 7 6 5 4 3 2 1
20 19 18 17 16 15 14 13 12 11

Printed in China

Contents

Biography Boxes

List of Tables and Figures

Tables

Figures

Acknowledgements

When this project was first discussed, it benefited enormously from the enthusiasm of Emily Salz at Palgrave Macmillan. Although Emily moved on before it came to completion, it would never have been possible without her support and commitment. During the time of writing many staff at Palgrave have been to some extent or another involved and, while it would be impossible to name all of them, thanks do need to go to Vicki Lee, Beverley Tarquini and Sheree Keep. However, the task of actually seeing the project through to the bitter end fell to Anna Reeve, and the authors would like to extend a particularly warm debt of gratitude to her, for her continuous enthusiasm for the book itself, her hard work on its behalf and her ability to apply just the right amount of gentle persuasion when it was most needed.

Both authors would like to thank David Woodman and Chris Bond, who have been supportive friends and colleagues since the idea for the book was first discussed, and gave us plenty of constructive criticism as it was being developed, as well as Yvonne Guerrier and Garry Marvin, formerly Dean and Assistant Dean (Research) at the School of Business and Social Sciences, Roehampton University, for their continuous encouragement. Many people offered us their expert advice in the writing of the specific sections within a book that does, after all, cover a rather broad range of disciplines and topics. However, we would particularly like to thank the following: Kevin Dobie, Stephen Driver, John Eade, Ulla Gustafsson, Jo Sibthorpe, Allen Simpson, Dave Tinham and Matthew Warren.

The author and publisher wish to thank the following publishers, organizations and authors for granting permission to reproduce copyright material: *Financial Times*, for Table 7.2, originally from M. Wolf, 'Countries Still Rule the World', *Financial Times*, 6 February 2002; United Nations, for Table 7.3, originally from *UNCTAD World Investment Report 2001: Promoting Linkages* (New York and Geneva: United Nations, 2001); *Foreign Policy*, for Table 7.5, originally from *The 2008 Global Cities Index* (*Foreign Policy*, 2008); and Gary Schmitt, for Table 8.2, originally from Kagan, Schmitt and Donnelly, *Rebuilding America's Defenses* (Washington: Project for the New American Century, 2000).

Every effort has been made to trace all copyright holders, but if any have been inadvertently overlooked the publishers will be pleased to make the necessary arrangements at the first opportunity.

Darren J. O'Byrne
Alexander Hensby

Introduction

John Tomlinson is a good writer and knows how to begin an article. As there is no better way of making the point we wish to make at the very start of this book, allow us if you will, to use Tomlinson's own words on the subject:

> To begin with let us agree – on this we *can* all probably agree – that 'globalization' is a rather unsatisfactory term for the phenomena we are attempting to describe and to understand. The reasons why globalization is such an unfortunate word are several. Because it invites overstatement and smacks of an overwhelming tendency to universalize, or at least to over-generalize. Because most of the processes and experiences it describes, though vastly wide and growing in their distribution, are hardly ever actually, *literally* global in their reach. And therefore because it invites close analysis to point out all the exceptions rather than to see the force of the trajectories involved. And because, as a response to this, the élan of the term quickly becomes dissipated once it is hedged about by necessary qualifications – for instance its general pairing with the opposing tendency to 'localization'. More significantly, because it seems to many to articulate – and even to distribute and enforce – the dominant cultural, economic and political discourses of the West. But most of all because it has been a victim of its own success: hardly mentioned before 1990, it is now a word, as Zygmunt Bauman (1998, p. 1) says, 'on everybody's lips, a fad word fast turning into a shibboleth'. (Tomlinson 2007: 148)

Well said! In this book we intend to provide a survey of much of the main literature which purports, whether explicitly or implicitly, to be about 'this thing we call *globalization*'. However, what we want to *do* with it is quite different. We want to make the claim that *globalization* is best defined as one particular form of contemporary global change; that much of the literature associated with it is not actually *about* globalization but about some other process which may or may not be contradictory to it; and that there is an intellectual validity to *all* of this literature, not within the study of 'globalization' because as Tomlinson rightly says this has been plagued with confusion, not least because the term is used differently in different academic disciplines, but as contributors to alternative paradigms within the interdisciplinary field of *global studies*.

With this as our goal, we have set ourselves the task of looking at this literature, from across the range of social sciences and related disciplines, in order to ascertain how respective contributions, whether from an anthropologist studying new diverse cultural forms within a locale, a political scientist exploring the dynamics of nation-state interdependence, or an economist praising the virtues of a single market, have sought to define their subject matter. They may or may not have referred to it as 'globalization' but what, actually, is the process they are describing? In trying to disentangle these contributions and setting them up as alternative paradigms, we have sought to develop a schema for comparing and contrasting models of global change which do not presume consistency of subject matter, which may in some cases be compatible and in others be entirely contradictory with each other but which, at least, *say something* worthy of engagement with. To this end we have pulled the term 'globalization' out of the metaphorical haystack within which it has got lost and reduced it to a simple definition: as the *process of becoming global*. This is a surprisingly important if simple and often overlooked point – *as a word*, if it is to mean anything, that is *all* this word can mean. It is not a thing in itself. We should not subject it to reification or essentialization, although many do. It ends in the suffix '-ization', suggesting it must be a *process*, and processes are defined by their 'end point', which in this case must be 'the global'. If that much is straightforward, then the questions we need to ask when interrogating such a process are clear-cut. What is it to be 'global'? How does one measure the extent of this 'globality'?

'Globalization', then, is treated as a process defined by a conception of becoming *one world*. Much of the literature which is associated with it, though, is not, actually, underpinned by this definition. Rather, it presents, explicitly or implicitly, a different process, the process of becoming something else. In the eight chapters that follow, we survey and interrogate eight different process-models which are presumed within this literature. *They do not say the same thing.* 'Liberalization' refers to the process of becoming liberal, read as the relaxing of borders for the easier flow between states of goods, money, labour, people, ideas, as well as the apparent triumph of the liberal values which advocate this. 'Polarization' refers to the process of increasingly apparent division between two extremes, namely, in this case, a rich world and a poor world. 'Americanization' refers to the process of becoming American, read as the imposition of American values worldwide through cultural, economic and political-military forms of imperialism. 'McDonaldization' is actually used here in a more metaphoric sense than a literal one, to refer to a process through which practices and values become standardized across the world. 'Creolization' refers to a process of increasing diversification, of new hybrid forms emerging from the continuous interplay of difference. 'Transnationalization' refers to a process of moving towards a new level, one *above* the nation-state (but not necessarily global), read usually in respect of new forms of economic power and political governance. 'balkanization' refers to a process of increasing division into units defined (objectively and subjectively) by their respective differences to one another.

We do not say that in introducing these eight paradigms we have exhausted all the possible models suggested within this literature. Nor do we say that they are mutually incompatible, that one has to accept one at the expense of the others. Rather, there is often much overlap between them and the 'reality' of the situation is likely to exist in all of them and none of them at the same time. Readers should keep this in mind when travelling through this book. These are models, analytical tools, even Weberian 'ideal-types', if you like, but they are not absolute and fixed articulations of social reality. The world is far more complex than that, but as social scientists we accept that in order to best understand the complexity one has to sometimes reduce it to a more simplistic form.

Part of the project of this volume, then, is to relocate the reading of this literature away from the unhelpful and almost labyrinthine study of 'globalization' and towards the emerging interdisciplinary field of 'global studies'. Global studies refers to the ways in which academic knowledge can help us understand the dynamics of the globe itself, but we need not presume this is a replacement for, or indeed incompatible with, the more established study of international relations. The core focus of international relations has always been the (mainly political and diplomatic) relations of nation-states to one another, a focus which neither presumes nor precludes any analysis of the location of such states within a global framework. Sociology, however, is in a different position, in so far as it is well-recognized that most of the 'founders' of sociology in the nineteenth century treated their subject matter – 'society' – synonymously with the nation-state. If, as Martin Albrow (1990) suggests, early sociology was 'universalistic' in its pretensions to scientific accuracy regardless of time and place, and later sociologies have been bound up in specific 'national traditions' and problems, and 'internationalism' in the sociological context can refer to the way specific dominant national traditions were exported and in some cases adapted to local use, then the 'globalization' of sociological knowledge brings with it obvious challenges: if the tools of the sociological trade were honed within a nation-state framework then are they applicable to the task of engaging with the problem of *world* society? Anthropologists have been faced with an even more difficult task (to which, it has to be said, they have risen admirably), given that a lot of traditional anthropology and ethnography has been about *local* cultures and practices, and it is dangerously easy to simply present the *global* as that sweeping tidal wave which threatens the precious local. Historians are perhaps better placed to adapt to the demands of global studies, in so far as there is a long-standing field of global or world history which does not use the nation-state as its central unit of analysis, whether associated with the cyclical and civilizational histories of Toynbee and Spengler or the socialist world histories of someone like Hobsbawm.

The task of global studies, then, is to bring together these and other voices in order to debate the processes and dynamics impacting upon all aspects of modern social life. It incorporates critical voices for whom this fundamental dynamic may not be 'globalizing' at all: to engage in global studies does not require one to possess a theory of 'globalization'. It is also inherently multi-disciplinary, and incorporates a range of research areas. Scholars working within global studies are interested in America's war on terror and in the global marketing and fan base of Manchester United, in the theory and practice of human rights and in the discrepancies in the distribution of wealth and life-chances between North and South, in the democratizing possibilities of global information and communication systems and in migration patterns, labour exchanges and friendship networks.

One might reasonably argue that there is nothing new about 'global studies' except the name, and that its history can be traced back long before Marshall McLuhan coined the phrase 'the global village', back to the ancients, and to the universalizing presumptions of many of the world's major religions. Each discipline would no doubt highlight its own historical contribution to this area. We are sure there is much truth in this, but in the current context it is not important. We welcome the publication of a volume 'Historicizing Global Studies' as a companion to this one, on *Theorizing Global Studies*. It would make fascinating reading. But our task is to address a contemporary literature associated with a relatively recent academic development. Perhaps the early signs of this came in the 1960s, but globalization as a contested idea really took off in the 1980s and by the 1990s it had become a 'buzz-word' for academics, activists, journalists, politicians, and business-people alike to attach to their respective theories, causes, concerns, policies, or strategies. Its crystallization as a legitimate academic field came in the UK with the establishment of the Global Studies Association (GSA). This was the brainchild of Paul Kennedy, a well-respected sociologist of development at Manchester Metropolitan University who organized a series of conferences on global themes at the turn of the century, from which, in 2000, the GSA was formed. Inspired by this, two years later in Chicago a North American branch of the Global Studies Association was formed, under the auspices of Jerry Harris, which brings together an eclectic blend of academics and activists at its annual conference.

The emergence of global studies exists not only in the imagination of academics. Global studies programmes are fast emerging at universities across North America and Europe. At the University of California at Santa Barbara, the relatively new global studies major has attracted over 700 students, making it the most popular undergraduate major. California State University at Monterey Bay and the University of Wisconsin have both a department of and a programme in global studies on their books. At Freiburg University in Germany, a two-year Master's programme in global studies is offered in conjunction with universities in South Africa and India. There are respected academic centres at the University of Minnesota, Johns Hopkins University and Manchester Metropolitan University, to name just three. The reputations of many longer-established centres committed to understanding the dynamics of global interdependence – such as the Braudel Center at the State University of New York, Binghampton, USA, or the Centre for the Study of Globalisation and Regionalisation at Warwick University, UK – speak for themselves. Leading journals, including *Theory, Culture and Society*, have dedicated much space to discussions of global cultural change, and other interdisciplinary journals, such as *Global Networks* and *Globalizations*, have emerged. More recently the Global Studies Network has been established to bring together the many research centres, academic programmes and specific-issue organizations working broadly within the global studies umbrella. Further information on all of the above and far more is easily available by typing 'global studies' into any Web search engine.

Clearly, then, global studies has come a long way in a short time. Perhaps its greatest accolade, evidence of its acceptance within the public as well as academic imagination, has been to be subjected to the wrath of the American right-wing commentator Robert David Johnson, who in 2004 saw fit to pen an on-line article attacking the Global Studies Association, the various global studies programmes in the US, and the whole concept of 'global studies' which, he argued, uses the language of promoting a necessary 'global citizenship' (certainly an interest of global studies) to promote an anti-American left-wing ideology (hardly!) (Johnson 2004).

Given its interdisciplinary origins and reach, it is understandable that there is no clear or single direction within global studies, and different emphases exist in different settings. The early Manchester Metropolitan University conferences focused largely on cultural aspects of global change, with later ones drawing on themes such as human rights and global civil society, reflecting the interests of the GSA's European members, who are largely drawn from sociology. In North America, by contrast, a stronger activist voice has been heard in debates over global inequalities and labour rights. At the 2004 conference of the GSA (North America), held at Brandeis University, many of the contributors were working within a framework associating current global dynamics with Americanization and neo-imperialism, reflecting the importance of such a framework within the broader global studies field of enquiry (hence the less than favourable comments on the GSA from Johnson). For the European in attendance, it would have seemed striking how little attention was being paid at the time to such debates within the European context; many leading European scholars, such as Leslie Sklair, Saskia Sassen, Ulrich Beck and Anthony Giddens, prefer to operate within what we call in this volume a 'transnational' framework.

This observation brings us neatly on to the purpose of this book, namely, *theorizing* global studies. If we are to accept that global studies has emerged as a significant new field of academic enquiry, how are we to theorize it? Is there a framework within which we can locate, compare and contrast the key contributors to the new field? If each discipline or field of study is to be defined by its theoretical schools of thought, what does global studies have?

One attempt to provide such a schema has been developed by David Held and his collaborators, presented in their influential book *Global Transformations* (Held *et al.* 1999), which uses as its core criteria the *extent* of global change suggested by the different contributors to the debate. Held and his associates divide these key contributions into three camps, the 'hyper-globalists', the 'sceptics' and the 'transformationalists' (a schema that has been uncritically reproduced in countless undergraduate and postgraduate essays ever since). The hyper-globalists are clearly a naive bunch. Their ranks are made up largely of neo-liberal economists (Kenichi Ohmae and the like) who wish to celebrate the extent to which we now live in a fully globalized free market economy, together with social and cultural theorists (Marshall McLuhan and Martin Albrow, for instance) who claim that new technologies have effectively reshaped social relations, bringing about the demise of the restrictive old world and ushering in a new world, a 'global village' or 'global age'. But if these hyper-globalists suffer from naivety, the sceptics suffer from an apparent lack of imagination, and come across as a dour bunch, rather stuck in the past. Sceptics would have us believe that there is 'nothing new under the sun', and in some cases that the world today is even less interdependent than it was 100 or so years ago. The sceptics are also a diverse crowd ideologically. Some are in the mould of the Old Left (Paul Hirst and Graham Thompson), others trained in neo-realist or neo-conservative thought more popular with the Right (Samuel Huntington). In between these rather extreme, ideal-typical straw positions stand the transformationalists, who, in the view of Held *et al.*, are champions of reason. Transformationalists accept that the world today is experiencing global change on a rapid scale, but deny that this constitutes any wholly *new* society or set of social relations; rather, it reconfigures and transforms existing social relations. Into this camp come a wide range of scholars, including Anthony Giddens, James Rosenau, Manuel Castells, Saskia Sassen and, of course, the authors themselves. A comparison of the three positions is presented in the table below:

This model is, of course, quite crude in its basic distinction between those who suggest 'full change', those who claim 'no change' and those who accept 'some change' but within existing frameworks. In fact, we could add a subgroup of the 'transformationalists' by singling out a range of contributors, mostly inspired by a blend of neo-Marxism and 'postmodern' theory, who set themselves the task of understanding contemporary global cultural and economic processes using a modified Marxian theory back in the late 1980s, many of them part of the 'New Times' school associated with the journal *Marxism Today* whose number included such otherwise quite distinct names as Stuart Hall, John Urry and David Harvey. The point of this schema for

Table 0.1   Hyper-globalists, sceptics and transformationalists

	Hyper-globalists	**Sceptics**	**Transformationalists**
Globalization defined as...	...reordering of the framework of human action	...internationalization and regionalization	...reordering of inter-regional relations and action at a distance
Globalization driven by...	...capitalism and technology	...states and markets	...combined forces of modernity
Globalization results in...	...a global civilization, a global free market economy	...regional blocs, state-controlled internationalization, possible clash of civilizations	...greater global interconnectedness and the transformation of world political institutions
Nation-state power is...	...declining or eroding	...reinforced or enhanced	...reconstituted or restructured

Source: Adapted from Held *et al*. (1999: 10).

us is that these contributors in each grouping are not classified according to 'standard' theoretical schools of thought, and in this volume at least are discussed in different chapters because they present a range of different models.

A second possible schema for classifying and contrasting theories of global change, which also defies conventional models of social theory, is to look at the *historical context* of any such transformation. This approach would distinguish between those who treat the process of contemporary global change (whether they call it 'globalization' or not) as a *long-term process*, which rather than replacing earlier debates around modernization and capitalism and other such driving forces in history should actually be viewed as *pre-dating* and even driving them, from those who see global transformations in contemporary contexts, as part of a clearly identifiable and recent *rupture* in the dynamics of history. For all the other differences between them, writers such as Roland Robertson and Immanuel Wallerstein belong to the former camp, while Anthony Giddens, David Harvey and Martin Albrow are among those belonging to the latter. Slightly outside of this distinction we can place those who have resisted treating global change as a single historical event and prefer instead to speak of multiple or competing projects of globalization. Leslie Sklair's work is a good example of such an approach, and another is Darren O'Byrne's application of the Habermasian distinction between 'system' and 'lifeworld' to the concerns of global studies (O'Byrne 2005). As with the previous system, these names belong, for us, in different chapters. Long-term theorists of global change are not of a like mind when it comes to saying what that process of global change actually is, and neither are those who adopt a more contemporary approach.

A third system we might apply would perhaps be more familiar to the reader, in so far as it would draw on the distinctions commonly used within most social science subjects. This would focus on the root *causes* of global change – capitalism, the state, values and so on. In this schema, we can go back to some of the founders of the social sciences as sources of inspiration – Karl Marx, Emile Durkheim, Max Weber and Adam Smith, for instance. Each of these writers was concerned with understanding and to some extent explaining the sweeping social transformations of the nineteenth or early twentieth centuries, and while their gazes were all locked on the same processes and transformations *per se* – the shift from a feudal to a capitalist economy, the shift from local, community-based social relations to more specialized, urban-based ones, the increasing centralization of political power, the growth of industrial technology and so on – each presented a different foundational explanation for these changes. For Marx, it was the economic dimension, the change to a capitalist mode of production, albeit understood in a directly politicized fashion, that mattered most, and from which all other processes derived. For Durkheim, the explanation lay more in the realm of socio-cultural activity, changing *ways of life*, patterns of social solidarity and social relations. For Weber, the increasing dominance of an instrumentally rational *way of doing things*, a formal and bureaucratic system of administration which gave rise to the nation-state and its associated legal and political institutions, was crucial, thus paving the way for a tradition of political-cultural, or institutional, analysis. For Smith, the economic dimension was inseparable from an ethical dimension of values derived from basic human nature. These founders of modern social science thus gave us the tools to help us understand social change. Theorists of global studies, as with all subsequent social sciences, have developed those tools to suit their field of study. There is almost nothing else to unite the approaches of Immanuel Wallerstein, Leslie Sklair and David Harvey, for example, except that they all acknowledge a debt to Marx, in that they seek to theorize global transformations within the changing dynamics of the capitalist economy. Roland Robertson, however, focuses on the *experience* of the world as 'one place' and thus on cultural patterns and ways of life, acknowledging the influence of Durkheim upon his work. Writers as diverse as Martin Albrow, George Ritzer, John Meyer, Robert Gilpin and Samuel Huntington all owe a debt to Weber, utilizing his wide range of analytical tools and theoretical propositions, including the role of the nation-state in framing the modern age (for Albrow), the process of rationalization associated with the centralized nation-state (for Ritzer), the cultural analysis of political institutions (Meyer), the centrality of the nation-state in the international political arena (for Gilpin), or the inevitability of conflict between competing interest groups (for Huntington). In contrast to such 'realists', Smith's liberal agenda from the nineteenth century provides the impetus for the likes of Kenichi Ohmae and Francis Fukuyama, who take it in distinct but associated directions. Yet again, this classification system is convenient but not definitive. Just taking those who are 'Marxian' as an example, we will see that the contributions of Wallerstein, Harvey and Sklair say very different things indeed within the context of global studies, and so are dealt with in different chapters of this book.

We leave it to the reader to use her or his preferred method of classifying the different theories contained herein. In doing so no doubt they will be influenced by the standard classification systems used within their disciplines – sociologists would look for Marxist, Weberian or Durkheimian traditions, international relations scholars would distinguish between realist, liberal and Marxist approaches and so on. Before global studies can develop its own range of theoretical schools of thought, it needs to have a clear idea about its own subject matter. This book is intended to be a contribution to that project. We thus present, as a central argument within the growing field of global studies, an overview of eight different processes which frame the theoretical and analytical writings of these different and noteworthy scholars. We leave it to the reader to map the similarities and differences of key names across the chapters, and in the conclusion we will endeavour to pull some of these themes together.

Globalization: The Global Village

1

1.1 Introduction

The term 'globalization' is used so freely by politicians and activists, journalists and academics, that it has become rather over-familiar. However, if one had never heard of it before and was asked to imagine what it might mean, one might come up with a simple enough definition. One would surely look at how the word is constructed – it ends in '-ization', suggesting a *process* or a *transformation* of some kind, so surely it means the *process of becoming global*.

That might seem fair enough, but what actually would it *mean* to 'be' global? What indicators are there to measure the extent of such a transformation – to ascertain how 'global' something is? Again, the answer, perhaps surprisingly, would be relatively simple: it would involve the extent to which the subject of the transformation – be it a corporation's marketing strategy, a television programme, an individual's lifestyle or identity, or pretty much anything else – can relate directly to the globe, unmediated by the nation-state.

Such a definition is curious, perhaps, because it allows us to conceptualize the process of 'globalization' at multiple levels. The globalization, for example, of *me as a person* would involve the extent to which I am connected directly to this 'globe as a single place', perhaps because I relate to it in respect of my identity-construction, seeing myself as a 'citizen of the world' rather than of any nation-state, or because I act in such a way as to recognize this relationship – maybe I am an active member of the global environmental movement, maybe I spend a lot of time travelling, maybe I have a family or friendship network which spans the globe but with which I am in immediate and constant contact. But the globalization of me as a person hardly constitutes a significant global shift. It is important then to distinguish between globalization as a generic process which can apply to anything or anyone, and *the globalization of the world* – that is, the extent to which the world itself is becoming global. That is not a particularly easy concept to grasp.

In this chapter, then, we are taking a very specific definition of globalization – as the process of becoming global – and distinguishing such a process from the alternative models of global change with which it is often confused. As Robbie Robertson says:

[G]lobalization is ... about human interconnections that have assumed global proportions and transformed themselves. If we focus on globalization simply as a modern strategy for power, we will miss its historical and social depths. Indeed, the origins of globalization lie in interconnections that have slowly enveloped humans since the earliest times, as they globalized themselves. In this sense, globalization as a human dynamic has always been with us, even if we have been unaware of its embrace until recently. Instead we have viewed the world more narrowly through the spectacles of religion, civilization, nation or race. Today these old constructs continue to frustrate the development of a global consciousness of human interconnections and their dynamism. (R. T. Robertson 2003: 3)

The key dynamics at play here are global *interconnectedness* and global *consciousness*. Although he does not make any such link explicitly, he could easily be citing his namesake, the sociologist Roland Robertson, who previously presented us with what subsequently became the most commonly used academic definition of globalization:

Globalization as a concept refers to both the compression of the world and the intensification of consciousness of the world as a whole. The processes and actions to which the concept of globalization now refers have been proceeding, with some interruptions, for many centuries, but the main focus of the discussion of globalization is on relatively recent times. In so far as that discussion is closely linked to the contours and nature of modernity, globalization refers quite clearly to recent developments ... But it is necessary to emphasize that globalization is not equated with or seen as a direct consequence of an amorphously conceived modernity. (R. Robertson 1992: 8)

So, for both Roland Robertson and Robbie Robertson (forgive us for this potentially confusing coincidence!) globalization involves twin processes: the physical process of interconnectedness, or 'compression', which implies that the world is getting smaller; and the awareness that we as individuals have of our relationship to the world as a single place. Both writers also emphasize that such a process has a very long-term history – and this seems perfectly reasonable, given that it refers to an evolutionary process of *becoming* rather than an actual state of affairs.

However, both also acknowledge that events and occurrences associated with 'modernity' have had a huge impact upon this long-term process. Other writers treat 'globalization' as an extension of or a consequence of

Table 1.1   The five phases of globalization

Phase I: The Germinal Phase (Europe: early 15th c- mid-18th c)	Growth of national communities; expanding scope of the Catholic church; accentuation of concepts of the individual and of ideas about humanity; heliocentric theory of the world and beginning of modern geography; spread of Gregorian calendar
Phase II: The Incipient Phase (mainly Europe: mid-18th century–1870s)	Sharp shift towards the idea of the homogeneous, unitary state; crystallization of conceptions of formalized international relations, of standardized citizenly individuals and a more concrete conception of humankind; sharp increases in legal conventions and agencies concerned with international and transnational regulation and communication; international exhibitions; beginning of problem of 'admission' of non-European societies to 'international society'; thematization of nationalism–internationalism issue
Phase III: The Take-Off Phase (1870s–1920s)	Formalization of the problematic relationship between national societies, individuals, 'international society' and humankind; early thematization of the 'problem of modernity'; increasing global conceptions of 'acceptable' national society; thematization of ideas concerning national and personal identities; inclusion of a number of non-European societies in 'international society'; international formalization and attempted implementation of ideas about humanity; globalization of immigration restriction; sharp increase in number and speed of global forms of communication; first 'international novels'; rise of ecumenical movement; development of global competitions (e.g., Olympics, Nobel prizes); implementation of world time and near-global adoption of Gregorian calendar; First World War
Phase IV: The Struggle-for-Hegemony Phase (1920s–60s)	Establishment of the League of Nations and then the United Nations; establishment of principle of national independence; conflicting conceptions of modernity (Allies vs Axis), followed by Cold War (conflict within 'the modern project'); nature of and prospects for humanity sharply focused by the Holocaust and use of the atomic bomb; crystallization of the Third World
Phase V: The Uncertainty Phase (1960s–90s?)	Moon landing; accentuation of 'post-materialist' values; end of Cold War and rise of the problem of 'rights'; widespread access to nuclear and thermonuclear weaponry; increasing number of global institutions and movements; sharp acceleration in means of global communication; societies increasingly facing problems of multiculturality and polyethnicity; conceptions of individuals rendered more complex by gender, sexual, ethnic and racial considerations; civil rights becomes a global issue; more fluid international system and end of bipolarity; enhanced concern with humankind as a species-community, particularly via environmental movements; interest in world civil society and world citizenship in spite of the 'ethnic revolution'; consolidation of global media system; Islam as a deglobalizing/reglobalizing movement; Earth Summit in Rio de Janeiro

Source: Robertson (1992: 58–9).

modernity, industrialization and capitalism (Giddens 1990; Sklair 1991, 2002). Still others see it as a process which ushers in the *end* of the modern age (Albrow 1996). These distinctions, large and small, will be addressed in this chapter.

One of the clearest attempts to produce a general mapping of globalization across recent history has been offered by Roland Robertson (1992: 58–9). His useful sequencing of five 'phases' is re-presented below in tabular form for the convenience of the reader, although much of the wording is verbatim:

Much could be done to develop this model, and of course to update it (not least in the light of the events of 11 September 2001, the invasions of Afghanistan and Iraq, and the 'war on terror', plus the global financial crisis). What remains useful, and interesting, about it is that it presents globalization in gradual rather than absolute terms, as a process involving real human experiences. In Robertson's mapping, the world becomes increasingly interconnected and thus 'smaller' because of a growing consciousness of it, while at the same time our consciousness of it is enhanced because it is becoming increasingly interconnected and compressed. In other words, globalization as a generic process and the globalization of the world are intertwined processes.

1.2 Compression: the growing interconnectedness of the world

Robbie Robertson's (2003) historical account of globalization claims that, while the drive to interconnectedness is as old as human civilization, the beginnings of a *global* interconnectedness can be traced to around 1500 AD, to the early mappings of the world, early European imperialism and the opening up of new trade markets. This, he says, is the 'first wave' of globalization. The 'second wave' emerged around 1800 and its catalyst was the industrial revolution, while its politics were driven by high imperialism. The 'third wave' is the wave of American globalism, beginning in around 1945, after the Second World War left much of Europe devastated and paved the way for the United States to emerge as the world's dominant power.

At a theoretical level, the concept of global interconnectedness is closely allied to the perspective of systems theory, as in the contributions of John Burton to the study of international relations and Niklas Luhmann to the discipline of sociology. Systems theory derives in part from the structural-functional analysis which was prevalent in the social sciences in the 1950s, the chief theoretician of which was Talcott Parsons, the eminent Harvard sociology professor. Across a series of publications Parsons provided a detailed blueprint for analyzing society in systemic terms. Society – and bear in mind that this tended to equate to *nation-state* society – was viewed in holistic terms, as a single entity comprised of multiple component parts, each of which performed a function that ensured the smooth continuation of the wider whole. Component institutions such as the education system, the political system, religion and the family, for instance, were defined by the role they played in satisfying necessary 'functional prerequisites'.

Structural-functionalism faded from the scene during the 1960s, as a new generation of scholars felt that its vision of society was static and conservative. For some critics, it was seen as too holistic, incapable of appreciating human experiences and motivations. For others, it was too consensus-oriented, presenting an image of the 'ideal' and fully functioning system as one of equilibrium, from which was derived the idea that any deviations from this – crime, poverty, unemployment and other such 'social problems' – resulted from some systemic malfunction and could be 'fixed' in much the same way that an illness of the body can be treated, or a broken machine can be repaired. Even more damning, perhaps, was the suggestion made by more radical scholars that the 'ideal' society presented by the structural-functionalists mirrored modern, industrial, capitalist, Western society. This was most apparent in 'modernization theory', which emerged from structural-functionalism. Modernization theory carried an often-implicit assumption that Western industrial societies represented a 'higher' stage of development to which 'under-developed' countries should aspire, and that international institutions should seek to boost the infrastructures of such countries to help them achieve such an aspiration. Such problems with modernization theory were highlighted by more radical critics, whose work we will discuss in Chapter 4.

Perhaps as a response to this, modern systems theory emerged from the ashes of structural-functionalism. In 1972 the Australian-born, British-based academic and public policy advisor John W. Burton recognized the importance of general systems theory to study of international relations in his textbook *World Society*, and in doing so explicitly called for an interdisciplinary approach to the subject. Recognizing that the emergence of institutions, problems and experiences that transcend the nation-state level has laid down a gauntlet to the traditional field of *international* relations, Burton proposes that the study of 'world society' is more appropriate because it is 'a much wider study than the relations of units within it' (1972: 19), and such a global perspective would enable us to 'ask questions that are more fundamental and important to civilization, and be able to assess better the relevance of our own national behaviour to the wider world environment' (*ibid.*: 21).

This is precisely the point at which the contributions of the German social theorist Niklas Luhmann come into play. Luhmann studied under Parsons but he grew disenchanted with his mentor's particular take on systems theory. Instead he developed a more theoretically subtle and complex variant which begins with the assertion that a system is defined not just by the functions of its component parts, but also by adaptation to its environment, and, ultimately, by communication. All systemic activity operates as a form of communication, and the system itself is the bordered structure within which this communication takes place. If we assume, following Parsons and traditional systems theory, that a nation-state society is a kind of system, then to speak of *societies* is effectively to speak of *systems* between which there is little or no communication. As a direct result of functional differentiation, which has defined the process of modernization, 'globalization' becomes, for Luhmann, almost inevitable, in that 'world society' is akin to a 'system of systems' (Luhmann 1990).

Such interconnectedness, read as it often is as a long-term, historical, evolutionary process, forms the objective dimension of the globalization of the world. Its associated subjective dimension, the recognition of the world, is the quality referred to as *globality*.

1.3   Globality: the evolution of global consciousness

As has been discussed, the historian Robbie Robertson distinguishes the history of contemporary globalization according to three 'waves'. The current wave, the phase of American globalism, is a post-1945 phenomenon. What is important to note is that for Robertson, in keeping with those writers who define globalization as a particularly modern thing, there is something quite distinct about this 'third wave':

> Its difference can be summed up in one word that suggests the emergence of something greater than the accident of interconnections. That word is globalism, meaning a conscious process of globalization or a set of policies designed specifically to effect greater global rather than international interactions. (R. T. Robertson 2003: 4)

The *novelty* of this 'globalism' is further explained:

> No such globalism existed under British hegemony in the nineteenth century. Britain rode the forces driving globalization but never pursued strategies designed to engender global relations. Its goals were always nationally or imperially focused. The same might be said of the United States, but its globalism set in place institutions capable, in theory if not in practice, of independently developing global policies. (*Ibid.*)

While much of the actual dynamics of this phase which, for Robbie Robertson, is defined by American globalism will be discussed in Chapter 4, the emergence of globalism as an ideology at the dawn of this phase is central to the thrust of this chapter. Again, this view is shared by Roland Robertson for whom globality is defined as a 'consciousness of [the problem of] the world as a single place' (R. Robertson 1992: 132). Roland Robertson clearly equates the contemporary phase of globalization to a heightening of globality.

In many respects, 'globality' is a far more useful term than 'globalization'. It is certainly more *concrete*. As a process, globalization is fluid, hard to pin down, impossible to observe with any accuracy and thus pretty much meaningless from a research point of view. *Globality*, by contrast, is a quality, the quality of being global (Albrow 1996), and thus entirely measurable. Globalization as a general process, applicable to anything, is itself measured according to the amount of globality its subject exhibits. Although so far we have presented it in subjective terms – and it is a subjective quality, in so far as it requires a subject – the subject need not be a person. For example, a corporation can be a subject exhibiting globality through its marketing strategies – Coca-Cola's classic campaign from the 1970s, the one about buying the world a Coke, was clearly aimed at a global audience, and thus consciously designed to sell the drink as a global product. Indeed:

> [Globality] appears increasingly to permeate the affairs of all societies and multitudes of people across the world. This is not simply a matter of an increasing awareness of the challenges of other cultures but also of what is very misleadingly called the 'global village'. In other words, it is not merely the rapid increase in 'knowledge' of global variety...that is at issue. What we have to acknowledge is that there is clear evidence of an even more direct concern with the theme of globality. (R. Robertson 1992: 132)

Globality, then, is *the* central concept in Roland Robertson's theorization of globalization. It is not unreasonable to say that Roland Robertson has contributed more than anyone to the theorization of globalization as a process (see, for example, R. Robertson 1990, 1992, 1995; Robertson and Chirico 1985; Robertson and Lechner 1985). Influenced by Parsons and in a large part by the classical sociologist Emile Durkheim, Robertson presents a culturalist analysis of globalization which, though originating in pre-modern Europe, has been heightened by modernization such that the second half of the twentieth century has seen a dramatic increase in the *extent* of globality.

It is not difficult to imagine the reasons for this. Robertson himself lists them in his survey of globalizing events during the later 'struggle for hegemony phase' and the 'uncertainty phase'. Following the events of the Second World War, the second half of the twentieth century can be described as an 'age of fatality; an age in which we are made all too aware of our own mortality' (O'Byrne 2003: 101). It may be a bleak observation, but the dropping of the first atomic bomb made possible the realization that the destruction of the world was an empirical possibility rather than just a matter of theology; that one's death might not be a personal event but rather form part of nothing less than the destruction of everything, which is a sobering and wholly globalizing thought. Commentators such as Zygmunt Bauman (1989, 1991), Ulrich Beck (1992), Anthony Giddens (1991) and Darren O'Byrne (2003) have all discussed the extent to which this post-war generation was the first to live with the threat of total destruction, not merely from the bomb but from all manner of 'manufactured risks' (Beck 1992), including global environmental destruction and the spread of AIDS and other globalizing diseases. Is it any wonder that such generations have appeared to abandon the false security offered by the nation-state, with its machinery of social control and the centralized means of violence rendered increasingly impotent in the face of such globalized threats, in favour of global social movements and campaigns? Environmental activism and a meaningful concept of global citizenship emerge as *very real* responses to the threats such populations face. We will look at these in more detail in the following section.

Biography Box 1:   Roland Robertson

Roland Robertson (1938–) made his name as a sociologist of religion and was one of the first sociologists to engage in the international dimensions of culture, with work published in the late 1960s. He was certainly one of the first to use the term 'globalization', in a series of journal articles and most significantly in his 1992 book *Globalization*. He was for many years based at the University of Pittsburgh and is currently Professor of Sociology and Global Society at the University of Aberdeen.

But of course, before moving on from the concept of globality, we must recognize that though the potential for increasing global consciousness most certainly has been facilitated by these (destructive) late-modern tendencies, it is far too sweeping a generalization to talk of the mass emergence of this in practice. Clearly, globality as a quality is far more prevalent in the richer 'core' countries than it is in the poorer 'periphery', and even within the core, it remains a luxury enjoyed more by the cosmopolitan middle classes than by the working classes. We might go so far as to say, following O'Byrne (1997: 76), that globality exists as a form of *cultural capital*, actively encouraged and thus transmitted in some environments but not in others. Globality is a distinctively middle-class form of cultural capital.

1.4   Welcome to the global age?

The globalization of the world, then, entails the growing interconnectedness of its various component parts (people, places and so on) coupled with an increasing awareness on the part of actors (individual, corporate etc.) of the world as a single stage upon which to perform. It was, famously, the Canadian communications professor Marshall McLuhan who popularized the phrase 'the global village' in his 1962 work *The Gutenberg Galaxy*. McLuhan had suggested that the rapid developments in communications technology, allowing the instantaneous flow of information around the world, had made possible the existence of a single, interconnected (but by no means standardized or harmonious) world.

Biography Box 2:   Marshall McLuhan

Marshall McLuhan (1911–80) is most famous for introducing the term 'the global village', as well as for his assertion that in an age of new media technology 'the medium is the message'. A Canadian-born communications theorist and professor of English at the University of Toronto for many years, his publications include *The Gutenberg Galaxy* and *Understanding Media*.

Since McLuhan introduced the term, casual commentators have happily made use of it to distinguish the *world of now* from the *world of then*. We have already discussed the extent to which the second half of the twentieth century was characterized by a heightening in both global interconnectedness and globality. Robbie Robertson speaks in historical terms of 'waves of globalization' but makes no claims that these represent distinct periods in broader global history. Roland Robertson identifies the globalizing factors which 'speed up' the process in the twentieth century, but is at pains to point out that these constitute a continuation of past events. Niklas Luhmann sees contemporary 'world society' as a 'system of systems' brought about by hyper-differentiation, but does not take his account down the route of postmodernism or epochal change. Numerous writers, primarily social scientists, have presented alternative accounts, unified in the belief that *to some degree or another* these changes do represent such a qualitatively different experience of the world as to constitute a *break from* the past. Naturally, there are disagreements over the *extent* of this disjuncture.

Two of the more radical statements in this respect have come from Howard Perlmutter (1991) and Martin Albrow (1996). While they have little else in common, both writers see globalization as a distinct and identifiable process ushering in a new period in history – for Perlmutter, the first 'global civilization', for Albrow, the 'global age'. In either case, these terms are used to identify a distinctly new form of society which cuts across nation-state boundaries, and is comprised of a web of transnational connections between people, networks and institutions. It is the result of the intensification of communications and interactions (Luhmann 1990), and of the relative decline in the role of the nation-state, which is replaced by the globe as a single unit of analysis as the key point of reference (Albrow 1996; Burton 1972; Bushrui, Ayman and Laszlo 1993; Modelski 1972; Perlmutter 1991).

Perlmutter's contribution is heavily indebted to postmodern theory (which we will say much more about in Chapter 6). Drawing on what was new terrain when this article was being written, the growing interdependence of the world, Perlmutter argues that not only are we approaching a truly global civilization for the first time in human history, but also, rather worryingly, 'we' (our leaders and our various institutions) are wholly under-prepared for this transformation. The core factor in this change, according to Perlmutter, is the emergence and increasing significance of a new set of values which are not reducible to 'industrial' or 'de-industrial' values. The actual character of this new civilization is uncertain – at least three possible directions are visible: the trend towards 'homogenizing Westernization' (see Chapters 4 and 5 in this volume), the trend towards 'unbridgeable cultural chasms' (for which, see Chapter 8) and the trend towards 'global dynamic syncretism' (more on which in Chapter 6).

A more theoretically detailed account of this transformation is contained in Martin Albrow's theory of contemporary epochal change. Albrow's work is incredibly wide-ranging in its historical detail, much of which is intended to reintroduce the 'history of epochs', according to which each such epoch is defined according to a core 'project'. Albrow is a sociologist deeply influenced through much of his career by the work of Max Weber, so it is unsurprising to see him turn to Weber in order to locate the central 'project' of the 'modern age'. This, he argues, is the emergence and growing dominance of the centralized nation-state. Weber wrote at length about the extent to which the world in which he lived (the world of the late nineteenth and early twentieth centuries, during which time the discipline of sociology was itself being formalized) was becoming increasingly characterized by the de-humanizing, faceless bureaucracy that accompanies the shifting of certain social relations and means of social control away from the immediate, the local and towards a distant, centralized machinery. Nonetheless, the nation-state was crucial in defining 'modern' progress – it represented the 'centralized means of violence', the machinery of law able to administer and execute an objectively rational and non-arbitrary system of social justice. With the formation of the nation-state as a political-legal institution comes the emergence of international society, as nation-states engage with one another, and through this comes the reinvention of the nation-state as a source of identity. In short, the nation-state is the key dimension of the modern age, the central unit of analysis, the space in which the everyday lives of individuals are acted out and against which they are made meaningful.

As the twentieth century drew to a close, various factors including territorial over-expansion – the 'contradiction of the modern age' – resulted in the de-centring of the nation-state from this core position. The emphasis he places on the declining role of the nation-state is by no means unique to Albrow's theory of globalization. What *is* significant is what this represents – for Albrow, if as Weber suggests the *modern* age is defined by the centrality of the nation-state, then, if the nation-state has been displaced, necessarily the modern age has come to an end. At this point it may be tempting to dismiss Albrow's analysis as an excuse for postmodern theoretical excesses, but Albrow is too clever a writer to fall into such a bottomless pit. Following the history of epochs, then the 'new age' which replaces the 'modern age' has its own distinctiveness, its own logic, its own project. If the postmodernists celebrate the end of modernity at both a substantive and a theoretical level,

Albrow maintains a 'modernist' stance while assessing the character of this *post*-modern epoch. At its core, he argues, is the concept of the globe itself, for all the reasons outlined by the other writers we have covered in this chapter. That being the case, we can refer to the age (or epoch) in which we live as the *global age*.

Biography Box 3:   Martin Albrow

Martin Albrow (1937–) has been for many years one of the leading experts on the sociological theories of Max Weber and published extensively in that field until turning his attention to the problem of globalization, undertaking a theoretical project which culminated in the publication of his tome *The Global Age* in 1996. He is founding editor of the journal *International Sociology* and has held professorial posts at Cardiff and Roehampton; he is currently Senior Visiting Fellow at the Centre for Global Governance at the London School of Economics and Political Science.

It is worth bringing in the work of Anthony Giddens (1990) here because he, like Albrow, identifies the contemporary phase of globalization as representing a qualitative shift from earlier modernity. In so far as he identifies the post-war globalism and the rise of communications and information technology as key drivers in this globalizing process, Giddens seems to have much in common with other writers so far discussed. His theorization of the *processes* of globalization is distinct, however: his central concerns are with what he calls 'time-space distanciation' (the separation of the logics of time and space) and 'disembedding' (the decreasing significance of place). Thus, for Giddens, globalization involves our changing relationships with these dimensions – space, place and time. What *results* is the emergence of a *transnational* level, which we will deal with in Chapter 7. It is, however, convenient at this stage to locate Giddens within the context of this section, because while he, like Albrow, clearly sees the current phase as a disjuncture from rather than a continuation of modernity's broader project, and thus stands in opposition to 'long-term process' theorists such as Roland Robertson, Giddens does not go quite so far as Albrow; he is not willing to create such a break with the past as to speak of epochal change. For Giddens, globalization does represent a disjuncture but it is a disjuncture *within* modernity's logic rather than from it. Modernity is defined by Giddens as constituting the inter-relationship of capitalism, industrialization, surveillance and military power. Each of these dimensions is still prominent under contemporary globalized conditions, except in a radically altered form. For Giddens, then, globalization's effect upon modernity is that it 'speeds up' modernity's logic, it takes it to its extreme, like a juggernaut out of control, and the resulting era can be best described as 'late' or 'reflexive' modernity. Again, we will return to this (and to other aspects of Giddens's writings on the subject, and also those of David Harvey, a major theorist who develops a similar theory of global change which is more Marxist in its orientation) in Chapter 7.

1.5   The practice of global citizenship

We have already introduced the central concept of *globality*, the quality of being global, and stressed that this quality can be exhibited not only by people but by other actors, such as corporations, who commonly make use of it in their marketing strategies. It is also the life-blood of many campaigning organizations, such as those concerned with disarmament, human rights and environmental protection, whose actions are motivated by a concern for the future of the planet regardless of nation-state borders.

The growth of such organizations and the causes they represent has encouraged some commentators to speak of the emergence of a new 'global citizenship'. So popular has this term been in activist, media and educational discourses that it has been rather stripped of its meaning – not unlike the term 'globalization' itself. If, though, we can sift through the rather casual and unsophisticated references to 'global citizenship' commonly used, we might find that a *meaningful* understanding of it provides us with an excellent case study of 'globalization in action'.

First of all, though, we need to make clear what global citizenship is *not*. O'Byrne (2003) makes a strong case for distinguishing global citizenship from what has for centuries been referred to as *world* citizenship by defining the former as 'world citizenship under the influence of globalized conditions' (2003: 118). World citizenship is not new – O'Byrne traces its development across history from Socrates to the Stoics, through the 'religious universalists' of the Middle Ages, to Kant and the 'moral universalists' from whom we get the modern idea of human rights (*ibid*.: 55–67; following Heater 1996). It is also not necessarily *global*. It does involve a recognition of a common humankind, but this recognition might be derived from the pursuit of empire (as with the Roman philosophers), the belief in one people under God (epitomized by Augustinian theology) or by a belief in the presence of abstract universal features of 'human nature' (as espoused by the early Enlightenment theorists and pursued by subsequent human rights scholars).

Global citizenship, by contrast, involves the purposeful intention of acting in a politically meaningful way on the global stage. It involves the construction of a political identity which is borne directly out of an unmediated relationship between the individual and the globe. In effect, it is the politicization of globality, and not only is it a pragmatic response to 'real' conditions, but it is also *performative* (Albrow 1996: 178):

> Global citizenship is world citizenship focused on the future of the globe...Global citizens are not ruling the state as Aristotle's citizens did, nor do they have a contractual relationship with it in the manner of modern nation-state citizens. In an important sense they are actually *performing the state*. (Albrow 1996: 177)

O'Byrne goes on to provide a clear example of just such a performance, in his account of the work of an organization called the World Government of World Citizens (the name is admittedly misleading in the context of the distinction between 'world' and 'global' citizens made above, but this cannot be avoided) and the exploits of an individual named Garry Davis. In 1948 former United States fighter pilot Davis had renounced his US citizenship in a public display in Paris and declared himself a citizen of the world. He was by no means the first person to do so, but it is the direction his declaration subsequently took that makes him an interesting case study. Davis decided that declaring oneself to be a world citizen would not be enough – for such a declaration to be meaningful, one would have to truly understand what is meant by 'citizenship'. It is clearly a *political* term, an expression of empowerment. Citizens have power and are actively part of the political process. Thus, *global* citizenship must involve an active recognition of the dynamics of power, rather than just a casual statement of solidarity or empathy with humankind as had been done many times before. In 1953 Davis launched the World Government of World Citizens. His philosophy was strikingly simple – if citizenship is about empowerment, and government is the servant of the people, then *we are the government*, and all that was required was to declare it so. In the nuclear age, as has already been discussed, the 'social contracts' between individual citizens and their nation-state governments are revealed as impotent. What Davis was effectively saying was that the only way to deal with the problems we as citizens face in such an age is to declare oneself a global citizen, to empower oneself on the global stage, to bypass the fallacy of nationalism:

> You take the words 'world' and 'citizen'...together and say that's what you are...[and] you're giving yourself a conceptual power...[T]he word 'world' is a conceptual word and 'citizen' is a power word. So you are re-empowering yourself on both levels, putting together concept and percept in terms of the problems of today. You can't say, 'I am a Buddhist and therefore I am meeting the problems of today head on', because you're not, or 'I am an American ...' What you are doing is taking the crystallizations of religion and nationalism and falling into their relativity...So you identify yourself as a world citizen...Identity, in political terms, is sovereignty, the exercise of inalienable rights. (Davis, cited in O'Byrne 2003: 150–1)

His World Government of World Citizens was not, then, designed to be an NGO campaigning *for* a world government – far from it, in fact. It was designed to serve *as* the government of the people, a world government in itself, and thus certainly *not* non-governmental, because, as Davis has pointed out in his own writings on the subject, non-governmental equates to powerless. Global citizenship is then not just reflected in Davis's personal commitments, his opposition to the divisive nature of nationalism and his belief in the undeniability of 'one world'; it is also reflected in the organization's practices. For example, through its administrative arm, the World Service Authority, it distributes 'world passports'. If a passport is somehow symbolic of one's allegiance to and membership of a nation-state community, then a world passport becomes a natural extension of this, but it is more than symbolic – the vast majority of nation-state governments have at some point accepted this passport as legitimate for the purpose of permitting entry across their borders. Not only does this highlight some striking inconsistencies in respect of border controls, but it also allows the organization to help people exercise what the organization perceives as being their fundamental right to cross borders, so it has a deeply pragmatic significance which is only made possible because of the globalized conditions of the second half of the twentieth century.

This, of course, is quite a distinctive example, and deliberately so. But the practice of global citizenship as the exhibiting of globality in an empowering way is by no means restricted to such cases. One might argue that environmentalism represents the most obvious form of this globality in practice. The modern environmental movement is, after all, operating by its very definition with the globe in mind. It is both a response and a contribution to globalization. Centuries of Enlightenment rationality and the scientific pursuit of 'progress' have resulted in what the sociologist Ulrich Beck refers to as 'manufactured risk', which is inherently global in its reach. Science and nature have become politicized as these consequences become apparent to us all. As Beck says, 'damage to and destruction of nature no longer occur outside our personal experience... instead they strike more and more clearly our eyes, ears and noses' (Beck 1992: 55). Furthermore, 'environmental problems are not the problems of our surroundings, but... are thoroughly social problems, problems of people, their history, their relation to the world and reality, their social cultural and political situations' (*ibid.*: 81).

According to Beck, the proliferation of risk has generated a feeling of perpetual uncertainty and insecurity among individuals across the globe, as well as an increasing distrust of scientific knowledge. Moreover, the perceived inability for individual nation-states to effectively deal with an increasingly global political field created a 'democratic deficit', leaving a political vacuum for alternative political cultures to prosper. For many social and political scientists, 'new social movements' have represented its special and essential product. Borne out of the 'expectations explosion' of the 1960s and 1970s, new social movements are distinct from political parties in that they speak of personal autonomy and identity politics rather than an instrumental subscription to totalizing, old-fashioned discourses. Whereas traditional political identities tend to be dictated by class or region, the politics of new social movements are universal in both their subject and relevance. Their capacity to attract supporters, however, comes from the effects of 'disembedding' and 'time-space distanciation' that Giddens (1990) speaks of. This reordering of space and time has a profound effect on individuals, freeing us of our short-sightedness, stunted knowledge and self-absorption, and allowing us to see, understand and experience the global level more clearly and directly than ever before.

Embodying this move towards global political consciousness are a number of international non-government organizations (INGOs) which include the World Wildlife Fund, Greenpeace International and Friends of the Earth. These organizations campaign for a range of environmental issues both on a local and global level and are made up of multiple national affiliate groups. Overall, environmental politics has grown rapidly since the 1960s, with the combined memberships of the 12 leading organizations in the US rising from an estimated 4 million in 1981 to 11 million by 1990 as the green movement gathered momentum (Bramble and Porter 1992: 317). As of 2003, there were some 1,781 INGOs with specifically global political goals.

Despite the success of the green movement, *direct* political victories of new social movements have been few and far between, with traditional political parties continuing to dominate most democratic elections. A more fitting legacy, at least, has been the generalized impact of helping to stimulate a greater global consciousness, so that individuals have been more pressed to 'think globally' over issues such as recycling and the purchase of environmentally friendly goods. The extent to which this emerging global consciousness represents an evolutionary process of *globalization*, however, is debatable, and subsequent chapters will shed different light on many of the processes, actors and relationships involved.

1.6 Global events, global experiences

Having identified the existence of a global level via interlinking processes of modernization, as well as ample opportunity for the expression of a global citizenship via shared political interests, we can now turn to *how* one might access and experience globalization. Alongside education, a key part of this process is the role of the media. Whereas for most people the ability to travel and experience the world is both expensive and time-consuming, the media effectively offers us a round-the-world ticket for free: via books, magazines, television and the internet, the media provides us with the knowledge from which we derive most of our understanding and 'mediated experience' of the world.

Of course, the rise of media and the printed word has contributed to the establishment of a consciousness beyond immediate physical territories for thousands of years. Globalization, however, has radicalized this process to the extent that distinctions of space and time are no longer as easy to denote. Indeed, through satellite television and the internet, individuals and groups are now increasingly adept at accessing and interpreting information from a wide range of sources, both historically (such as the reproduction and broadcast of past events) and spatially (through vivid and detailed photographic reproductions of different cities and landscapes). Such is the power of media technologies that individuals across the world are now able to simultaneously experience events beyond the physical reach of the vast majority. In essence, globalization has allowed for the possibility of *global events* – events that are intrinsically global in their reach, audience and impact.

As Thompson (1995) reminds us, this is not entirely new. Media, from the printed word to the internet, has been used in order to give symbolic forms a degree of fixation, so that they can be stored and reproduced for a wider audience. But the intensification of media production in the past 60 years has transformed how we *experience* culture, which brings with it profoundly *social* consequences. Marshall McLuhan, already introduced as the man who coined the term 'global village', understood this well: 'Today, after more than a century of electric technology, we have extended our central nervous system itself in a global embrace, abolishing both space and time as far as our planet is concerned' (McLuhan 1964: 11).

Since the 1960s, the opening of this 'global village' has established broader and more structural social consequences, both in how knowledge is accessed and identity is constructed. First, media reproduction plays a significant role in rationalizing and rearticulating history. Photographs, literature and television dominate our experience of and engagement with certain places, people and moments in history. This creates a 'mediated worldliness', as media shape our sense of place in the world, and what lies beyond the sphere of our personal experience. For example, world-famous landmarks such as the Eiffel Tower, the Pompeii ruins, the Empire State Building and the Taj Mahal gain a 'mediated familiarity', as they have been photographed, filmed and reported on from a multitude of different media outlets over history. The accessibility of images portraying these landmarks can give us a sense of knowledge and interest, but also stimulate inspiration, empathy and identity. As a result, we might feel that we know, understand and have feelings about a place without having ever physically been there ourselves.

So, as we can see, the globalization of media raises and extends our understanding of society, as the consumption of symbolic forms change the way we view ourselves, and our understanding of the rest of the world. But media can also be *interactive*, in that it can alter distinctions between 'public' and 'private'. As a result, everyday private actions such as shopping or sitting in the park become public if they are filmed and then broadcast as part of a news story. Moreover, private conversations and recordings might undergo a similar transformation if they are deemed to be in the 'public interest'. Once a media form becomes public, it can be consumed by a plurality of recipients, using different points of receipt, and at different times in history. This invites a potentially infinite number of understandings, interpretations and opinions, and thus can be difficult to control. Through the mediation via images on television, of, say, Aboriginal peoples living in Australia, its audience gains an insight into other people's lives, and how they differ from our own. This, too, can be politicized, as we develop personal affinities and concerns for other individuals and populations that we may never meet. On the other hand, the mediation of violent and threatening action may extend our own quasi-experiences, and provoke strong political interests, be they human rights or protectionism.

There is, of course, a mediator involved in this process, which raises the important question of how and to what extent our interpretation of particular scenes and events are being shaped by its presentation. The potentially infinite number of different and contrasting interpretations might be dangerous to those associated with the media form, and as a result control may be sought as to how they are presented. This becomes especially significant during media events that invite political and moral debate, such as acts of war or violence, global poverty and human rights abuses. Such events, presented globally and instantaneously via the media, give greater opportunity for a 'globalized empathy' and communitarian responsibility, for stimulating a shared sense of *humanity* which transcends ethnic and national boundaries.

Of course, acts of charity, philanthropy and benevolence have taken place for centuries, often associated with either religious duty or good moral citizenship. The opening up of these acts and organizations to globalization, however, was a more awkward process as, despite the beginning of a media-assisted global visibility, nation-states continued to limit financial aid and welfare to their own territories, or at least those belonging to international coalitions and governing bodies such as the World Bank and the United Nations. Under this model, charitable pledges were largely controlled by governments, apparently reflecting the nationalistic and short-sighted interests of its citizens. By the latter twentieth century, however, awareness of international crises and political campaigns such as the civil rights movement, the Cold War and the campaign for nuclear disarmament, as well as the aforementioned rise in environmentalism, had signalled a political consciousness beginning to extend beyond national and local interests.

Yet crucial to achieving global empathy is the capacity to present events with a cognitive framework to aid the *understanding* of their importance and relevance, and also possibilities for responsive *action*. This is not an inevitable part of the package when news events are reported to a global audience. As Chouliaraki (2008) notes, global events that appear to be presented as 'adventure' are counterproductive to fostering global empathy as the singular and abstract placing of events (i.e., 'boat accident' in India, or 'biblical floods' in Bangladesh) via largely factual and context-free one-minute reports only succeeds in alienating viewers and blocking feelings of pity towards distant sufferers (*ibid.*: 375). In contrast, 'emergency' news stories, which produce a demand for action on the suffering, were more successful in eliciting concerted responses from its audience. These became more prominent in the 1960s through the news broadcasting of crises surrounding war, notably the proliferation of refugees in the aftermath of the Bangladesh Liberation War and the Vietnam War in the early 1970s, and provided individuals with readily available grounds for protest and activism.

For those more concerned by the humanitarian rather than political side of such international crises, the emergence and expansion of international social movement organizations and advocacy groups such as Amnesty International, Oxfam, UNICEF and Human Rights Watch provided a suitable outlet. These organizations were created in order to raise awareness over human rights issues with a view to pressurizing governments into providing more aid. As part of this process, these groups began to participate in fundraising benefits, with the intention of creating a media 'event' that could be reported prominently across the globe. Perhaps the first of this kind was the 'Concert for Bangladesh', organized by UNICEF and the former Beatle George Harrison, which took place in New York City in 1971. This was followed in 1982 by the Nuclear Disarmament Rally, where an estimated 750,000 people marched to Central Park, New York, to protest against nuclear weapons.

Yet perhaps the first truly global empathy event occurred shortly afterwards in response to the Ethiopian famine of 1984–5, in which over 1 million people died as a result of catastrophic harvests and a national government preoccupied by civil war. In the same year, a BBC news crew was the first to document the famine, with Michael Buerk describing 'a biblical famine in the twentieth century' and 'the closest thing to hell on Earth'. The report shocked Britain, motivating its citizens to bring world attention to the crisis in Ethiopia. In January 1985 the RAF carried out its first air-drops, delivering food to the starving people. Other countries including Germany, Poland, Canada, USA and the Soviet Union were also involved in the international response.

Yet the public response to the crisis continued to outweigh the actions of national governments, as organizations such as the Red Cross, Amnesty International and UNICEF had to buy grain on the open market in order to help those suffering. Among those who had been watching the BBC reports was the singer Bob Geldof, who responded by co-writing the hit single 'Do They Know It's Christmas' and organizing a simultaneous 'Live Aid' series of concerts in 1985. In total, the event was watched by an estimated 400 million viewers, across 60 countries, and raised over £150 million for famine relief. With the 'global level' now truly opened up, further globally broadcast concerts and telethons were set up, including recently Live 8 in 2005, the Concert for Diana in 2007 and the World Aids Day Concert in 2007.

Taking global interconnectedness further still, the 2004 Asian tsunami arguably represented the biggest and most collectively spontaneous act of global empathy event yet seen. Occurring during the Christmas period, the disaster was broadcast across the world, almost spontaneously provoking widespread donations and benefits. The *Guardian* newspaper reported on 6 January 2005 that 'a tsunami of human solidarity is sweeping across the surface of the globe in response to the physical tsunami that has ravaged the shores of the Indian Ocean', with private donations in Britain reaching about $90 million and worldwide public aid pledges surpassing $3 billion in barely a week. Overall, it was argued that the Asian tsunami had probably provoked 'the biggest humanitarian relief operation in history'.

However, the scale and depth of public engagement with the disaster brought with it several complications over the politics of global empathy. First, although charitable donors may have contributed on the assumption of a fully coherent level of global governance and regulation, the reality was far more complex. Like Live Aid before it, the lack of coordination of aid (with aid and donations being irregularly contributed and not always of practical use), as well as the sometimes inefficient or even nefarious states and leaders that received a high proportion of the funds, suggested that, in practice, the global level represented an ideal type to be bought into and taken advantage of. Taking a more Marxian perspective, one could argue that spontaneous acts of charity in the Western world satiate the desire to be recognized as a 'good moral global citizen', while at the same time indirectly benefiting from the structural power relations that allowed such disasters to either occur, or damage parts of the world to the extent that they did. Certainly, the sudden upsurge in global empathy hardly crystallized into any concrete condemnation of global social inequalities.

Second, many commentators claim excessive and competitive donor responses threaten less dramatic but equally important relief efforts elsewhere. Enriqueta Bond, president of the US Burroughs Wellcome Fund observed that, 'while everyone opens up their coffers for these disasters, the ongoing toll from malaria, AIDS and tuberculosis is much larger than these one-time events', and that 'we would do more good to invest in prevention and good public-health measures such as clean water' (quoted in Butler 2005). Tony Blair, then UK prime minister, also expressed concern that tsunami aid might detract from other areas of the world in need of relief, warning that Africa suffers 'the equivalent of a man-made, preventable tsunami every week' (*ibid.*). This leads to a third and final point that the conflicting interest groups, together with self-interested parties and the ecstatic media coverage of global disaster events had contributed to 'compassion fatigue'. This phrase was used in the media to describe the 'overexposure' of charitable causes directed at the general public throughout 2005, the tsunami of 2004 being soon followed by the series of Live 8 concerts to campaign for action against poverty, and another major natural disaster – Hurricane Katrina – which wrecked havoc upon the poorer territories of the United States in August 2005. If one could agree that the emergence of globalized empathy provided key foundations for the creation of a global citizenship, one can nevertheless argue that there is still much to do in terms of building genuinely *global* interest groups to carry this forward.

As the previous case study illustrates, by providing individuals with images of, and information about, events that take place in locales beyond their own immediate physical territory, the media has the capacity to stimulate or intensify varieties of different opinions and even collective action. For 'distant sufferers' this may stimulate acts of empathy and compassion; for acts perceived to have a more immediate and direct impact, global events might instead stimulate feelings of personal fear, uncertainty and insecurity. This becomes especially sensitive when it comes to the media coverage of war: such is the persuasive power of media representation of enemies, allies, the innocent and the guilty, it has been often argued that modern day warfare now consists of a war on two fronts – the war as it is fought against the enemy and the war as it is portrayed and reported on television.

The visibility of war and conflict has been developing and expanding over a number of years. Whereas the immediacy and reach of media reportage in the First and Second world wars had been extremely limited, the advent of television during the 1950s consumer boom transformed how war and conflict was to be consumed. This effect manifested itself during the Vietnam War, where America's first major interventionist military campaign was given day-to-day coverage on television via on-the-spot news reporters broadcasting live to national and global audiences. This added significant visibility to the stages, methods and different protagonists of war: as Thompson notes,

> the vivid images of napalm attacks, wounded soldiers and civilians, screaming children and frightened refugees, as well as reports of US military setbacks and rising death tolls, fuelled the controversy in the United States concerning the legitimacy of the intervention and provided individuals with readily available grounds for protest. (Thompson 1995: 114–5)

By the first Gulf War in 1990, the American government took measures to limit negative news coverage, as access to the front line for journalists was strictly controlled by military authorities (*ibid.*: 115). Moreover, the war saw both sides making conscious efforts to use media coverage to its advantage and portraying positive images of success, reason and innocence in their campaigns. This strategic and creative use of media was picked up on by the French cultural theorist Jean Baudrillard (1995), who went as far as to assert provocatively that the Gulf War 'did not take place'. Although not denying that conflict or the deaths of innocent civilians occurred, his point was that the importance of portraying the war positively to a global audience overrode the actual events themselves. In other words, narratives were constructed by both sides to fit around the image of war, which did not necessarily correlate to reality. Baudrillard argues that the Western media helped to propagate the notion of an ongoing conflict by endlessly recycling images and scenes of war to disguise the fact that very little action actually took place. By the end of the war, beyond the deaths of hundreds of thousands of soldiers and civilians, very little had changed – nobody won the war, nobody lost the war. The only victor, it seemed, was the television viewer.

Such practices in constructing global events were put into perspective on 11 September 2001, when the World Trade Center and the Pentagon were subjected to terrorist attacks. The attacks, almost immediately broadcast live across the world, arguably represented the most deliberate and strategic orchestration of a 'global event' that the world had yet witnessed. The planning was meticulous, from the two-year training for the terrorists to earn their pilots' licences, to the carefully sequenced nature of the attacks so that media coverage would be instantaneously broadcasted worldwide. Such was the scale and impact of the event that al-Qaeda did not even need to initially claim the event as its own – the goal of transforming global consciousness and provoking greater fear and uncertainty had truly been achieved.

For the sociologist Zygmunt Bauman, 9/11 represented the 'symbolic end of the era of space', arguing that a terrorist assault on one of the best-known landmarks in one of the world's best-known cities live on television 'gave flesh to the heretofore abstract idea of ... the wholeness of the globe' (Bauman 2002: 87). Like environmentalism, the emergence of global terrorism suggested that physical territories and national boundaries were no longer protective as attacks could take place anywhere, and at any time; this would be proved in subsequent attacks in Madrid, London, Bali and Istanbul. The ability to remain 'resourceful, distant and aloof' was compromised as Bauman notes how the events of 11 September 'made it obvious that no one ... can any longer cut themselves off from the rest of the world' (*ibid.*: 88).

If 9/11 represented a defining moment of globalization in its ability to create 'global events', and as a consequence stimulate an increasing global 'commonality of fate', it perhaps also represented the model's first significant cracks. As Baudrillard wrote in his 2002 essay *The Spirit of Terrorism*, 9/11 was an intrinsically global event in that it did not simply represent a 'clash of civilizations or religions', or even a riposte to the 'spectre of America'. Rather, it represented 'triumphant globalization battling against itself' (Baudrillard 2002: 11); Baudrillard sees 9/11 as the high-water mark of globalization as a hitherto unassailable and evolutionary force. The idea of becoming 'one world', operating under a single consciousness and mode of exchange, has been unquestionably challenged and, with this 'global level' now established, the battle is over who, or what, defines globalization today.

1.7 Conclusion

In this chapter, we have sought to present a *strong* theory of globalization, not as some 'thing' in itself, or as a generic term appropriate for use in any scenario of global social change, but specifically as the process of becoming global. Thus, globalization can occur at multiple levels. We can witness the globalization of a particular marketing strategy, whose target audience is nothing less than the world itself. We can acknowledge the globalization of individuals' self-identities and citizenships, indicators of which include the extent to which their political actions and orientations relate directly to the globe rather than through the level of the nation-state, which can of course take a 'soft' form (everyday environmentalism) or a 'hard' form (the case of Garry Davis being a good example). We have seen how identification with the world is heightened by particular 'global events', such as the Live Aid concert, the 2004 tsunami, or the terrible events of 11 September 2001, all of which serve to bring us closer to the 'one world' we all share. We have also seen how the *world itself can be globalized*, although, as Robertson insists, the outcome of such a process is far from clear.

The central factors in this discussion have been *globality* – the quality of being global, of engaging directly with the globe – and the physical *interconnectedness* of the world. When discussing globalization as defined in this chapter, whether at the very personal, micro-level, or at the level of the world itself, or indeed anywhere in-between, these factors come into play. Globality especially proves useful as an indicator of the extent of globalization, a measurable quality. Rather than seeing globalization as a single, almost unstoppable force, a 'thing', our definition of it allows for multiple globalizations to co-exist, and for different aspects of our lives to be relatively more or less 'globalized'. Those who think that we live in a global marketplace because of free trade might present the case for the economy to therefore be relatively globalized compared to, say, the political system, or culture; others may feel that increasing levels of globality have resulted in a considerable degree of cultural globalization while the economy, like the political system, remains heavily nation-state biased. These are all, effectively, judgement calls.

There are numerous criticisms of this approach, of course. Many would say, with good reason, that to treat globalization merely as an empty process which needs to be applied to something to have any meaning, is to ignore the power dimensions contained therein. Such critics may argue that it makes no sense to speak of 'cultural globalization' or the 'globalization of self-identities' in isolation from 'economic globalization', and that 'globalization' does represent a totalizing process which manifests itself in multiple forms. Thus, to understand its dynamics, we need to adopt a more critical perspective. We should ask, who is driving this process of globalization? What are its contours? How was it created? Who dominates? Who is accountable? Who can change it? Many who ask such questions suggest that this 'globalization' is better called by a different name, perhaps 'Westernization' or 'Americanization'. However, it is worth pointing out that the idea of globalization presented in this chapter is capable of accommodating such rival frameworks: 'Americanization', for example, can be treated as a recent phase in this long-term cultural evolutionary process (Maguire 1999; R. T. Robertson 2003).

Let us now move from globalization as a relatively apolitical process to this slightly more contestable terrain: to a series of far more ideologically driven interpretations of contemporary global change, many of which are often referred to as 'globalization' but which do not necessarily involve a process of becoming global. During the course of these subsequent chapters we shall be returning to a lot of what has been discussed already, and perhaps presenting it in a different light.

Liberalization: A Borderless World

2

2.1 Introduction

One of the most prominent models used to describe the contemporary global lay-offs condition is the model that we shall refer to as 'liberalization'. It is important to qualify our use of this term to describe the model in question, because in lay terms the model is probably better known by a different name. To the eternal frustration of countless academics, it is commonplace for public commentators – including journalists, politicians and also activists – to refer to this as 'globalization'. Now, having already introduced and discussed, in the previous chapter, a more precise definition of 'globalization', it should become evident that what has been discussed in that chapter, and what is being described in this more popular usage of the term, are actually quite distinct models, even if there is a necessary amount of overlap. The 'globalization' model presumes that the globe itself has become or is becoming a meaningful stage upon which individuals and institutions act, or practices are acted out. This necessarily entails the erosion of the nation-state as a core point of reference. The more popular use of the term, however, focuses specifically on the alleged erosion of boundaries *between* nation-states. While this allows, it is argued, for a freer flow of goods, resources, people, ideas, capital, etc. across these dwindling borders, it does not, significantly, imply a direct relationship with the globe *per se*. The former model situates the globe in a 'strong' capacity, the latter in a 'weak', incidental capacity. It is for this reason that we refer to this latter model not as 'globalization', but as 'liberalization'. A clear statement of this model is provided by its proponent, the business strategist Kenichi Ohmae, in his own, rather distinctive, style:

> On the political map, the boundaries between countries are as clear as ever. But on a competitive map, a map showing the real flows of financial and industrial activity, those boundaries have largely disappeared. Of all the forces eating them away, perhaps the most persistent is the flow of information...Today, of course, people everywhere are more and more able to

get the information they want directly from all corners of the world. They can see for themselves what the tastes and preferences are in other countries. (Ohmae 1990: 18–19)

The term 'liberalization' is not without controversy, but it serves a double purpose here, because it is not only accurately descriptive of what its advocates claim is actually going on – for liberalization in this sense, one might also refer to the *relaxation* of restrictions, the processes 'eating away', in Ohmae's words, at those boundaries – but it also highlights the relationship between this model of global change and the 'liberal' (and 'neo-liberal') tradition in political theory, and with a particular set of values that are described as 'liberal'. It is hardly surprising that Ohmae equates the relaxation of border restrictions with a welcome decline in government controls – liberals have always been disapproving of too much state intervention.

In the popular usage, the model described here is used almost exclusively in reference to economic transactions. Its advocates, from Adam Smith through Milton Friedman to Ohmae, are talking about the strategies for relaxing restrictions on trade. It is used in reference to the 'free market', to the globalization of capitalism. In that respect, at least, the use of the term 'globalization' is consistent with how we have used it in the previous chapter, in so far as capitalism, as an institution and a practice, operates on a stage – capitalism's 'stage' is called the market – that is nothing less than the globe itself. But the globalization of capitalism and the liberalization of restrictions are different things. It is necessary to be clear about this when studying the perceived or actual processes of contemporary global transformation. In truth, most who champion this model are concerned primarily with the autonomy of the market – its 'invisible hand', in Smith's famous phrase. Their arguments are usually positioned at the nation-state level, which is to say they may suggest that ending restrictions on trade between nation-states is good for those national economies. This is a value judgement, even if its advocates support it with evidence, and the liberalization model is not only an important model within global studies in a descriptive sense, it is also important as a normative position. As such, it has its critics as well as its supporters. Numerous are those whose publications are grounded in the premise that at the descriptive level this is an accurate model of global processes, but at the normative level it is an undesirable one. Such contributions to the debate are equally littered with evidence to counter that of the opposition – evidence that this so-called 'free market' necessarily involves unequal exchange, that it benefits richer nation-states and is harmful to the interests of less-rich ones. Most contributions, from either side of the debate in fact, tend to take as read the *reality* of the process they are describing. There is only a small, but still a significant, body of literature taking the model to task on descriptive rather than normative grounds.

For the purposes of this chapter, then, it is necessary to interrogate this debate in respect of both its descriptive and normative assertions. To do so, we need to first understand the theory of the marketplace. We then need to examine how this theory has come to be so intertwined with the subject matter of *global* studies, and for this we need to appreciate the so-called Washington Consensus and recent policies of the World Bank and the International Monetary Fund. Having done this we are in a better position to tackle the descriptive and normative claims made within the debate. We shall begin with an overview of what we can call the *liberal* theory of trade, which itself needs first to be understood within the broader ideology of *liberalism*.

2.2 Liberalization and liberalism

The claim that 'globalization' equates to a process of 'liberalization' in which national boundaries are opened up to allow for the freer and easier flow of capital and ideas between countries takes us, of course, to a belief that is central the liberal tradition in politics and international relations. This is the belief – espoused by classical liberal thinkers such as Immanuel Kant, Thomas Paine, Adam Smith, John Stuart Mill, and Richard Cobden – that free trade between countries effectively reduces the possibilities of war and actively promotes the spread of democratic values and what we would today call human rights. Thus, the term 'liberalization' carries a dual meaning: on the one hand, it refers to the 'easing up' of border controls which makes such exchanges possible and, on the other, it refers to the process by which the world itself is 'becoming liberal'.

Naturally, the two overlap considerably, as both are bound up within the complex yet coherent body of thought that is liberalism. To put it crudely, the philosophy of liberalism, from John Locke onwards, begins with a simple commitment to the *freedom of the individual*. For Locke, this commitment, justified by an appeal to philosophical anthropology via the social contract, manifests itself in its political form: that individuals must be free from (unnecessary) state intervention; that the role of the state and its institutions must be to serve the people and that state intervention in people's lives must be minimal. This political form of liberalism gave rise to a particular, Western interpretation of human rights – that is, that human rights are the possessions of all individuals, that they cannot be denied by states, and that they amount to safeguards upholding an individual's right not to be arbitrarily or unnecessarily 'interfered with' by the state (not to be tortured, not to have their freedoms denied through slavery, not to have their privacy denied, not to be denied the chance to express their beliefs and opinions). In other words, for the liberal, *human* rights are essentially synonymous with *civil* rights.

What underpins this political liberalism is an inherent individualism, and it is precisely this individualism that gives rise to the two other 'core' liberal values – capitalism and democracy. As liberals from Smith onwards have tried to tell us, capitalism as a system is best left to its own devices, away from state interference, which means that, at the level of the individual, I should be free to engage in economic activity, to trade, to invest and to benefit from any gains made from such activities. Locke's own philosophical anthropology saw humans as essentially enterprising and commercial creatures, competitive yet cooperative. Democracy (which of course was not necessarily a priority among many early liberals, including Kant) emerges merely as an extension of the liberal belief in the primacy of the individual over the state, extending the liberal commitment to civil rights to incorporate basic political rights of involvement as well. Thus, for the liberal, I am a citizen, entitled to a life of privacy left largely untouched by the public realm of law and politics; I am a consumer or producer, a trader in the marketplace which, equally, sits outside the formal political realm; and I am, within that realm, a voter, exercising my power and authority over the state in the fairest (and most individualistic) manner possible.

Thus, the model of globalization-as-liberalization is inherently underpinned by the philosophy of liberalism. Liberalization is the process through which borders between states are being eroded, allowing for an easier flow of capital, goods, ideas and people. In the process of liberalization, the nation-states themselves remain, but with their regulatory powers largely diminished (Ohmae 1994), they exist primarily as political entities increasingly subservient to the 'invisible hand' of the marketplace (both economic and ideological). Liberalization thus entails both the globalization of the marketplace, the opening up of economic activity through the breakdown of trade barriers, and a kind of benign homogenization, as the ideologies of capitalism, democracy and the protection of civil and political freedoms are exported around the world, rendering it increasingly interdependent. Within Global Studies, of those espousing the belief in globalization as liberalization, the former is associated with numerous neo-liberal economists, of whom Ohmae (1990, 1994) and the British Conservative Party politician John Redwood (1994) are among the most significant, while the former is associated primarily with the political theorist Francis Fukuyama (1991).

2.3 The theory of the free market

The definitive position on the necessity of the global marketplace is usually attributed to Adam Smith. Smith was an eighteenth-century economist and moral philosopher whose huge and immensely influential text, *An Inquiry into the Nature and Causes of the Wealth of Nations* (1776) is considered to be the crucial statement of classical liberal economics. Ultimately, and in true liberal fashion, Smith saw it as an economic defence of individual liberty and self-interest.

Smith is famous for introducing the term 'the invisible hand', although this has largely been popularized by his followers rather than Smith himself. The theory derived from this term can be summarized as follows. Individuals tend to act out of self-interest, which means that, in theory, the market is volatile. However, in fact, the nature of market exchange, based on principles of supply and demand, ensures its stability. It is inherent in the nature of market capitalism – the invisible hand of the economy – that equilibrium is ultimately reached and problems of production and consumption overcome. The end result of this self-stabilizing economy is beneficial to society as a whole. Any attempt by the state to regulate the economy will in fact be detrimental to the market's ability to repair itself, and thus to society, so it should leave it alone – *laissez-faire*.

In so far as Smith's work is read as a critique of state intervention in the market, it follows that the market should be allowed free reign to expand into new areas. For Smith, the marketplace is *inherently* potentially global. It is, in any case, in the nature of capitalism (not a term Smith uses) to seek out new markets after exhausting old ones. This was the view presented by Karl Marx, who was heavily indebted to Smith. Marx saw capitalism very much as a hungry beast expanding its reach (Lenin famously took this aspect of Marx's thought and devised from it his theory of imperialism). Smith emphasized the positive aspects of market liberalization, Marx the negative ones, but in both cases, in very different ways, a similar reality was being described.

Smith's observations are largely taken as read for classical or liberal (and neo-liberal) economists, but the apparent realization of the liberal ideal of a truly *global* marketplace, an economy not regulated by state interference, has required a more precise restatement of those observations. While we will discuss the historical context of this in the next section, it is worth drawing attention here to some recent arguments in support of global capitalism.

Possibly the most frequently cited such defence has come from the Japanese nuclear engineer-turned-management consultant Kenichi Ohmae. In a series of significant publications, including *The Borderless World* (1990), *The End of the Nation-State* (1994) and *The Next Global Stage* (2005), Ohmae has presented the case for unfettered trade between nations, and for the freedom of corporations to respond to perceived consumer demands worldwide. A cursory glance through the Introduction to *The Borderless World* lays Ohmae's position quite clear:

> There is a role for governments – to protect the environment, to educate the work force, and to build a safe and comfortable social infrastructure. When governments are slow to grasp the fact that their role has changed from protecting their people and their natural resource base from outside

economic threats to ensuring that their people have the widest range of choice among the best and the cheapest goods and services from around the world – when, that is, governments still think of and act like the saber-rattling, mercantilist ruling powers of centuries past – they discourage investment and impoverish their people. Worse, they commit their people to isolation from an emerging world economy, which, in turn, effectively dooms them to a backward spiral of frustrated hopes and industrial stagnation. (1990: x)

Ohmae is an unrepentant globalist, for whom the fully borderless world is both inevitable and desirable. In matters of economic growth, the nation-state has outgrown its usefulness. There are clear parallels between Ohmae's passionate defence of global capitalism and the more sociologically informed accounts of the demise of the nation-state presented in the previous chapter as indicative of the 'globalization' model. Ohmae sits firmly in this camp, equating (by his own admission, somewhat prematurely and abstractly) multinational corporations to global citizens, obedient to the demands of consumers around the world, helping to build and manage this new economy which, in the spirit of Smith, can only be beneficial for (global) society. Needless to say, commentators less sympathetic to these arguments present the motives of multinational corporations in quite a different light.

Biography Box 4:   Kenichi Ohmae

Kenichi Ohmae (1943–) is a Japanese economist, a consultant on business and corporate strategy and the author of numerous books and articles on the role of business in the modern world. He is celebrated as the greatest champion of the virtues of the new global economy.

2.4   The 'triumph' of liberal democracy

So far, we have largely discussed liberalization in economic terms, in respect of trade and financial deregulation, but the philosophy underpinning the process of liberalization, the liberal philosophy defending individualism free from state intervention, takes on a significant political aspect as well.

In such philosophical terms, one of the most widely discussed, and controversial, defences of the liberalization model has come from Francis Fukuyama, first in an article he wrote in *The National Interest* in 1989 called 'The End of History?' (Fukuyama 1989), and subsequently in a more detailed volume called *The End of History and the Last Man* published in 1991 (Fukuyama 1991).

Fukuyama's claim is that, with the fall of the Berlin Wall and the end of the Cold War, 'History' (spelled with a capital 'H' for reasons that will be outlined below) has effectively come to an end. Liberal democracy has 'triumphed' against its last remaining ideological alternative. During the twentieth century, liberal democracy saw off the challenges of monarchism and fascism, and ultimately Soviet-style communism, to reign supreme as the incontrovertible ideology. Thus, 1989 saw the culmination of 200 years' worth of increasing liberal democratic dominance – Fukuyama suggests that whereas in 1790 there were only three liberal democracies of note (the United States, Switzerland and France), by 1990 there were 61 (1991: 49–50; following Doyle 1983: 205–35). The 'end of History' does not mean the end of historical events, of course, as Fukuyama is at pains to explain; rather, it means that the *cycle of history*, the Hegelian dialectic, has reached its conclusion. The eighteenth-century German philosopher Georg Hegel conceived of History as a series of stages, each of which contained its own contradiction, and from each such contradiction would come the seeds of the next stage that would supplant the previous one. Hegel's historical idealism presented the modern nation-state as the final stage in this evolutionary process, the one lacking in internal contradiction, the 'end of History'. Karl Marx followed in this tradition. Perceiving each stage in history as being defined according to its economic infrastructure, its mode of production, he sought to illustrate not only how the capitalist mode of production was borne out of the internal contradictions in the feudal epoch, but also how the irreconcilable contradictions within capitalism – namely, the inevitability of conflict due to a recognition of the polarization of wealth and the necessity of exploitation which made it work as a system – would result in an emergent class consciousness among the exploited, and usher in a new stage of communism, which, free of contradictions, would represent the end of History.

Taking his lead from Hegel, Fukuyama suggests that not only does liberal democracy have no remaining challenges without, it also lacks any contradictions within, and as such it stands alone, unopposed, at the top of the mountain, at the end of History. In Fukuyama's thesis, it is capable of overriding any internal conflicts because it is grounded in a combination of core ideologies: liberalism which protects individuals from state tyranny through the promotion of civil, political and religious rights; democracy, which involves citizens in the decision-making process and thus prevents the rise of authoritarianism; and capitalism, which ensures economic stability.

Fukuyama suggests that this 'triumph' of liberal democracy at the end of the Cold War effectively consigns the need for warfare to the waste bins of history, a position shared by John Mueller (1990). Such a belief has its origins in Kant's theory of perpetual peace, although Fukuyama clearly takes it in a different direction. There are clearly numerous flaws in Fukuyama's argument, but there are also many misinterpretations of it. Fukuyama himself has come to reassess what many critics felt was his undue optimism. He has pointed, for example, to developments in bio-technology positing a challenge to our understanding of what it is to be 'human', and that this might undermine liberal democracy. Perhaps more obviously, commentators have suggested that the resurgence of religious fundamentalism is incompatible with the principles of liberal democracy, and that Islamic fundamentalism, in particular, has become a major alter-native to the 'Western' way of life. This criticism leads directly to the sug-gestion, made by Samuel Huntington, that the contemporary world is not defined by the triumph of liberal democracy but by a 'clash of civilizations', by diversity and inevitable conflict occurring between different cultural blocs. From a different perspective, some feel that it is naive to presume that capitalist liberal democracy does not contain any contradictions – neo-Marxists such as Jurgen Habermas, Claus Offe and James O'Connor have put forward strong arguments to show that late capitalism is undergoing a period of crisis, while environmentalists consider the effects of rampant and unopposed capitalism on the environment as an obvious indicator of an inherent contradiction in its logic. And the French philosopher Jacques Derrida (1994) has angrily criticized Fukuyama's thesis not only for being naive and arrogant, but also for ignoring the levels of poverty and injustice still prevalent within the liberal democratic societies Fukuyama is so keen to praise.

Whatever the strengths and weaknesses might be of Fukuyama's thesis *per se*, the relationship between this perceived 'triumph' of liberal democracy and the liberalization of borders for economic purposes is significant. As one astute commentator has observed, while the process of 'liberal democratiza-tion' in previously authoritarian countries has occurred largely in spite of rather than because of the United States and its allies, the spread of such political values as free elections and civil liberties around the world is easily co-opted so as to add legitimacy to the underlying liberal project of economic liberalization (Bello 2004: 10).

Biography Box 5:   Francis Fukuyama

Francis Fukuyama (1952–) is an American public intellectual most famous for his controversial 1991 book *The End of History and the Last Man*, which was based on an 1989 article in *The National Interest*. He is currently Bernard L. Schwartz Professor of International Political Economy and Director of the International Development Program at the Paul H. Nitze School of Advanced International Studies at Johns Hopkins University in Baltimore.

2.5   Neo-liberalism and the 'new global economy'

Global liberalization as we recognize it today has its roots in the late 1970s and the rise of neo-liberal markets. However, most global theorists would argue that the concept of a globally integrated market is not a new one. Owing in part to a history of liberal economics spanning across three centuries, it has been argued both by Bello (2004) and Hirst and Thompson (1999, 2002) that flows of merchandise trade, capital investment and labour migration in the late nineteenth and early twentieth centuries were all comparable with those of today. Hirst and Thompson argue even that financial integration was greater during this earlier period, with levels of capital export from the major lender countries incomparable to the present context (Hirst and Thompson 2002: 248).

This earlier phase of global economic integration was ended by the outbreak of the First World War, and was followed by a period of national protectionism involving considerable state involvement in the international economy. After the Second World War, much of the West experienced a 'golden age' of social and economic prosperity. In the most part, this followed the economic philosophy of 'Keynesianism', inspired by the ideas of British economist John Maynard Keynes. He argued that market economies are intrinsically unstable and possess the potential to suffer prolonged periods of economic depression, as had been experienced in the United States in the 1930s. Keynes saw that a system of 'managed capitalism' would be more effective in which the government would be responsible – through higher taxation and public spending – for providing a minimum level of social and economic support for its citizens. As a result, government-owned and managed public services and industries including state education, housing, healthcare and employment schemes were set up as part of the modern 'welfare state'.

In practical terms, Keynesian economics was characterized by a necessity to maintain a stable and efficient domestic market. For this task, governments undertook interventionist policies such as restraining aggregate demand through strategic increases in income tax or interest rates. This allowed governments to control inflation, sustain full employment and provide a basic provision of welfare on a national scale. Economically, state regulation had been supported by the Bretton Woods system of monetary management, which established the rules for commercial and financial relations among the world's major industrial states.

Keynesian economics arguably marked the high-point of socialist 'organized capitalism', being both a system of economic corporatism and a mode of moral government with the aim of achieving collective justice and the creation of a 'good society'. However, by the 1970s, Keynesianism was faced with a number of crises. First, the United States pulled out of the Bretton Woods system of fixed exchange rates in 1971, initiating the collapse of the Bretton Woods system and the market 'floatation' of national currencies. Second, owing to disputes over involvement in the Yom Kippur war, the Arab-based oil consortium OPEC quadrupled the price of oil in 1973–4, highlighting the West's global dependency on international trade. Compounding matters further, both of these shocks took place amid growing concern over escalating costs in welfare provision among Keynesian states. With heavy industry in decline, workers operating via trade unions campaigned for governments to protect employment from falling demand. This was made more difficult by the inflexibility of state-controlled industries, as significant sectors of the economy were entirely separate from the international market, which prevented them from attaining any 'natural' market value and competing internationally. As rising unemployment placed added strain on welfare budgets, governments responded by printing more money, causing rapid inflation. The resultant period of 'stagflation' suffered by capitalist economies in the 1970s dealt a crushing blow to the credibility of Keynesian economics, as the ability of national governments to control and manage the economy was called into question.

While the 1970s represented a period of economic instability for Western nation-states, opportunities for money-making were developing elsewhere. Lash and Urry (1987) observe how, independent of nation-state regulation, emerging private 'offshore' financial markets were facilitating trade between private shareholders and capitalists. The opportunity to earn quick, 'stateless' money gradually encouraged more and more European banks to open up their own currencies to the new opportunities of the international exchange markets. This, in turn, initiated an expansion of international branch networks, the formation of international banking groups, and the establishment of industry-funding bank consortiums.

The successes of competitive financial markets soon gained the interest of national governments. Attracted to the enormous potential for money-making free from the weight of corporatist welfare responsibility, Ronald Reagan's Republican administration from 1980 and Margaret Thatcher's Conservative government from 1979 were pioneers of drawing up economic policies that complemented the market-centred competitive rationality of offshore markets. With governments sweeping away many of their financial restrictions, banks set up financial centres in London, New York and Tokyo, enabling them to shift their activities from Keynesian 'custodial' banking to market-driven 'competitive' banking. This, too, was enabled by the new advances in capital mobility, as new transportation, communication and production technology enabled capital flows to increase their velocity beyond the means of the traditional 'paper economy'. All in all, this marked a significant 'disorganization' of capitalism and the birth of a new private, unrestricted and global enterprise culture (*ibid.*).

For Reagan and Thatcher, inspiration for their *laissez-faire* approach would come from neo-liberal economics, developed in particular by the 'Chicago School' of economists led by Milton Friedman and inspired by Friedrich von Hayek. As one might expect, neo-liberals built on classical liberal philosophy, with its prioritization of individual freedom over state interference, with

Smith being held in particularly high esteem. They tend to have less time for Locke, except in respect of his defence of private property – neo-liberals are not so easily convinced by the benign picture he paints of human nature which gives rise to his liberalism, preferring a quasi-Hobbesian, even social Darwinist philosophical anthropology which justifies their belief in society as little more than a marketplace in which self-serving individuals compete in a contest for the survival of the fittest.

As political policy, neo-liberalism can be characterized principally in terms of its political commitment to the free market and the 'rolling back' of the state's role in economic and social life. More specifically, governments should first liberalize their monetarist policies and provide a more realistic currency valuation by limiting government borrowing, printing less money and cutting 'supply-side' deficiencies such as welfare spending. By opening up the economy to competition and market forces, national economies would be better placed to benefit financially from the new unregulated capital investors in the private sector.

Second, governments are expected to liberalize their employment policies. In the case of the United Kingdom, for example, declining industrial productivity in the 1970s had caused trade unions to adopt more 'militarist' tactics in order to protect employment. The shifting of political power towards trade union groups was seen by the new Conservative government as obstructive to the free play of market forces. Thatcher held the view that employers should only pay wages equal to the market value of what workers produced, and embarked on a systematic set of policies restricting and ultimately liquidating the powers of the trade unions. This view was echoed in the United States, where the reorganization of the economy was also led by the emergent financial sector. According to William K. Tabb (2001), there were 'lean and mean' reorganizations that downsized corporations with massive lay-offs and plant closings – such ruthless tactics in economizing would set the precedent for mobility among multinational organizations (*ibid.*: 55).

Third, governments are encouraged to dismantle the collectivized utilities of the welfare state through privatization. For neo-liberals, this is both politically and economically desirable as it reduces the burden of state provision and expenditure, as well as giving opportunity for domestic assets to compete independently on the global market. There are moral and popular dimensions – for example, privatization is seen as fundamental in reclaiming 'freedom' for businesses, as they are viewed as superior in running industries over the state, and would buoy private ownership among small investors and provide a new impetus for a fully liberalized enterprise culture. This presupposed a philosophical as well as economic justification to neo-liberalism: according to Eric Evans, the Conservatives sought to 'make people stand on their own feet and replace a dependency with an enterprise culture' (Evans 1997: 122). Thatcher's own view was blunter still, publicly stating in 1975 that 'everyone has the right to be unequal' (Johnson 1991: 232).

After initial stutters, neo-liberal states began to prosper in the late 1980s, enjoying low unemployment, low inflation and almost continuous economic growth. By the 1990s, the support for neo-liberal economics had extended beyond traditional right-wing parties. In his 1994 State of the Union address, Democrat President Bill Clinton described the global market as the key to the US economic future: 'it means jobs... for the American people – low deficits, low inflation, low interest rates, low trade barriers and high investments' (Brecher and Costello 1998: 15). Succeeding the Conservatives in 1997, Tony Blair's British Labour government would also continue to pursue a neo-liberal agenda, albeit under the aegis of so-called 'Third Way' politics. In 2005, Blair wrote that, in today's global economy, 'success will go to those companies and countries which are swift to adapt, slow to complain, open and willing to change', and that 'the task of modern governments is to ensure that our countries can rise to this challenge' (*Newsweek*, November 2005).

2.6   The neo-liberal agenda

Underpinned by universal notions such as market rationality and freedom of the individual, the conversion of liberalism from a theory of the state to a theory of the globe is perhaps an easy one, returning us essentially to Ohmae's 'borderless world' image of a single, free market. In theoretical terms, the free market is a fundamentally just and inclusive system of exchange: by removing 'irrational' barriers (such as tariffs) that constrain the natural process of fair exchange, the market will be able to freely generate the most wealth. This logic dates back to David Ricardo's classical liberal theory of 'comparative advantage', where it is argued that if each nation were to specialize in those activities in which they were most productive, the total wealth would be increased. Implicit in this theory is a *laissez-faire* role for governments focused on enabling and assisting market actors so that the comparative advantage can be successfully found, and profit maximized.

However, it is important to note that fundamental to the creation and maintenance of a free market economy – in particular one that now operates on a global scale – is universal participation, so that the greatest wealth of commodities and resources are made available for the competition and consumption of all. This places individual nation-states into a wider network of global actors where relations of production, exchange and consumption take place outside the borders of governance and regulation by a single state. In a nutshell, for all of its anti-interventionist rhetoric, liberalization nevertheless requires a degree of global governance. This brings us to consider two key institutions of global economic governance: the International Monetary Fund (IMF) and the World Bank.

Both institutions were created in 1944, with the United Kingdom and the United States as their key stakeholders. The responsibility of the IMF was to regulate global markets and exchange rates in order to maintain economic stability and avoid depressions. This involved the maintenance of global aggregate demand, which was realized through providing loans for countries in need of balancing their accounts. The World Bank, on the other hand, was initially created to help fund the rebuilding of Europe after the Second World War, though it has since expanded its duties more generally towards development projects, particularly in the Third World.

According to the economist Joseph Stiglitz (2002), the founding of both organizations was based on a Keynesian recognition that markets did not always work well, and that failing economies often had adverse social effects, from unemployment to food shortages. As a result, the IMF – an institution funded through taxation across the world – incorporated the need for collective action for economic stability on a global level. This responsibility intensified in the 1970s after the abolition of exchange rates, giving the IMF the responsibility of managing the exploding international debt crisis, affecting the Third World in particular. By the beginning of the 1980s, however, both institutions had begun to follow the neo-liberal turn of Reagan and Thatcher, shifting dramatically their rationale away from promoting global economic stability towards that of capital market liberalization.

In light of this shift, the IMF's new strategy for tackling Third World poverty was to devise 'structural adjustment' programmes as necessary conditions for new loans, whereby debtors would be forced to adopt neo-liberal policies such as cheapening costs of production, removing restrictions on foreign investment and privatizing state enterprises. These principles would later form the basis of a full-blown standard reform programme promoted by the IMF, the World Bank and the United States Treasury, known informally as the 'Washington Consensus'. Its name was coined by the economist John Williamson (1990, 1997) who saw it as prioritizing ten key principles for market liberalization: fiscal discipline, appropriate public expenditure, priorities from subsidies to pro-growth services, tax reform to reward enterprise, market-determined interest rates, liberalization of trade barriers such as licensing and tariffs, abolition of barriers to foreign direct investment, privatization of state utilities, the abolition of regulations that impede market entry and free competition, and legal security for property rights. Many of its ideas were designed initially to specifically assist development in Latin America, which had suffered in particular from irresponsible government overspending and rampant inflation. However, such was the perceived universality (not to mention irreversibility) of neo-liberalism, that it was deemed that the standard Washington Consensus reform package should theoretically be of economic benefit to any country in the world. Over the next decade this would start to be put into practice.

2.7   The benefits of liberalization

Classical liberal economics holds that the market increases standards of living through its own rationality: markets facilitate competitive trade, trade enhances economic growth, and growth reduces poverty. In essence, entry to the market is a significant step towards financial prosperity. By this reckoning, *global* liberalization should offer an unprecedented opportunity to reduce poverty and share the world's resources.

The link between liberalization policies and living standards, however, is much contested, with an array of statistical projections offering wildly different interpretations, making it an open debate as to whether global poverty has decreased or increased, whether global inequality has decreased or increased, or even if the global economic market is at all responsible for any of these trends. In general, interpretations of these trends fall into two camps: those who see liberalization as spreading worldwide opportunity for economic growth and prosperity, and those who see liberalization as essentially 'polarizing' the global economy into two separate worlds of rich and poor. The latter argument will be explored in more detail in Chapter 3: here, we shall discuss the arguments for the perceived social and economic benefits to the global market.

The World Bank economist David Dollar (2005) is among the most fervent advocates of liberalization, offering compelling statistical evidence of its overall social and economic benefits. Dollar argues that since 1980 poor countries have actually grown faster than rich countries. This is matched by the fact that in China and India poverty (at the $1-a-day standard) fell from 1 billion to 650 million between 1978 and 1998. Poverty also fell in Bangladesh, Indonesia and Vietnam as growth rates increased. In contrast, poverty rose in Africa where growth lagged, though this was outweighed by the dramatic reductions achieved in Asia, driving global poverty down by at least 200 million since 1980 (Dollar 2005: 108–9).

Dollar links poverty reduction to growth, which, in turn, he understands in terms of whether a country has integrated fully into the global market. He points to developing states such as China, Mexico, India, Indonesia and Malaysia that have shifted their economic policy from inward-looking to outward-looking and have reaped the benefits. This has been made possible by countries abandoning traditional raw material exports in favour of manufacturing, with Bangladesh now producing clothes, Thailand producing computer peripherals and China producing electronics. These exports from the developing world are often part of multinational production networks, where manufacturing costs tend to be much lower than in the West. This might suggest exploitation and the heightening of north–south economic dependency, but Dollar counters this by inviting us to draw comparisons in living standard between globally integrated developing economies and those which keep their borders closed: whereas integrationist economies have produced growth and reduced poverty, he claims that there is not one example of an isolationist country recording higher living standards today than it did 40 years ago (*ibid.*: 123).

The successful liberalization of a national economy infers a practical as well as economic shift. Entrance into the global economy requires careful assessment of which areas of trade should prove productive: this may expose some firms to the harsh realities of global competition, but the argument is that liberalization is advantageous in both eliminating low-productivity firms and stimulating market innovation and flexibility. This is made possible through the global transfer of *knowledge* that liberalization provides, meaning that countries in possession of the right *ideas* are more likely to prosper economically. Seen in this way, post-industrial liberalization is more democratic in the opportunity it provides than any prior global trade system: whereas traditional growth theory rested on the assumption that nations were poor because they lacked valuable objects like raw materials and industrial infrastructure, today countries can close the 'idea gap' themselves by sending students abroad to study, connecting to the internet, allowing the investment of foreign firms and investing in the latest equipment and technology (*ibid.*: 118).

This implies that liberalization provides *moral* as well as economic benefits, a view strongly supported by the economist Jagdish Bhagwati. Within liberalization, Bhagwati (2004) argues, are ethical and moral processes which provide more genuine 'trickle-down' opportunities than its critics would suggest. First, he argues that the emphasis placed on knowledge as liberalization's most valuable resource has begun to reduce child labour. This has been achieved through higher incomes for families brought on by open markets – such as rice growers in Vietnam – which have reduced the need for the meagre supplementary income of child labour and has spurred parents to keep their children in school.

Second, liberalization incorporates a rationality that is market-oriented rather than based on potentially irregular cultural norms and values such as nepotism, elitism or traditionalism. In economic terms, Bhagwati argues that this has helped reduce gender equality, as firms competing globally can no longer afford to indulge in pro-male prejudices such as wage discrimination. Once exposed to the global market, firms that indulge in gender prejudice are going to be at a competitive disadvantage against firms that hire and pay men and women without this prejudice. Such economic reasoning has already seen reductions in the gender wage gap in the United States, a trend Bhagwati believes will continue to extend worldwide. This market-rational approach to gender has also initiated a wider reflexive reorientation of cultural values in which women are encouraged to break free of traditional cultural values and be opened up to the opportunities of modern global society. Bhagwati gives the example of Japanese wives of businessmen being exposed to ideas about women's rights and equality in the West, and soon becoming 'agents of social reform' in their own country.

In sum, both Dollar and Bhagwati claim that moral and ethical successes are endemic to liberalization processes, thus inviting it to be justified as a *social* rather than simply economic theory. Moreover, these moral virtues recall the classical liberal philosophies of some 150 years ago: Bhagwati sees all of the above cases as signs of a virtuous social model described in 1848 by John Stuart Mill:

> It may be said without exaggeration that the great extent and rapid increase in international trade, in being the principal guarantee of peace in the world, is the great permanent security for the uninterrupted progress of the ideas, the institutions, and the character of the human race. (Mill, quoted in Bhagwati 2008)

2.8   The limits of liberalization?

Although liberalization, at least on a theoretical level, resembles something of a smooth and logical transition towards an economically ordered and morally virtuous globe, its implementation at a social level reveals a number of potential conflicts. Although liberalization carries with it its own system of values – namely a faith in the power of market equilibrium and individual freedom to improve people's lives – the extent to which the world is capable of running effectively according to these principles is open to debate.

The famous Hungarian political economist Karl Polanyi (2001) is a key critic of liberalism. He believed that economics has two separate meanings – one that is *formal*, where exchange is determined by rational decision-making, and one that is *substantive*, where exchange is informed by social and environmental factors, and thus open to the peculiarities of socio-cultural interaction. In pre-industrial societies economic exchange was defined openly according to the latter definition. The rise of industrial capitalism, however, initiated a transformation of exchange relations under the auspices of the former, meaning that markets were promoted not merely as practical 'accessories' to economic life, but also as the rational self-regulating forum for all exchange processes. Via the commodification of labour, land and money, the market effectively subordinates the very *substance* of society itself to its own formal laws.

Like Marx, Polanyi saw markets as inseparable from their social and cultural contexts, meaning that attempts to liberalize the economy should be seen as intrinsically *political* in its consequences. At a basic level, market rationality gives social objects a 'fictitious' market-determined value that might be far removed from its use value. At a broader level, Polanyi highlighted the possible effects of a market left to its own devices, in particular, the effects of economic crises on the working-class poor. From this, Polanyi posed a provocative question: should economic crises be seen as an unavoidable part of a 'naturally flowing' market, and therefore a price worth paying for the wealth and freedoms of wider society, or are they moral outrages about which something must be done?

Taking this question into a global context, Hirst and Thompson (1999) contend with Dollar and Bhagwati's view that a liberalized world economy produces mutually beneficial economic relations. At a macro level, it can be argued that trade, investment and financial flows continue to be concentrated in the triad of Europe, Japan and North America, leaving a Third World, or 'Global South' lacking in basic entitlements. This power imbalance is compounded further by the enduring hegemonic power of the US economy, for it remains 'the only possible guarantor of the world's free trading system against politically inspired disruption'. Effectively, they argue that 'the openness of global markets depends on American policy' (Hirst and Thompson 1999: 14), meaning that any advocacy of economic liberalization from the IMF and World Bank is blurred by the self-interest of its elite actors.

The question of whether the global free market reproduces hegemonic power structures will be addressed in more detail in the next chapter, but it remains of interest here to consider the practical considerations of developing countries when adopting liberalization policies. In order to benefit from liberalization, national authorities are expected to balance transparent financial accounting with prudential regulation and financial stability. However, if such measures were to impose an additional cost to multinational corporations, and thus negatively affect their international competitiveness and profitability, they might be tempted to take their business elsewhere. This then imposes a dilemma on the national authorities: do they risk losing major capital investors in order to maintain economic stability through public expenditure, or do they relax their supervision over the financial sector even further? As power relations appear synonymous with economic relations in the liberalization model, the latter choice appears the more attractive, but at what cost?

The fear for economists such as Jeremy Brecher and Tim Costello (1998) is that corporations, when seeking suitable locations to invest in, have the capacity to hold nation states to ransom by demanding minimal supervision and regulation in order to maximize their profit. This, in turn drives workers, communities and countries to compete to lower labour, social and environmental costs – thus forcing them into a 'race to the bottom'. This scenario infers competition between nation-states to attract the investment of global corporations by offering the lowest prices and the greatest freedoms. And due to the unavoidable need to constantly save and economize, nation-states might have to reduce environmental protection, wages, salaries, healthcare and education so as to remain competitive – initiating a 'downward levelling' of environmental, labour and social conditions.

The social consequences of downward levelling are not limited to low-skilled labour either – increasingly, jobs in the professional sector, from nurses and plumbers to teachers and call-centre workers are being opened to market forces, with the intention of cutting costs through lower salaries.

This leads to a loss of job security that is felt in both the north and south as corporations, acting in the interests of 'competitiveness', replace union seniority systems and stable job structures with 'flexibility', 'short-termism' and 'downsizing' via subcontracting through temporary employment agencies. Such employment instability has been felt across the globe, as employment becomes increasingly homogenized into a single market. As Princeton economist William Baumol put it, 'it is not that foreigners are stealing our jobs, it is that we are all facing one another's competition' (quoted in Brecher and Costello 1998: 21).

2.9 Liberalization on trial: the global financial crisis of 2007–8

Whether one is an advocate or a critic of liberalization, one cannot deny the far-ranging impact that the social and economic integration of the world creates. In other words, the perceived *benefits* and *risks* of liberalization are genuinely *global* in their impact. For Ohmae and Bhagwati, the benefits lie in the free market's capacity to disseminate greater opportunity for individuals, both on an economic and a moral-cultural level. On the flipside, however, the risks caused by liberalization, such as downward levelling and 'boom and bust', have an equally global reach. And in a global society of mediated visibility and communication, these risks have the potential to put the validity of a market society under the spotlight in a way hitherto unseen in the history of liberal economics. By far the most pertinent example of this phenomena, demonstrating the greatest impact, is the global financial crisis of 2007–8, an event described by political theorist Andrew Gamble as 'one of the most dramatic and extraordinary financial crashes in the history of capitalism' (Gamble 2009: 5).

Economic slumps and financial crises are nothing new to the history of global capitalism; indeed they are a central tenet of classical liberal economics: according to Ricardo, crises are an unavoidable product of the capitalist business cycle. This view was studied further by Marx, who argued that the self-interest of profit-seeking market agents causes a detachment of market value from production value, with the need to maintain high demand leading to overproduction and, inevitably, economic slump. Both Marx and Polanyi voiced concerns over the social consequences for a fully marketized society, noting how the poor would invariably bear the brunt of any economic downturn with each crisis driving down wages and causing mass unemployment as the capitalists sought to protect their surplus. This was exemplified most famously in the United States, where the financial prosperity of the post-war 'Roaring Twenties' was followed by the Wall Street Crash of 1929 and the Great Depression of the 1930s.

For all this apparent endemic instability, however, the rise and dominance of neo-liberalism and financial markets in the late twentieth century, accompanied by steady economic growth, led many to consider whether global capitalism had finally reached something resembling equilibrium. As Gamble observes:

> At the height of the boom it seemed possible, against all historical evidence to the contrary, that this time it might really last for ever. The era of boom and bust had finally passed away, and the global economy was now so sophisticated, so flexible, so interdependent, that its breakdown was now unthinkable. It performed miracles of coordination every day, and the fact that no-one properly understood how they were accomplished only added to the marvel and the mystery. (Gamble 2009: 2)

Such causes for optimism had already come with a recent reminder of liberal capitalism's fallibilities: the 'marvel and mystery' of the global economy had induced a financial slump some ten years before the 2007–8 crisis with the East Asian crisis of 1997. In this case, despite decades of steady growth in East Asian 'tiger' economies such as Japan, South Korea and Malaysia, the IMF pushed aggressively for their stronger integration into the global economy via the recommendations of the Washington Consensus (Masuyama 1999; Lee 2003; Chang 2007). In 1997, uncertain steps towards financial liberalization had heightened fear of risk among investors, contributing in part to a 'bank run' as investors feared a downturn and withdrew their funds. This fear of risk exacerbated the downturn into a full-blown crisis. Stiglitz (2002) claims that the role of liberalization in the crisis was a nefarious one, as the IMF's attempt to manage the crisis actually compounded the scale of the crisis, exchanging rescue packages of capital investment for further economic liberalization reforms. This suggests that the IMF's key concern was to contain the crisis's global impact by effectively propping up the global economy through bailing out overseas investors over social welfare, a decision which would cause riots and demonstrations in Indonesia. This nevertheless failed, as the contagious fear of risk propounded through the interconnectedness of global markets served to drag down investment confidence across the world regardless. Such was the scale of mismanagement in the IMF's macroeconomic policy that the *Wall Street Journal* would later argue the East Asian Crisis would be better titled as the 'IMF Crisis'.

Echoing Marx and Polanyi, Stiglitz argues that the IMF policies in East Asia provided a clear illustration of the practical defects in unfettered financial liberalization. But these defects nevertheless failed to significantly grab the headlines in the West, as neo-liberal markets continued to produce economic growth and could thus continue behind their veils of marvel and mystery. Its ever-deepening complexities, however, would be exposed in the global economic crisis of 2007–8, arguably giving the limits to economic freedom an all-new visibility in the West.

From the 1980s onwards, financial liberalization in the United States had enabled local and regional markets and investors to be connected to other local and regional markets and investors across the world, creating a high-speed global marketplace with more competitors, greater investment choice and the opportunity for greater profit. This opened up savings and loan institutions to a new world of global buyers and sellers, aided by the free-flowing nature of capital movement. As already seen, this had been assisted by governments' willingness to liberalize their monetarist policies in order to stimulate investment and growth by issuing tax cuts, privatizing public assets and deregulating the financial sector.

The housing market would become a principal arena for investors. House prices in the US had been rising since the 1990s, as banks had taken advantage of low interest rates to maximize the number of mortgages it could fund. This booming market would prove attractive for financial investors, as mortgage lenders and commercial banks could group loans together as 'collateralized debt obligations' and then sell them as mortgage-backed 'securities' on the open market. From 1999 these securities could be traded by banks and commercial lenders, following the US government's repeal of the Glass–Steagall Act. In another symbolic act of liberalization, the act, which had originally been set up after the Wall Street Crash of 1929 to prevent the investment of debt into the stock market, was now deemed obstructive to the fast movement of capital brought about by the global free market. By lifting these restrictions, financial organizations had the freedom to use borrowed money to supplement further investment and make faster transactions and short-term profits.

Two events would further inflate the housing market. First, in 1997 the US government allowed 'subprime' mortgages to be securitized and resold competitively. These mortgages belonged to low-income families with poor credit histories and thus represented potentially riskier returns for investors. However, banks were able to justify giving these securitized packages top 'AAA' credit ratings. Such opaque valuing was achieved free of independent regulation, and subprime securities quickly became desirable trading chips for investors. This made the overall mortgage market even more lucrative, encouraging banks to take on further subprime mortgage applications.

Second, the market would become even more crowded when the 'dot com' bubble of online businesses burst in 2000. This created a mad dash for investors in search of safe and profitable markets to reinvest with, and the US housing market seemed to provide suitable refuge. This had the twin effect of cushioning the impact of the dot com slump while causing an even greater surge in the housing market: in ten years, house prices in many leading economies increased by more than 75 per cent, and in some countries including Britain, Australia and Spain, they more than doubled (Gamble 2009: 3).

But growth in the housing market rested on valuations that were becoming increasingly divorced from reality. Subprime mortgage securities were essentially repackaged debt and were securitized initially on the basis that the housing market would continue to rise. Such hubris would be compounded by the fast and free-flowing market, as these securities would then be bought, repackaged and resold many times under the same reasoning, resulting in its selling price becoming more and more removed from its actual financial content. To make matters worse, further US liberalization reforms in 2004 enabled investment banks to leverage their transactions even further in order to keep up to speed with profitable investment opportunities. This opened up a chasm between the amount banks *claimed* to be earning, and the amount of capital they physically *owned* at any one time: investment banks could now hold as little as 1.6 per cent capital against these investments, or $16,000 per million they claimed to have earned (Rolet 2009).

By 2006, subprime mortgage lending had swelled to $600 billion – 20 per cent of total mortgage originations – of which 75 per cent was securitized (Aalbers 2009: 36). Many of these packages had been bought and sold for a high profit, earning investors large bonuses from their employers while distributing the costs (and consequences) across the entire global market. Of course, the successful payment of these mortgages would depend both on low unemployment levels and the continued growth of housing prices, arguably a perilous and unrealistic equilibrium. 2006 provided the tipping point when interest rates in the US rose above 5 per cent. For many subprime owners mortgages were now unaffordable, leading to an increase in defaults and foreclosures. As house prices began to fall, the systemic risk from which securitized mortgage asset selling was built upon slowly began to filter through the system, generating a 'credit crunch' in 2007 as banks reduced the availability of loans and rapidly increased their interest rates to maximize returns. As the bottom fell out of the US housing market it soon became clear that securitized mortgage packages were effectively worthless, leaving banks with no way of ascertaining the real value of many of the assets they had once so freely added to the balance sheets. This growing realization led to major losses posted by banks, with each triggering further collapses across the markets. In July 2007 the IMF predicted that the losses of the financial crisis were expected to exceed $1 trillion. The crash reached its climax in October 2008 when markets across the globe were forced to temporarily close as failing banks were either frantically sold off at cut-down prices or nationalized by governments. Others, including most notably the US firm Lehman Brothers, were left to collapse altogether. The crash's victims also extended beyond financial service firms: in the case of Iceland, its whole economy was built on the financial sector, resulting in the government declaring the entire country effectively bankrupt. By January 2009, the IMF had predicted the worst recession for advanced economies since the Second World War.

Like 1929 and 1997 before it, the financial crisis had profound social consequences for those on a low income. For many homeowners, the initial credit crunch resulted in foreclosure as they found themselves paying high monthly payments for a property rapidly decreasing in value. In cities and neighbourhoods where employment and housing prices were at their most perilous the crash saw the abandonment of whole residential districts, with homes in Detroit being reportedly sold for as little as $1 (McGreal 2010). This, too, has its own severe social spillover effects with homeowners either ditching their properties, or even burning them down so as to get out of mortgage repayments (see also Immergluck 2009).

To sum up, one might see the nationalization and government bailout of a number of leading investment banks as providing both an ironic and symbolic end to 30 years of continuous macro liberalization programmes worldwide. Governmental bailout packages for the banking sector have been issued across Western Europe, China and the United States, with collective figures estimated to be as high as $3,000 billion (Maccartney 2009). Much like the recovery packages issued during the Asian crisis, however, these arguably represent more an effort to 'prop-up' the global economy than reform it entirely, as state funds have been used to restore liquidity to market trading across the globe. Much has been said of a renewed commitment to financial regulation by the G20 leaders, but the extent to which this can be imposed without impeding the free-flow of global capital remains to be seen. Once again, the IMF is expected to play a central part in economic recovery programmes. Liberalization may have seriously faltered, but much of its ethos remains deeply embedded within the structures of world financial markets.

2.10   Conclusion

Recalling the image of a 'global society' depicted in Chapter 1, one might argue that the theory of liberalization represents its natural economic expression: a system by which each actor is an equal participant on the 'global stage' that is the free market. Put another way, the economic freedoms afforded by liberalization can be seen to complement the fluid architecture of a global society increasingly removed from regionalized political and cultural divisions. As a result, advocates of this theory argue that if liberalization does not represent at present the reality of global economic relations, it should at least represent its *ideal*. Those who criticize the model, demanding fixed regulations, are accused as failing to see the bigger picture: the free market prioritizes the many over the few, and by allowing the global market to operate according to its own rationality it will be at its most effective in producing the greatest good for the greatest number.

The productive engine driving this 'bigger picture' is, of course, the capitalist system: the pursuit of profit is seen to generate wider economic growth through the creation of new commodities, and the openness of the market encourages healthy competition between producers, thus driving up economic standards. In this sense, the global extension of liberal capitalist markets is a natural one, with Marx observing as long ago as 1848 that capitalism is always looking out for new commodities and new consumers to expand the market. Yet this is seen as a moral as well as economically rational process, with greater social benefits and opportunities emerging out of the slipstream of global liberalization: after all, poverty represents, among many things, a population deprived of the opportunities to work and consume and ultimately bolster global market productivity even further. Whether you come from a rich country or a poor country, these freedoms and opportunities promised by liberalization are hard to resist: after all, who wouldn't want to be free?

However, like any process that is ultimately *social* in its consequences, liberalization remains accountable to its participants. Not only do the vagaries of market fluctuation have potentially damaging social effects – causing mortgage foreclosure, the loss of life-savings or unemployment – they are seldom the fault of the actual victims, occurring instead as the unintended product of a chain of unmanaged economic transactions. The financial crisis of 2007–8 arguably marked a sea-change for the perception of the global economy: its failure was a televisual 'global event' in which the media was able to clearly identify winners and losers, with the latter given greater capability to hold the former up to scrutiny.

This newfound visibility to the global marketplace raises new and interesting questions about the validity of liberalization as its 'ideal type'. At a most basic level, we may ask whether a global market society can ever actually exist in practice. In order to function correctly, the model requires a number of key presuppositions, namely self-regulating markets, rational actors and a fair and level playing field. But the unevenness of how, when and where liberalization has been implemented across the globe indicates that a global market, as it stands now, is too messy and irrational to fully resemble its theoretical ideal type. Moreover, the unequal distribution of knowledge and resources across the globe make fair and equal participation an unlikely fixture. This may also lead us to question *who actually benefits* from liberalization: does it represent a consensus view of how a global economy should operate or has it been constructed to favour certain actors over others? For critics of neo-liberalism it has long been recognized that the origins of the major global economic institutions such as the World Bank and the IMF are entwined with the origins of modern liberal democracies in the West, with the United States and Britain taking particular precedence. Indeed, such is the depth to this close-knit relationship – where, for example, the president of the World Bank is hand-picked by the president of the United States – some critics have preferred to view liberalization as nothing more than a new imperialism, led by the hegemonic powers of the West. We shall expand on these debates in more detail in Chapter 4.

In summary, despite its palpable faults, liberalization as both an ideological force and an economic reality cannot be underestimated. Its advocates continue to believe that when implemented correctly, liberalization is capable of initiating a progression towards a more equal, just and even peaceful global society. Beneath the rhetorical trappings of 'freedom', however, one might question the extent to which one should endorse a system prone to periodic failures responsible for such damaging social consequences. Yet, despite the calls for a systematic overhaul of the global economy following the recent financial crisis, reforms have tended to be corrective rather than radical as the fundamental elements of liberalization remain structurally embedded within the systems of global economic trade. What recent events have at least succeeded in causing, however, is a 're-politicization' of the neo-liberal agenda, whereby the future of the global economy is subject to closer public scrutiny than ever before. This at least means that liberalization should no longer be seen as an inexorable, uncontested process, though the extent to which it can be successfully tamed through greater regulation and accountability in practice remains to be seen.

Polarization: Rich World, Poor World

3

3.1 Introduction

Underpinning the liberalization model is the assumption that the contemporary global economy is defined by the relaxation of trade borders between countries and, thus, by the extension of free trade. However, as we have seen, its critics present an altogether different scenario: they suggest that, rather than allowing for more widespread economic development, the economic policies attached to this model are inherently biased towards the already rich north or west. What emerges is a system of exploitation which helps the rich get richer and the poor get poorer; in other words an ever-expanding gulf between rich and poor. Thus, the definitive feature of this 'new' and 'global' economy is the stark division it propagates between north and south. Accordingly, ours is very much a divided world.

The activist and academic Walden Bello (2004) presents a detailed archaeology of contemporary north–south relations in terms of a long-term strategic plan to undermine the power of the so-called Third World *and* those institutions, including the United Nations itself and the Bretton Woods institutions, especially the World Bank, which were perceived by right-wing political advisors in the USA and elsewhere as being complicit in supporting the 'Third World agenda'. From the beginning of the 1980s, Bello lists such factors as: the replacing of the liberal Robert McNamara as president of the World Bank with a more conservative successor; rewriting the ideology and policy of the World Bank away from local reconstruction and towards economic reform, via policies of 'structural adjustment'; reinventing the General Agreement on Tariffs and Trade (GATT) as the more hard-line World Trade Organization (WTO) with a clear agenda to regulate international trade in the interests of the northern industrialized countries; marginalizing the role of the prominent United Nations agencies involved in global economic development, including the Economic and Social Council and the UN Development Programme, and effectively dismantling the United Nations Conference on Trade and Development (UNCTAD); and handing more power to the so-called G7, the group of seven leading industrial countries (*ibid.*: 40–54). The result of all of this restructuring, Bello claims, was the marginalization of the south in respect of the management of the international economic system.

Perhaps the clearest summary of this problem, though, comes from the editors of an influential volume from the early 1990s, for whom this problem of the 'new world order' is best defined as 'globalization-from-above':

> Globalization-from-above extracts resources from the natural world and from local communities in order to increase the wealth and power of the wealthy and powerful. It concentrates that wealth and power in organizations which use their control of people and resources to expand their domination and to fight each other. It transfers power and resources from the natural world to human domination, from communities to elites, and from local societies to national and transnational power centers. (Brecher, Brown Childs and Cutler 1993: xi)

However, from the same volume, another excellent summary of the argument, highlighting the weaknesses of the 'dominant discourse', is presented in the chapter by Vandana Shiva:

> The 'global' in the dominant discourse is the political space in which the dominant local seeks global control, and frees itself of local, national, and global control. The global in this sense does not represent the universal human interest; it represents a particular local and parochial interest which has been globalized through its reach and control ... [The] most powerful countries dictate global affairs, but they remain narrow, local and parochial in terms of the interests of all the world's communities. (Shiva 1993: 53–4)

It is worth including Shiva's quote here in this introduction as a warning not to equate the politicized opposition to the perceived polarization brought about by processes of 'globalization' and 'liberalization' with a call for some kind of simple 'return to the local'. The parochialism of localization is equally problematic. We will conclude this section by returning to Shiva and a related contribution by Walden Bello, whose respective concepts of 'Earth democracy' and 'deglobalization' are seen as alternatives to the dominant discourse. However, we first need to understand, in more descriptive terms, the nature of the relationship between the 'rich and powerful' world and its subaltern.

3.2   Core and periphery: the structuralist approach to global development

Understanding the nature of the dynamics between the north and the south, or the global rich and the global poor, requires the adoption of an approach to economics and development studies which can be called *structuralism*. Not to be confused with the French philosophy of the same name, which had its roots in linguistics, this kind of structuralism emerged in the 1950s through the work of Raul Prebisch (1949, 1950, 1959) and the Economic Commission for Latin America, and in the earlier work of Celso Furtado (1964), and was taken up by the school of 'dependency theory' led by Andre Gunder Frank and other Latin American scholars (see, for example, Frank 1967, 1975; also Cardoso 1977; Furtado 1969). Structuralism rejects the orthodox liberal idea that the world market results in equal exchange and mutual benefit, drawing instead on indigenous perspectives in Latin America which distinguish between the powerful central economies and the weaker peripheral ones. Structuralists emphasize the need to locate national economies (such as those in Latin America) within the broader system dominated by the major industrial powers (the United States, primarily). Structuralists reject the claim that national economies are uniform, and that under-development is caused by deficiencies in those national economies themselves. Indeed, in under-developed countries, a differentiation of interests emerges. Rejecting the ahistorical basis of modernization theory, structuralists seek to adopt an historically specific approach to understanding development issues. Early structuralists such as Prebisch proposed industrialization, protected by appropriate tariffs, as a solution, believing it would enable poorer economies to achieve stability and semi-autonomy within the interdependent system.

Structuralists such as Prebisch were significant, then, in shifting the focus of development away from national economies and towards the broader world system, but they tended to retain a liberal commitment to industrialization, and a preference for reformist policies at the national level, and did not pursue the core-periphery distinction to its logical end – that is, that the causes of under-development reside firmly within capitalist expansion itself. This mantle, and with it the demand for the radical reconstruction of the world system itself, was taken up by Frank and the dependency theorists in the 1960s. Frank's basic position – following that of the American Marxist economist Paul Baran (1957) – was the application of traditional Marxian theory to the problem of under-development in the 'Third World'. Baran had recast the Marxian concept of 'surplus' to focus on the realization and exploitation of economic surplus in the Third World within the context of the wider economic system, which, he claimed, was no longer 'progressive' as it was driven by monopoly rather than competition. This resulted in a polarization of the world economy into a dominant 'metropolitan centre' and its subordinate 'peripheral satellites' (Frank 1967). So, rather than being a purely internal problem equitable to a kind of stunted modernization which could be overcome through investment and the sensible management of the country's social and economic infrastructure, under-development for Frank was seen in structural and dialectical terms, the product of unequal power relations. In short, we cannot understand, never mind treat, the problem of under-development in one country without recognizing that some countries are poor *precisely because* some countries are rich, and *vice versa*. This is Marx's theory of exploitation applied to the global scale.

What Frank and the other dependency theorists introduced to the literature was an appreciation of the extent to which capitalism is a structural condition which exists across borders. Frank's work was mainly concerned with Latin America, but his theoretical analysis is equally applicable to other parts of the global south. Whether or not a country has (in traditional Marxian terms) entered into the capitalist mode of production is irrelevant; the countries of Latin America and elsewhere are *part of the capitalist system* because they exist in a dialectical relationship based on exploitation with the richer, 'advanced' capitalist countries. The 'problem' of the Third World is not, to put it plainly, one of *under-development*, but one of *capitalist* under-development. Betraying their roots in Marxism, dependency theorists have tended to advocate socialist revolution in peripheral countries, but they often maintain, as a pre-requisite for this, that such countries must 'opt out' of the world capitalist economy (Baran 1957; Frank 1972).

Baran and Frank's emphasis upon the exploitative and structural nature of global development is echoed in Immanuel Wallerstein's 'world-systems' approach. Wallerstein (1974) takes his lead from Frank's insistence that poorer nation-states are not under-developed in the traditional sense, but rather locked into subordinate peripheral positions *vis-à-vis* the wealthier countries within the world capitalist system. For Wallerstein, the modern world-system is a capitalist system characterized by a single division of labour and defined by the power relationship between the industrially advanced countries (which Wallerstein calls the 'core') and the under-developed ones (which he calls the 'periphery'). Core countries are defined both by their advanced economies and by the political and military power which they utilize to maintain their hegemony. However, 'core' and 'periphery' (or, indeed, 'semi-periphery', a term Wallerstein later introduced to refer to states which both exploit and are exploited, and which are often in transition between the extremes) are not static categories. Nation-states shift across the spectrum, and core states undergo *hegemonic cycles*. In the formative years of the modern world-system, the dominant European powers, England, France, Spain, the Netherlands, occupied the core, but in more recent times many of these old world imperial centres have slumped into the semi-periphery. The United States of America, Wallerstein suggests, entered into the core in 1890.

The modern world-system, which is an *economic* totality, replaced the earlier form of systemic interconnectedness which was the 'world-empire' form (primarily a power relationship derived from political and military supremacy and sustained by cultural dependency, characterized by the paying of tribute from the colonized regions to the imperial centre). While Wallerstein traces the beginning of the modern world-system to around 1600 in Europe, there is considerable disagreement among world-systems theorists about the precise origins and historical periodization of the modern world-system (Amin *et al.* 1982; Chase-Dunn 1989, 1999; Frank and Gills 1993; Hopkins and Wallerstein 1982; Wallerstein 1974, 1979, 1980, 1983, 1989). Even so, they are united in forming a significant contribution to the field of global studies, in that they see contemporary global dynamics as an extension of the historical world capitalist system. Most, but not all, world-systems theorists reject the use of the term 'globalization'. Their concern is primarily with interstate relations within a structural framework, the world-system as a 'global social formation' (Chase-Dunn 1989, 1999) – that is, the economic and political dynamics between core and peripheral countries (and, more recently, 'semi-peripheral' countries). Thus, the modern world is not 'globalized' but interconnected, and this interconnectedness has been a feature of human society since the dawn of capitalist modernity, perhaps even before. So, world-systems theorists such as Wallerstein take the structuralism of Prebisch and its Marxian-inspired variant of Baran and Frank and reconstruct it in global historical terms, albeit at the expense, some would say, of its capacity for reform. For sure, Wallerstein lacks the confidence of Frank and others in the possibility of subordinate countries 'opting out' of the world economy, which is too strictly established, and thus in the potential for a socialist revolution at the nation-state level, although he does present a rather vague call for the overthrow of the capitalist world-system and its replacement with a socialist alternative (at the world-systemic level).

Although distinguished by their respective emphases on reform or revolution, 'opting out' or total overhaul, the writings of Prebisch, Frank, Baran, Wallerstein and others have, taken as a whole, helped to establish structuralism not only as a major perspective within economics and development studies, but – especially Wallerstein – in global studies as well. Whether or not one subscribes to it, there is no better theoretical assessment of the view that 'globalization' equates to *polarization*, a view which is supported, not always with as much theoretical sophistication, by many academics and activists involved in the debate. Of course, it does need to be said that, despite their obvious sophistication in parts, such theoretical models as presented by these writers have been accused of over-simplifying the structural conditions of the world. Their emphasis on *inter*-national structural divisions tends to result in less attention being paid to, on the one hand, *trans*-national economic institutions and, on the other, *intra*-national inequalities resulting from the global economy. As a theoretical framework it is easy to see polarization purely in terms of rich and poor *countries*, the north and the south, although of course this need not be the case: an even more sophisticated polarization framework could easily accommodate an analysis of such economic distinctions within a given nation-state, the south within the north and *vice versa*, as it were. Indeed, recognition of this complexity is present in the Marxian and non-Marxian literature on polarization alike. Even so, due to its perceived limitations, the polarization framework (especially its Marxian, structuralist variant) has come under attack from the political left as well as the right, and we will return to these at the end of this chapter. But for the meantime, let us consider the *reality* of the framework being proposed.

Biography Box 6:   Immanuel Wallerstein

Immanuel Wallerstein (1930–) is a historical sociologist and economic historian, and the pioneer of world-systems analysis in the social sciences. He was the founder, in 1976, of the Fernand Braudel Center for the Study of Economies, Historical Systems and Civilizations at the State University of New York, Binghampton, which he remained the director of until 2005. His three volumes of *The Modern World System* constitute one of the most ambitious and important contributions to the social sciences of the age.

3.3   The reality of polarization: trends in global poverty and inequality

One can argue that to speak of polarization as an empirical 'reality' is to enter into a direct critical dialogue with those who speak of liberalization as an empirical 'reality'. In other words, both models offer an opposing diagnosis of the same phenomena – global economic integration – and how it impacts upon living standards in the Third World. Consensus has at least been reached in acknowledging that global economic integration is an empirical reality, and that this gives greater weight to the view that poverty and inequality are issues of *global* concern. Such views have been held by the IMF and the World Bank since their inception (see Chapter 2), and both institutions today see an increasingly interconnected global economy as providing unprecedented opportunities to tackle Third World poverty, to the extent that they have termed it 'the single greatest challenge of the century' (Kacowicz 2007: 565).

However, this common consensus begins to badly falter as soon as questions are asked as to the *actual* effect global economic integration has had on Third World poverty so far. Unsurprisingly, theorists of liberalization see it as spreading economic growth across the globe, enabling developing nations to become competitive players in the global marketplace. Theorists of polarization, however, see liberalization as an imperialist project developed to protect and extend the interests of the core elite under the sanctity of 'free trade' philosophies and their perceived (yet ultimately minimal) trickle-down effects. Such disagreements are widened further by the lack of consensus over how poverty should be defined and measured: datasets on poverty can be inferred to prove global poverty increase, global poverty reduction, or even global poverty stability.

We may begin by returning to the perceived successes of liberalization. As we saw in Chapter 2, its advocates see global economic integration as having helped significantly reduce global poverty: using World Bank statistics (2001, 2004), Dollar (2005) and Wolf (2002b) both argue that 200 million fewer people live today in absolute poverty compared with 1980. Not only is this trend viewed as a historically unprecedented reversal of fortune for the global poor, it is one that can be attributed to increased economic growth brought about by global financial liberalization. This is justified on the basis that economic growth provides more jobs and investment in infrastructure and social welfare. Aware of its miserly connotations, Bhagwati (2004) prefers to describe this phenomena as more of a 'pull-up strategy' than a 'trickle-down effect', as increased investment opportunities and market competition provides 'aspiration and hope' to the global poor, instead of despondency or envy brought about by more nepotistic, state-dominated economics.

So how do theorists of polarization contend with such claims? First, theorists of polarization take issue with how downward poverty trends are both calculated and interpreted. Certainly, there are questions about whether poverty should be measured by population number – which due to higher birth rates in the Third World shows unstable trends even in the World Bank's calculations – or as a percentage of the world population. The latter measurement tends to provide a more consistent support to the liberalization thesis, but even this is contested by Reddy and Pogge (2003), who claim that the percentage of the world population living below $1 a day was about 8 per cent higher in 1998 than the World Bank's own calculations.

It has also been argued that using the $1-a-day standard on its own is too narrow a definition of poverty, and one that relegates the significance of flows, relations and dynamics between regions and elites. According to Paul Spicker (1999), a more dialectical and multifaceted definition of poverty should instead be invoked, taking into account variations in available resources and entitlements as well as relational issues such as exclusion and inequality. Some degree of inequality in a global capitalist economy is of course inevitable, though narrowing the gap between rich and poor remains a key objective for the World Bank. Broadly speaking, there is consensus over the general *scope* of inequality relations since 1980, but there is much disparity over the actual *direction* of change. According to Dollar (2005), global inequality (measured by the GINI index) reduced from 0.67 to 0.64 between 1980 and 2000, a 'modest' yet symbolic trend reversal, and one that again is attributed to global liberalization. This decline has also been supported in studies by Sala-i-Martin (2005) and, to a lesser extent, Bourguignon and Morrisson (2002). The economist Branko Milanovic (2005), however, disagrees with this analysis, arguing that these calculations have incorporated too much guesswork where data is scant, and employed 'artificial smoothing' to ensure consistently downward trends (for more detail see Milanovic 2005: 173–9). Unsurprisingly, his own calculations reveal a different picture: also using the GINI index, Milanovic agrees that global inequality stood at 0.64 at the end of the millennium, but argued instead that it represented the end-point of a significant upward curve, with international inequality being as low as 0.44 in 1950. As of 1998, global inequality can be transferred into a dollar-ratio of 320:1 which he describes as 'probably among the highest, or perhaps the highest, inequality level ever recorded' (Milanovic 2005).

Widening relations of inequality produce a 'twin peaks' model of global income which provides the striking image for Wallerstein's theory of core–periphery relations. Milanovic sees an increasing divergence between rich and poor nation states, arguing that there has been a decline in the number of rich countries (measured by GDP) between 1960 and 2000, resulting in an increased concentration of global north states among the remaining rich states. More striking has been the cutting out of middle-rank 'contender' states: out of the 22 countries Milanovic identified to be within striking distance of joining the core group of rich states in 1960, by 2000 only Singapore and Hong Kong had actually succeeded, with the rest dropping out as contenders altogether. In sum, Milanovic sees a clearly observable polarization of rich and poor states, with the rich non-Western states of 1960 now making up today's contenders, and the non-Western contenders of 1960 now languishing in the Third or Fourth World. At a global population level, Milanovic provocatively concludes that polarization is creating a 'world without a middle class': in defining this category according to those whose incomes fall between 75 and 125 per cent of the world median, Milanovic locates a middle class that makes up only 17.4 per cent of the world population, as of 1998 receiving only 6.5 per cent of the total world income (Milanovic 2005: 130). This view is supported to some extent by Wade's (2001) 'champagne glass' model (see Figure 3.1), whereupon the richest 20 per cent of the world population account for 82.7 per cent of the total world income. Liberalization may be seen to give promise of opportunity, but wealth continues to be concentrated in familiar regions.

So how do we understand these global divergences of income? Bhagwati (2004) contests the usefulness of identifying transnational class groupings as they ignore the varying social and political context of a country's economic performance: in other words, economic failure might be caused by a *lack* of global economic integration, rather than exist as a consequence of it. Milanovic acknowledges this view, and identifies a variety of reasons for the 'failure' of contender states to join the core elite, varying from the effect of civil and international wars, political instability caused by domestic conflicts and uprisings. Nevertheless, he also identifies as a cause the difficulties experienced in opening up a country's economy to the global market. As a result, we can see that the question of how, and to what extent these failures are attributable to the neo-liberal global economy is a contentious issue. More contentious still is how, and to what extent, struggling states should be handled by the global economy – in other words, what should be done?

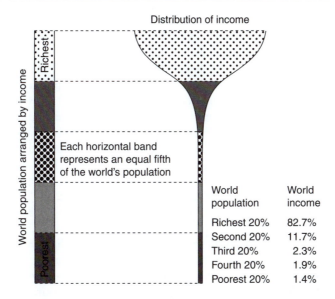

Figure 3.1   Robert Wade's (2001) 'champagne glass' model of world income distribution

Theorists of liberalization argue that there are more substantial and far-ranging social benefits to a fully integrated global free market than a system of isolationist state-economies. Many of these opportunities for prosperity come through economic growth, which, rather than being little more than an aggregation of self-serving venture capitalists, is integral to Third World prosperity. At a structural level, monopolization and economic success functions as an 'engine' of productivity through developments in technology that can be utilized by both the north and the south. At a social level, Bhagwati (2004) sees world economic growth as incorporating greater social responsibility and ethical behaviour, arguing that the added *visibility* in matters of poverty and destitution make unavoidable the need for billionaire tycoons to do 'social good'. Bhagwati illustrates this point with Microsoft founder Bill Gates's sustained and substantial commitment to charitable work, which both produces an enormous volume of economic benevolence to rival that of many a nation-state and helps promote the importance of ethical responsibility for figures of wealth and influence.

Theorists of polarization, on the other hand, see liberalization as ultimately limited in its redistributive potential for it goes against the basic rules of capitalist competition: as Gilpin (2001) argues, states and companies will always seek to maintain a relative advantage over their nearest competitors. Instead, we should consider the motives not just of capitalist actors, but the entire liberalization project. At a political level, Petras and Veltmeyer (2001) see global economic integration as representing an imperial project, in which the Washington Consensus serves as an 'ideological tool' for capitalist elites to construct a global economy that protects and enhances their own interests (*ibid.*: 12). The Korean economist Ha-Joon Chang (2007) agrees, likening the 'unholy trinity' of the IMF, the World Bank and the World Trade Organization (WTO) to 'Bad Samaritans' for relentlessly prescribing liberalization programmes to developing countries despite their highly questionable success rates. Far from operating as independent and impartial regulators of the global economy, Chang explains how the internal governance structure of the World Bank, IMF and WTO severely biases them towards the interests of the core elite. With decisions made according to the share capital that a country has, the rich countries collectively control 60 per cent of the voting shares. As the largest shareholder, the United States effectively has the power of veto in relation to key economic decisions (Chang 2007: 34–5; see also Buira 2004).

At a wider structural level, liberalization has exacerbated already-existing social and economic gaps between states by reinforcing what Joseph Schumpeter calls a process of 'creative destruction' where those in possession of the tools of global capitalist accumulation – wealth, resources, knowledge and mobility – are able to exploit the developing world through cheap labour and the mining of its resources, potentially causing a 'race to the bottom' as mentioned in the last chapter. The result is increased poverty and widening relations of inequality produced by a system designed to reward a small 'corporocracy' of financial markets and corporations that rule the world (Derber, quoted in Dallmayr 2002: 145).

3.4 Polarization as north–south relations

Theorists of polarization point to a number of structural relations caused by global economic integration in which the south has become dependent on and answerable to the amoral fluctuations of the free market. For many countries in the global south, entry into the global market has resulted in economic 'failure', whereas others have become economic 'winners'. Identifying causes of such divergence is a sensitive issue: Mehdi (2006) contends with accusations that neo-liberal markets are underpinned by a Darwinian natural selection and 'survival of the fittest', but questions the extent to which rational economic calculations can be invoked to explain economic 'failures'. To illustrate, Mehdi cites the example of the economist Martin Wolf who argues that the challenge for the global economy 'is to help the failures do better', a contentious diagnosis implying that 'those whose economies were damaged by harsh conditionalities of IMF, years of exploitation of their mineral resources by rich countries in the past, with the same exploitation still going on by the multinationals…are to blame for their estates' (Mehdi 2006: 137). This leads theorists of polarization to question whether liberalization really presents countries in the global south much opportunity to become anything other than economic 'failures'. For Latin America and sub-Saharan Africa, the opening up of national economies to the IMF model was seen to represent a compromise of national interests in favour of those of the global free market, producing disastrous social consequences.

The fortunes of Latin American economies had been precariously placed for some time, as countries including Brazil, Argentina and Mexico secured a glut of high-interest loans to aid industrialization and infrastructure programmes in the 1960s and 1970s. The weight of borrowing had been made possible by their continuous economic growth, but following the world economic downturn and stagflation crisis at the beginning of the 1980s the fall in prices and demand for developing country exports, as well a sudden upturn in world interest rates, caused a region-wide debt crisis leaving the region owing $66 billion by 1982. The IMF and the World Bank saw the crisis as largely attributable to irresponsible government overspending and the failure to control inflation, and responded by issuing structural adjustment programmes to prioritize debt repayment and liberalize economies under the tutelage of the Washington Consensus. As a result, the 1980s became known as a 'lost decade' for Latin American economies, as attempts to repay debts were rapidly outpaced by the spiralling rate of interest, leaving the region owing $698 billion by 1998. At the same time, liberalization programmes such as cuts to public spending, privatization of assets and opening up markets to foreign direct investment (FDI) were implemented to create a 'pull-up' effect for failing economies. Instead, theorists of polarization saw this as compounding Latin America's problems, as its economies were restructured to serve the interests of the global economy instead of a population rapidly slipping into poverty. Privatization and FDI initiatives would generate massive profits for foreign investors, but were achieved with the assistance of investment-friendly tax breaks, meaning that the countries themselves received little from such wealth-creating enterprises. Forced to prioritize its repayment of skyrocketing debts while at the mercy of the freedoms enjoyed by foreign investors, the 'relief'-driven Washington Consensus served more to underline the region's inescapable dependency on the global market and its bank creditors and investors in the global north.

Assessing the effects of the debt crisis, the South Centre, a policy think tank for the developing world, found that liberalization had significantly damaged socio-economic conditions for a large part of the region, and was responsible for a widening of the north–south gap in market-generated wealth and income. Regardless of the region's initial debt problems, the Centre concluded that liberalization policies were not in the interests of the global south and had favoured instead the 'dynamic and powerful countries' of the global north. Ultimately, they argued that 'a fully liberalized regime...would not necessarily promote widespread growth and development or take account of developing countries' preoccupations' (South Centre 1997: 2). Compounding matters further, the Centre also contended that the East Asian economies – the perceived 'success stories' of liberalization and resultant example for Latin America to follow – had in fact deviated significantly from the Washington Consensus programme, and had maintained 'draconian import controls' to protect their home markets. Ironically it was only in the 1990s that the pace of liberalization would accelerate in East Asia, a move that would prove a contributing factor, at least in part, to the 1997–8 financial crisis (see Chapter 2).

Adding to the legacy of unfettered liberalization strategies in the 1980s, Bello (2009) has argued that prioritization of debt repayment and implementation of liberalization programmes in both in Latin America and the Far East has contributed to a contemporary global food shortage. Among the aims of IMF liberalization policies was to produce a large-scale globally integrated capitalist market for industrial agriculture, one that would provide greater overall efficiency and prosperity. In sub-Saharan Africa, bank policies pushed governments to cut or eliminate fertilizer subsidies, decontrol prices and privatize in order to open up local food systems to the global marketplace. These reforms implemented a model of industrial agriculture used first and most effectively in Brazil. However, according to Bello, the Brazilian model 'is not one that should elicit much enthusiasm from anyone'. He explains:

> The Brazilian agro-enterprise is part of a larger system of global industrial agriculture marked by large agribusiness combines, monopolistic trading companies, long-distance transportation of food, and supermarkets catering largely to the global elite and upper middle class. This globalized system of production has created severe strains on the environment, marginalized large numbers of people from the market, and contributed to greater poverty and income disparities within countries and globally. (Bello 2009: 10)

Questions as to the priorities and efficiencies of a global industrial agricultural system were also asked in the case of the Philippines: much like Latin America, the IMF's structural adjustment programmes prioritized debt repayment, resulting in reduced investment in agriculture. The industry was dealt a further blow when the Philippines' entry into the WTO in 1995 forced the cutting of tariffs. Having seen its own agricultural sector crippled by liberalization, the government was placed in the absurd position of having to import at competitive global prices the very same food it used to produce itself more cheaply. In sub-Saharan Africa, Bello argues that the IMF's micromanagement of many of its economies in the 1980s had the effect of doubling poverty levels in the region. Moreover, failure was deemed to be the countries' fault due to their inability to compete effectively in the global agricultural market. Bello cites one significant and hopeful act of resistance in the case of Malawi, which in 2006 rejected the IMF's programmes in favour of subsidizing its own agricultural production, a move that caused an instant improvement in lowering poverty relations. Yet theorists of polarization see these market-dependencies as difficult for struggling countries in the global south to resist. Ultimately, their fate is dictated by the requirements of the global market: a market that invariably prioritizes profit-making – in this case, through supplying multinational supermarkets in the global north – above the less-lucrative issue of human need.

3.5 Polarization within the nation-state: the case of Russia in the 1990s

Theories of polarization, following Wallerstein's original model, have traditionally viewed economic divergences occurring between nation states and regions, thus producing a clear north–south divide. Yet this stands as structurally oppositional to liberalization's fluid and flexible notion of global free trade – capital ultimately has the capacity to transcend regional contexts, meaning that economic prosperity should not, at least in theory, produce a *regional* polarization of economic power. Add to this the argument made by liberalization theorists that economic prosperity today depends more on the access and implementation of ideas, rather than on natural resources, should core–peripheral relations not in fact be in a position of constant flux?

The answer is, perhaps, yes and no: Wallerstein's original world-systems approach does allow for movement between core and periphery, as in the case of Japan, but he argues that the hegemonic balance of global economic power has remained largely unchallenged. Others are not so sure, arguing that the north–south divide offers a crude and increasingly outdated way of understanding the flows of global polarization. Yet this does not necessarily mean the end of polarization as a process: rather, it has been argued that the new global division of labour cultivated by the IMF and the World Bank has simply 'reorganized' patterns of global inequality and exclusion, whereupon humanity has been divided into a 'new architecture' of winners and losers which cuts across territorial boundaries (Held and McGrew 2007: 133).

This transformation has not gone unnoticed by Wallerstein himself, who argues today that world-systems theory not only polarizes nation-states; rather, core–periphery should be seen also as a relationship of production, meaning that polarization can take place *within* as well as *between* individual states. This does mean, of course, that some countries – such as the United States – can still be predominantly core-like in their economic processes, with others remaining largely peripheral. Nevertheless, Wallerstein's point is that the rise of the capitalist world economy comfortably precedes and transcends the supremacy of any individual nation-state, as monopolies always have the capacity to self-liquidate (Schouten 2008). What remains integral to global relations, however, is the capitalist system itself.

Perhaps the most pertinent case of intrastate polarization is that of post-communist Russia. Fukuyama (1991) saw the demise of the Soviet Union as marking a watershed moment in modern history, as the liberal-democratic nations of the West finally lost their key ideological competitor. Having endured the inconsistencies and market stagnation of state-regulated economies while the rest of the world reconnected to market liberalism, the fall of communism initiated a breakneck race in the early 1990s to create a Western-style democracy and free market in Russia (Hoffman 2002; Silverman and Yanowitch 2000).

Central to the IMF's recommendations for transforming post-Soviet collectivist states into free market economies was a tactic known as 'shock therapy'. By suddenly releasing the price and currency controls while simultaneously withdrawing state subsidies and trade restrictions, shock therapy is said to provide a motor for competition, via the ensuing scramble for ownership and profit. Economist Jeffrey Sachs pointed to the relative successes of the economic liberalization programme undertaken by post-war West Germany in the late 1940s, where shock therapy had the effect of kick-starting the German economy.

In January 1992, the Russian economy freed prices on all goods and services. Six months later laws were passed granting the immediate privatization of 80 per cent of state enterprises, from pencil factories to oil refineries. As the privatizations unfurled, President Boris Yeltsin announced on 20 August 1992 that Russia was about to become a stakeholding society. Every citizen was to be issued with a voucher worth 10,000 roubles (the equivalent of an average monthly wage) that they could exchange for shares in the companies that employed them, or in any other former state enterprise. Yeltsin pledged that there would be 'millions of owners rather than a handful of millionaires' (Levy and Scott-Clarke 2004).

Yet shock therapy would prove to have divisive social consequences, as, for all Yeltsin's rhetoric, the people remained unschooled and largely ignorant of venture capitalism, having endured many years of collectivism, food shortages and economic strife. As a result, many saw the voucher as a glorified banknote instead of a valuable investment, and chose to exchange them for money or supplies, often at wildly varying valuations. As a result, entrance into Yeltsin's stakeholder society would prove to be a non-starter for most of Russia's citizens. Instead, privatization led primarily to asset stripping and monopolization from so-called 'oligarchs' – the small Russian elite of opportunistic entrepreneurs who possessed both the knowledge of the true value of their purchases and the economic capital to quickly monopolize their ownership (see Hoffman 2002).

Significantly too, the oligarchs were able to capitalize on the green and underdeveloped nature of Russia's economic infrastructure. According to Stiglitz (2002), the liberalization programme as advocated by the IMF was largely culpable. For most of the Western nations wishing to start a market economy, the basic market institutions of capitalist trade were already in place to build from. By contrast, post-communist Russia required the whole-sale creation of market institutions: its banking system had no experience of market competition, having been restricted purely to garnering savings and providing the funds for the country's central planning agency. Similarly, its legal system had no experience of legislating for commercial disputes, non-payment of loans, bankruptcy procedures and the upholding of 'fair' competition, meaning that the hurried implementation of shock therapy went crucially unaccompanied by a safety-net of legal accountability. This opened the doors for illicit practices to be implemented by managers inside firms, notably the wiping out of ownership records of minority shareholders from the voucher scheme while siphoning off company assets for personal gain. Compounding matters even further, the oligarchs recognized that the Russian economy was both unstable and overvalued and decided instead to transfer their riches to offshore bank accounts, or invest it in the booming US stock market (Stiglitz 2002: 144). As a result, billions of dollars generated by pri-vatization was transferred overseas, leaving a gaping vacuum of real capital in Russia's economy.

As expected, the monopolization of unregulated capital had a significant polarizing effect on Russia's population, with more than 50 per cent of chil-dren living in families in poverty by 1998. Recalling Milanovic's findings, shock therapy effectively liquidated Russia's middle classes, as rapid inflation both wiped out their savings and shrunk the real value of their wages. With their standard of living now lacking in support from education and healthcare authorities, emigration for many represented the only chance of salvation.

One can of course observe that any transition from communism to a mar-ket economy would result in some increase in inequality. However, it can also be argued that within the IMF's recommendations for shock therapy was the naive assumption that a society raised on the principles of communism with no inherited wealth or inequality as a starting point would create a sound socio-economic basis for a more egalitarian and meritocratic market economy. In practice, there would be no such level playing field.

3.6 The anti-global capitalism movement

What, then, is to be done? We have already established that structuralist theo-rists have presented different suggestions on how to combat systemic polari-zation. Prebisch called for controlled industrialization as a means of achieving reform. Frank advised peripheral countries to 'opt out' of the system as a pre-requisite for a socialist revolution at the national level. Wallerstein suggested that nothing less than the overhaul of the entire system, and its replacement with a socialist world-system, would do the trick. Yet these are perhaps famil-iar alternatives which arguably retain a preoccupation with Marxist notions of state-dominated collectivism and are thus seen by many as increasingly incompatible with the contemporary context of trans-territorial, free-flowing global networks. By contrast, the freedoms afforded by liberalization argu-ably provide a 'better fit' to the fluid architecture of global society today. This view complements Fukuyama's claim to an 'end of history' following the collapse of the Soviet Union (and by proxy, Marxist politics in general), as it was seen that liberal democracy now stood triumphantly as the uncontested model for building a safe and prosperous global society.

Yet the cases of Latin America, sub-Saharan Africa and Russia all suggest that liberalization's own solutions to poverty and inequality have created more problems than they managed to solve. At a structural level, we have seen the argument made for widespread, systemic polarization where the fate of the global poor is at the mercy of a fluctuating, amoral global mar-ket. The market itself is of course prone to failure, but has nevertheless been ring-fenced by nation-states and institutions such as the IMF and the WTO, which are convinced by its virtues. For critics of capitalism, the safeguarding of liberalization reveals hegemonic motives: with unelected global economic governing bodies acting on behalf of economically powerful governmental actors, it is no wonder that the global economy has polarized rich and poor. As a result, this 'democratic deficit' is said to provoke a greater need for organized resistance than ever before. Yet as ever with radical politics, there has historically been a problem identifying the actual *agent* of change. For sure, structural overhaul of any kind must involve the subaltern itself, but can it begin and end with the south?

For many, the new era of global resistance to neo-liberal capitalism for-mally announced itself in December 1999 at meeting of the WTO in Seattle (Tabb 2001; Castells 2004; Santos 2006). The meeting was abruptly shut down as a result of the actions of around 70,000 demonstrators. Provocative and anarchic protests were met with heavy-handed policing leading to vio-lent confrontations, the use of teargas and baton rounds, providing dramatic media images that were broadcast across the world. Although similar acts of protest had already taken place throughout the 1990s, Seattle represented a new radicalized activism hitherto under the radar for the majority of the world's population, yet one capable of publicly discrediting the neo-liberal project for all of the world to see.

Unlike traditional protest organizations, the movement is rather amor-phous both in its politics and its membership, and has been called many things: the global justice movement, the alternative globalization movement, the movement of movements, even (misleadingly) the 'anti-globalization' movement. Supporters have hailed it as an emerging new superpower, a manifestation of what Richard Falk (1993) called for when he spoke of a 'grassroots surge' of 'transnational militancy', but one that is also distinct from past movements, rejecting the intellectual vanguardism of the 'old left' in favour of an anti-hierarchical network of cross-global activist groupings. According to the Notes from Nowhere collective (2003: 16), the movement 'is in constant flux...swaps ideas and tactics across oceans, shares strategies between cultures and continents, gathers in swarms and dissolves, only to swarm again elsewhere'. The sociologist Boaventura de Sousa Santos (2006) characterizes the movement as a form of 'insurgent cosmopolitanism', as its broad and diverse membership is not dominated by any one class or institution (see also Cleveland 2003). As a result, traditional left institutions such as labour unions operate now alongside a wide range of fellow opponents to global injustices including indigenous movements – notably the Mexican *Zapatistas*, seen as a principal inspiration for many in the movement: peasant groups; anarchist direct action groups such as Black Block, SmashEDO and Reclaim the Streets; students and intellectuals; NGOs and social movement organizations such as Greenpeace; and organized forums and networks such as People's Global Action and the World Social Forum (WSF) (see Santos 2008). As the list implies, the movement incorporates sub-groups from the global south as well as the global north, thus giving greater credence to the belief that the movement is no vanguard acting on behalf of the repressed but an authentic voice of the world subaltern itself.

Politically, the movement is said to be united not by an unrelenting commitment to a single ideological narrative but rather by a more simple common belief that 'another world is possible' (which is also the WSF's slogan). Such ideological openness incorporates a wide range of sub-movements ranging from the more 'corrective' approaches to global capitalism such as Make Poverty History and Oxfam's Make Trade Fair campaign, to the more radical anti-corporate activities of direct action guerrilla movements. This of course infers a number of ideological tensions, but theorists of the movement claim that this does not undermine the movement's overall objective to pressurize governments and NGOs for greater social and economic justice: ultimately, the movement is united enough in its opposition to neo-liberal capitalism to continue generating acts of protest *à la* Seattle. Radical thinkers Hardt and Negri (2005) characterize the movement as a global 'disunified multitude' requiring the avoidance of fixed utopias to allow the movement to campaign effectively on range of global themes. These include the economic polarization of the global north and south through interest-fuelled debt dependencies, as exemplified by the pre-millennial Drop the Debt campaign; environmental politics and the absence of multinational corporate responsibility; the lack of labour protection brought about by the amoral fluctuations of the global free market; the rights and freedoms of indigenous populations as popularized by the Zapatistas and Ecuador's CONAIE; and the economic monopolization of the market by multinational consumer brands as described in Naomi Klein's influential polemic, *No Logo* (2000).

Just as the flexibility of its political agenda is deemed to be a sign of strength rather than weakness, the apparent absence of organizational structure is also seen to enhance the movement's effectiveness. This is justified on the basis that a political project as amorphous and multifaceted as neo-liberalism can only be effectively fought by a movement which is itself similarly amorphous and multifaceted. Crucially, what binds the movement together is its interconnectedness through communications technologies, with the internet creating new opportunities for groups and individuals to connect locally, nationally and globally: inspired by the 'informational' guerrilla tactics of the *Zapatistas*, the internet provides unprecedented opportunities for the movement to gain further solidarity by spreading media-literate and eye-catching messages across the world. Interconnectedness of course also offers greater opportunities for the creation of mediated events to help draw attention to the movement. This capacity was evident in the Seattle protests: rather than being masterminded by a central planning group, the *breadth* of the event itself was largely the unplanned outcome of a multitude of interrelated and intercommunicative sub-groups all turning up to demonstrate on behalf of their own specific cause (i.e., as labour union workers, farmers or environmentalists), but also to protest collectively as mutual opponents of neo-liberal global capitalism. The end result is a movement that could mobilize itself anywhere across the globe at any time, with each and every sub-group a small yet significant 'node on the network' of the anti-global capitalist movement.

As expected, the landmark success of Seattle paved the way for a succession of comparable demonstrations, particularly at global governance events including the World Economic Forum meeting in 2000, the 2001 G8 summit in Genoa, the 2005 G20 summit in Gleneagles and, most recently, the G20 summit in London in the aftermath of the credit crunch in 2009. With the dramatic, televisual nature of these protests making them prominent 'global events', the mass media has increasingly become a key arena in which protest politics are played out. Yet this has also created new problems for the movement's intention to promote its message. Since Seattle, the unpredictable and sometimes destructive nature of these protests has resulted in increasingly aggressive police tactics, resulting in the death of a protestor at the Genoa demonstrations in 2001. In this case, both the police and protestors claimed provocation by the other, though the resultant media stigma attached to the movement's 'militant' factions as akin to a 'dangerous folk devil' (Rosie and Gorringe 2009). This caused a great deal of soul-searching among activists within the movement, arguably exposing the fragility of its unison under the broad banner of 'global justice'.

Such characterizations were certainly out in force during the London G20 protests in 2009, though the death of an innocent bystander as an indirect consequence of unprovoked police violence shifted much of the spotlight away from the stigmatized 'anarchists' and towards heavy-handed policing strategies. Amid the chaos and finger-pointing, it became harder to deduce whether the actual message of the movement's reason for protest had been successfully put across to the general public. With protestors having to rethink how it balances effective activism with maintaining a positive media image it can be argued that the movement – at least in its present configuration – faces a somewhat uncertain future.

Biography Box 7:   Naomi Klein

Naomi Klein (1970–) is a Canadian activist and author who burst onto the scene with the publication of *No Logo* in 2000, which many people hailed as the manifesto for the emerging anti-global capitalism movement. She has followed this up with numerous critical commentaries on the war in Iraq, the global financial crisis and environmental disasters.

3.7   An alternative? Deglobalization

Associated with this movement are numerous academics as well as activists, some schooled in the Wallersteinian tradition but not all necessarily so, who seek to replace the dominant, polarizing model of the 'new world order' with a democratic 'one world community' committed to international law, human rights, environmental justice and grassroots sustainable development: a 'globalization-from-below':

> Globalization-from-below...aims to restore to communities the power to nurture their environments; to enhance the access of ordinary people to the resources they need; to democratize local, national, and transnational political institutions; and to impose pacification on conflicting power centers. (Brecher, Brown Childs and Cutler 1993: xv)

Walden Bello restates this commitment in more striking terms: what is required, he tells us, is not some mere adjustment *within* the system, for that would 'be merely marginal...(and) might merely postpone a bigger crisis' (2004: 107). Bello would hardly be convinced by Legrain's insistence that economic globalization if handled properly benefits rich *and* poor and that what is ultimately required is a *better* globalization, one which involves active participation from governments *contra* the market fundamentalism of the liberalization model (Legrain 2003: 326). He calls instead for an entire *paradigm shift*, drawing inspiration from Thomas Kuhn's famous work in the philosophy of science. 'A vision of a new world may be entrancing,' he says cautiously, 'but it will remain a vision without a hard strategy for realizing it, and part of that strategy is the deliberate dismantling of the old' (Bello 2004: 107–8). What, then, would such a strategy for ending the system of rampant trade liberalization actually entail? Bello is insistent that for the anti-global capitalism movement to have any real influence, it must work with the southern delegations to the financial institutions to secure their shared interests; it must work with national movements in the south and the north to maintain the pressure on their respective governments; and it must continue to organize visible mass protests (*ibid.*: 111). Then, following this *deconstruction*, it must involve itself in the active *reconstruction* of the global economy, through the advocacy of what Bello calls *deglobalization*. It is worth reproducing in full what he means by this, because despite what it seems to suggest, this is not a proposal for 'opting out' in the tradition of the dependency theorists of old:

> Deglobalization is not about withdrawing from the international economy. It is about reorienting economies from the emphasis on production for export to production for the local market.

- Drawing most of a country's financial resources for development from within rather than becoming dependent on foreign investment and foreign financial markets;
- Carrying out the long-postponed measures of income redistribution and land redistribution to create a vibrant internal market that would be the anchor of the economy and create the financial resources for investment;
- De-emphasizing growth and maximizing equity in order radically to reduce environmental disequilibrium;
- Not leaving strategic economic decisions to the market but making them subject to democratic choice;
- Subjecting the private sector and the state to constant monitoring by civil society;
- Creating a new production and exchange complex that includes community cooperatives, private enterprises and state enterprises, and excludes TNCs;
- Enshrining the principle of subsidiarity in economic life by encouraging production of goods to take place at the community and national level if it can be done at reasonable cost in order to preserve community. (*Ibid.*: 113–14)

Biography Box 8:   Walden Bello

Walden Bello (1945–) is one of the most pre-eminent scholars to have emerged from the Philippines. Professor of Sociology and Public Administration at the University of the Philippines Diliman, he is also the Executive Director of Focus on the Global South, a Bangkok-based NGO which he helped to form in 1975. He is rightly considered to be one of the most important analysts of the limitations of global capitalism but is equally well-respected for his work as an activist, and he has combined the two in such publications as *Deglobalization* (2004) and, more recently, *The Food Wars* (2009).

Bello's approach is supported by Vandana Shiva, a major environmentalist, feminist activist and theoretician from India. Shiva has promoted the idea of 'Earth democracy' and has made clear the case that the current discourse on the 'global' is not synonymous with the 'planetary':

> The way the 'global' has been structured, the North (as the globalized local) has all rights and no responsibilities, and the South has no rights, all responsibilities. 'Global ecology' at this level becomes a moralization of immorality. It is empty of any ethics for planetary living. It is based not on concepts of universal humanity, but on universal bullying. (1993: 58–9)

Shiva thus foregrounds the ecological dimensions of global transformation more explicitly than Bello. At the heart of her analysis is a distinction between two categories of the 'global': that of the dominant discourse, which even if it acknowledges ecological damage is so bound up in imperialistic projects that it cannot effectively deal with such problems, and the empowering 'ecological category'. The challenge ahead, she claims, is to rethink the discourse on the environment, away from the current 'lopsided view' according to which the 'construction of the global environment narrows the options for the South, while increasing them for the North' (*ibid.*: 57). Solutions can only come from shifting the northern discourse away from 'green imperialism' towards 'green environmentalism'.

Biography Box 9:   Vandana Shiva

Vandana Shiva (1952–) is an Indian-born environmental activist and feminist and one of the pioneering names in the eco-feminist movement. She is the author of numerous books and articles, including most recently *Earth Democracy* (2005) and *Soil, Not Oil: Climate Change, Peak Oil and Food Insecurity* (2008).

3.8   Conclusion

In this chapter we have surveyed a range of contributions to the most public of all the debates concerning 'globalization', namely, whether that which has been called a 'new global economy' or a 'global marketplace' characterized by free trade is global at all, never mind new or free. Writers such as Hirst and Thompson, discussed in the previous chapter, clearly question the extent to which contemporary capitalism is any more 'global' than its nineteenth-century ancestor. Wallerstein and others have developed theoretical models inspired by Marxism to show the dynamics of exploitation in relative, structural terms. Wallerstein's 'core–periphery' model parallels the popular distinction that is made by left-wing academics and activists, not necessarily

Marxian, between the prosperous north and the exploited south. For such writers, including Bello, 'globalization' in respect of the economy is a myth, the reality is the increasing polarization of north and south, and the solution is a strategically executed process of *de*-globalization. Of course, as we have attempted to present in this chapter, polarization need not be limited to north–south relations – it is perfectly logical to consider it as a reality within a nation-state.

The polarization framework is thus introduced as a direct challenge to the assumptions contained within the liberalization framework, which is championed by right-wing liberals, enthusiastic advocates of free trade. But the 'debate' as intimated here is not so clear-cut as it might seem: it is by no means a simple case of either/or. Some critics on the left engage with the literature on liberalization without presenting polarization as an alternative. Similarly, some commentators challenge the assumptions made by those within the 'polarization' camp without necessarily resorting to a familiar pro-liberalization line. As Philippe Legrain (2003: 10) suggests, (economic) globalization need not be synonymous with privatization or deregulation, two staples of the liberalization argument, and if the liberalization model favoured by the New Right is neither an entirely accurate description of reality nor an entirely desirable one, that does not in itself negate the case for economic globalization in some form, which, after all, he suggests, 'cannot possibly be to blame for the wretched poverty of many African subsistence farmers. They don't trade, so they can't be harmed by it' (*ibid.*).

Of course, whether he is correct in this is precisely the issue under debate. The 'polarization' framework is an inherently moral one, but it can also be a practical one, and the question needs to be asked (and the answer not assumed!): if the global economy is one of inequality, *who* is harmed by it and, at the same time, *who* benefits from it? Bello, who is a passionate and articulate defender of the cause, makes clear the case for deglobalization as a strategy for re-empowering the local above and beyond any strategy for developing more transnational regulatory bodies (2004: 115). There are those, even on the left, who would say that he has somewhat missed the point. Certainly, many have accused Wallerstein and his collaborators of misunderstanding entirely the nature and dynamics of global capitalism. Wallerstein's model of the world-system, of 'core' and 'periphery', takes nation-states as its central actors. Not all north–south distinctions do the same: Bello, and many of the other writers associated with 'the movement', leave the question of actual power rather open, and probably do so deliberately, as they see little point in distinguishing between the economic and political power of nation-states *vis-à-vis* transnational corporations or indeed transnational regulatory bodies. They are, effectively, all part of the same *problem*. But for some sophisticated modern Marxists, that is not good enough: to address the problem of polarization one must first address the dynamics of capitalism, which, in its contemporary phase, is dominated by corporations and institutions which transcend nation-states, including transnational corporations which operate using transnational practices in an international division of labour and are often managed by members of a transnational capitalist class (Frobel, Heinrichs and Krey 1980; Sklair 1991; 2001; Villamil 1979). For such writers, if polarization is a problem, then it is one that is intrinsically bound up in the way late capitalism operates. We will return to such critiques, and discuss the alternative model of global society they either explicitly or implicitly present, in Chapter 7.

Americanization: The New American Empire

4

4.1 Introduction

In the last chapter we looked at the Marxian-inspired (but by no conventional means Marxist) work of Frank and Wallerstein. Neither of these writers speak directly of 'Americanization' or 'American empire'. What they do is introduce us to a way of seeing the world which focuses on *power relations*. Later writers, not necessarily located within the dependency or world-systems schools, have continued this general emphasis but with a more specific focus: rather than speak of the 'core', they target the single dominant world power, the 'last remaining superpower', the United States, to show how *it* exists in a power relationship with *the rest of* the world. Such writers often refer to this structural condition as one of American *imperialism*, and suggest that terms like 'globalization' and 'liberalization' serve merely to mask the reality of American political, economic and cultural power (Chomsky 2003; Gowan 1999, 2002; Harvey 2003; Hudson 2003; Panitch 2000; Panitch and Leys 2003; Panitch and Miliband 1991; Petras and Veltmeyer 2001). For such scholars, the nation-state, or at least one nation-state in particular, remains central to our understanding of the global condition, as it protects its national self-interest and asserts its authority over the rest of the world.

This view is very much in vogue in contemporary global studies, particularly in the light of the American 'war on terror', the invasions of Afghanistan and Iraq, the defiance of UN resolutions, and the neo-conservative influence upon the Bush presidency. However, the 'Americanization' framework is not limited solely to the political-economic sphere. Commentators have for some time preferred terms such as 'Americanization' and 'cultural imperialism' to 'cultural globalization' when describing how American cultural values and practices have been exported to other parts of the world, largely through American-owned media (Tunstall 1994; Tomlinson 1991; Bourdieu and Wacquant 1999). The concept of Americanization has even taken a stronghold in the sociology of sport (Kidd 1991; Klein 1991; McKay and Miller 1991).

This chapter will trace the origins of the Americanization debate, particularly in cultural and media studies, before examining its recent application to the field of international politics. The primary argument in this tradition is that – whether it is through the exporting of cultural-ideological products which 'reproduce' American values, or through the more overtly repressive means of political-military coercion – US involvement overseas is creating a culture of dependency and the US itself has effectively become the imperial capital. Whether or not it is appropriate to speak of 'empire' in this context is central to this debate.

4.2   The theory of American empire

The concept of imperialism is far from new in the Marxian lexicon. In his book *Imperialism: The Highest Stage of Capitalism*, V. I. Lenin identified how the capitalist economy contained within the borders of a nation-state would become stagnant in the era of monopoly capitalism, wherein mergers and monopolies threaten the drive for competition which fuels it. Capitalism is ever a hungry beast, seeking out new markets wherever it can find them as soon as old ones have been exhausted. So, although empire-building and military conquests pre-date modern capitalism, the current form of imperialism (Lenin was writing in 1916) is historically specific, in so far as it represents the strategic project of meeting the expansive desires of capitalism.

What certainly *is* relatively new is the desire by scholars often from the traditional left to locate contemporary debates around 'globalization' within the framework of imperialism (see, among others, Amin 2001; Gowan, Panitch and Shaw 2001; Harvey 2003; Petras and Veltmeyer 2001; Went 2003). This debate was partly inspired by the publication of Hardt and Negri's ground-breaking *Empire* (2000). These authors, arguing from a post-Marxist perspective, describe the current global dynamics of power as a 'decentred' empire governed by a multiplicity of powerful agents including the United States, the G8 and the various transnational corporations. Today's 'empire', they claim, is transnational and hybrid, so far removed from earlier models of imperialism as to warrant a new intellectual armoury to make sense of it. Clearly with this 'postmodern' challenge in mind, in their introduction to the 2004 *Socialist Register*, Leo Panitch and Sam Gindin suggest that Marxism needs a new theory of imperialism to take into account the new stage of (global) capitalism. They suggest that, while for many years the concept of imperialism drifted off the agenda for many on the political left, contemporary conditions demand:

> a new theorization of imperialism, one that will transcend the limitations of the old Marxist 'stagist' theory of inter-imperial rivalry, and allow for a full appreciation of the historical factors that have led to the formation

of a unique American informal empire. This will involve understanding how the American state developed the capacity to eventually incorporate its capitalist rivals, and oversee and police 'globalization' – i.e. the spread of capitalist social relations to every corner of the world. The theory must be able to answer the question of what made plausible the American state's insistence that it was not imperialistic, and how this was put into practice and institutionalized; and, conversely, what today makes implausible the American state's insistence that it is not imperialistic, and what effects its lack of concealment might have in terms of its attractiveness and its capacity to manage global capitalism and sustain its global empire. (Panitch and Gindin 2003: 4)

This is precisely the challenge that David Harvey takes up in his 2003 contribution, *The New Imperialism* (Harvey 2003). Harvey is quick to point out that American imperialism is not in itself a new thing, but the contemporary form of it is quite distinctive. There have, though, been many such forms since the United States assumed its absolute global hegemonic position after the Second World War:

American imperialism...has lurched in unstable fashion from one vague...conception of empire to another. If Bush the younger betrays a certain Napoleonic impulse...Clinton's approach...more resembled that of the Ottoman empire at its height...soft power was preferred to hard, and the rest of the world was treated with considerable multicultural tolerance...The construction of American power under Roosevelt, Truman, and Eisenhower right through to Nixon, on the other hand, mirrored the subordinate client state approach of the Soviets rather than anything else, with the difference that Japan, unlike Hungary or Poland, was left free to develop its own economy provided it remained politically and militarily compliant with US wishes. (Harvey 2003: 6)

The contemporary phase, Harvey argues, can best be defined as a phase of *capitalist* imperialism. Traditionally, empire building has been driven by the logic of *territory*, but in capitalist imperialism it is dictated by the logic of *capital* (Harvey 2003: 27; following Arrighi 1994). These logics have traditionally existed in a contradictory, dialectical relationship with one another (Harvey 2003: 30), and while the logic of capital comes to the fore in capitalist imperialism, it does not do so in any straightforward way and where necessary the territorial logic resurfaces (*ibid.*: 33). Harvey asserts that the classical phase of bourgeois imperialism from 1945 came to an end in around 1970, to be replaced with a new *neo-liberal* imperialistic project. In this respect, Harvey's analysis overlaps somewhat with that of Hardt and Negri (2000) who suggest that America's project of 'European-style' imperialism came to a premature climax with defeat in Vietnam. The key difference is in respect of what followed – for Hardt and Negri the emergent decentred empire, for Harvey the neo-liberal ascendency. However, according to Harvey, even this project reached its point of exhaustion and went into decline at around the turn of the millennium. Having successfully established its hegemonic role through a half-century of bourgeois military and political imperialism, cultural imperialism and subsequently capitalist imperialism, for much of that time largely directed to staving off the threat of the Soviet Union, American imperialism found itself at the dawn of the new millennium in unstable waters. President Bush, incited by the architects of the Project for the New American Century, found it necessary to 'flex military muscle as the only clear absolute power it [i.e., America] has left' (*ibid.*: 77). As Noam Chomsky states, in similar vein, American's imperialist strategy is based on abandoning any commitment to, and undermining the legitimacy of, international law as a policy goal (Chomsky 2003: 28). The blueprint for this new imperialism was contained in the Bush administration's National Security Strategy of 2002, which 'declared the right to resort to force to eliminate any perceived challenge to US global hegemony' (Chomsky 2003: 3). Harvey's point is well made (as is Chomsky's), and although he himself does not present the example, the difference between the one form of imperialism and the other can be clearly identified if one contrasts the 2002 Iraq War with the previous Gulf War of 1990: if the 1990 war was primarily a war for economic interests, a neo-liberal war, which had favourable ideological consequences, the 2002 war was a heavily moralistic and imperialistic project, driven by the perceived need to protect a way of life, albeit with favourable economic consequences, a neo-conservative war (see O'Byrne 2004 for more on this).

Biography Box 10:   Noam Chomsky

Noam Chomsky (1928–) is one of the most famous intellectuals of the late twentieth century. Although his disciplinary background is in the area of linguistics, and he continues to serve as the Institute Professor of Linguistics at the Massachusetts Institute of Technology, it is as an activist and an outspoken critic of American foreign policy, articulated in such works as *Hegemony or Survival* (2003), that he is best known. The contributor to numerous documentaries and films, he is celebrated as the greatest champion of the American libertarian left. In 2005 the British magazine *Prospect* named him as the leading living public intellectual in the world.

4.3   The making of modern America

It probably seems inconceivable to us that any other nation-state could stake as strong a claim to determining the order of globalization as the United States. This arguably has much to do with the country's unique history as a young and inherently *modern* superpower, consciously founded with the intention of creating an 'ideal' society built upon a free and just political system and sound moral fortitude. Moreover, aspects of 'Americanness' and American character (Rauchway 2006) are recognizable motors within the engine of global change, from its desire to singularize the world economy under free-market values, to its promotion of democratic values and consumer culture. In order to understand America's relationship to the dynamics of global change, we must now turn to its history and origins.

Writing in the late nineteenth century, the French political thinker Alexis de Tocqueville (1968) noted that America's status as geographically isolated from, yet inherently and dynamically interconnected to Europe had given it a unique and enviable position to take the political and philosophical values of democracy, equality and meritocracy – chained by centuries of elites and traditions in the 'old world' – and apply it to a new and open land. Like many, de Tocqueville saw the origins of American values and labour ethics in its unique and peculiar history. Following early European expeditions of the fifteenth century, its population swelled as the British, French and Spanish colonists obtained royal charters to establish new settlements across America's vast territory. Initial groups migrating from Britain were mostly religious puritans and separatists and came with the intention of establishing towns and states that adhered to their own strict moral code. The result was the establishing of 13 colonies along the east coast (including Boston and Philadelphia). Spain, too, established Florida on the east coast, and later ventured north of its colonial territory from Mexico and Latin America to take the pacific coast. In the middle, France established the large colonial territory of Louisiana, which, although sparsely populated, incorporated 15 of today's states running from Mississippi to the northern territory of Canada, with Quebec as its major trading centre.

By the mid-eighteenth century, European empire building was faced with a number of problems. On the one hand, maintaining and defending territorial occupation was proving to be a costly business – for the French, the Seven Years' War resulted in the loss of Canadian possessions to the British, whereas Britain was itself had been seriously drained of financial resources as a consequence. On the other hand, the Anglo-American colonies had been enjoying a prosperous economy and their own democratic systems of local government. They would grow increasingly wary of Britain's attempt to strengthen its control over the North American empire, this being stoked considerably when it was agreed that debt from the war with France would be funded by excessively taxing the colonies themselves. This provoked acts of rebellion to British law (notably the 'Boston Tea Party' of 1773) and calls for freedom from empire, culminating in the War of Independence in 1775. American grievances over the restrictions to freedom imposed by its colonial masters, together with a faith in Enlightenment ideas of nature and contract, inspired Thomas Jefferson's famous 'Declaration of Independence'.

The eventual overpowering of the British forces resulted in victory for the patriots and the granting of independence to the United States at the Treaty of Paris in 1783. Yet independence required structural unity, and the pragmatism of joining together such disparate territories with the shared objective of freedom from empire rule masked a lack of common interest both economically and geographically. Echoing Enlightenment political thought, the federalists' response was draw up a social contract – a constitution – which was to be instituted by the people, for the people. James Madison, the Constitution's main architect, advocated a strong national government which possessed legislative, executive and judicial powers, but one that was also constantly limited by and accountable to internal checks and balances. This carefully constructed compromise of freedom and security, supported by the unique governmental systems of the Senate and the House of Representatives, was sufficient for 17 eastern states to ratify the Constitution by 1803. Its famous preamble runs as follows:

> We, the people of the United States, in order to form a more perfect Union, establish justice, insure domestic tranquility, provide for the common defense, promote the general welfare, and secure the blessings of liberty to ourselves and our posterity, do ordain and establish this Constitution for the United States of America.

The argument has been made by a number of commentators that within the American Constitution and its definitions of legitimate sovereignty lay the necessary foundations for American imperialism, and potentially *Americanization* on a global scale. The historian Anders Stephanson (1995) argues that the evolution of American national identity – illustrated by its Constitution – has been marked by values such as freedom and liberty that are unusually universal in their reach. There is some conjecture, however, as to the origins of such guiding values. For Michael Hunt (2009), this represents a classic republicanism and an emphasis on Enlightenment values of progress, efficiency and control. This economic rationalism was an essential part of America's early expansion, as colonists quickly set up vast tobacco farms along the east coast as a means of setting up profitable trade relations with Europe. More nefariously, this was also expressed in the mass importation of slaves (notably omitted as subjects of the Constitution) from Africa to the British colonies from the early seventeenth century. Such values certainly underpin much of America's technological and consumerist imperialism today, as well as a commitment to a single economic world order with no 'rogue markets' or anti-capitalist ideologies to contend with.

For others, such as Stephanson and the historian Walter Hixson (2008), America's national ideology is bound up in 'messianic' tendencies, notably a Calvinist Protestant ethic of productive power with the intention of demonstrating the existence and divinity of God. The sober puritanical Calvinist denominations would later give way to newer groupings that placed far less emphasis on a 'trained and learned ministry', instead developing a 'universal salvation' more in tune with the political democracy of the Constitution (Jenkins 2003: 84).

The truth perhaps lies somewhere in the middle. Although Enlightenment rationalism and Calvinism both entail mutually oppositional models of emancipation, this curious paradox has arguably equipped American ideology with a belief in its own political virtue and sense of progress, and a moralist, missionary impulse in relation to itself and the rest of the world. Echoing Weber's theory of capitalism, this creates a particularly dynamic form of US sovereignty, arising not from (in the words of Hardt and Negri) the 'regulation of the multitude', but rather 'as the result of the productive synergies of the multitude'. Power is therefore 'not something that lords over us but something that we make', meaning that 'the emancipation of humanity from every transcendent power is grounded in the multitude's power to construct its own political institutions and constitute society' (Hardt and Negri 2000: 164–5). This ethic of productivity and the control of outside forces infers a specific *imperial expansionism*, which due to its constitutional embeddedness impacts ideologically upon citizens and politicians alike. The imperial nature of American nation building is clearly argued by Hardt and Negri:

> Liberty and the frontier stand in a relationship of reciprocal implication: every difficulty, every limit of liberty is an obstacle to overcome, a threshold to pass through. From the Atlantic to the Pacific extended a terrain of wealth and freedom, constantly open to new lines of flight. (*Ibid.*: 169)

American imperialism has arguably entailed two separate processes – one inland, and one outland. The first phase began with the seizure of lands from indigenous North American Indian tribes, whose people were considered more a 'particularly thorny element of nature' (*ibid.*: 170) than a population also worthy of liberty and constitutional rights. This was then followed by the establishment of a designated terrain for republican democracy – essentially the initial states of America. This territory would almost double following the United States' purchase of Louisiana in 1803 (subsequently to be divided into 15 individual states) giving vital trade access to the port of New Orleans and the opportunity to push for further expansion Westwards.

One can see that empire building was certainly integral to this expansion, with President Munroe reporting to Congress in 1822 that 'extent of territory...marks...the difference between a great and small power' (R. T. Robertson 2003: 134). Yet this empire building was unique in its productivity and rate of expansion during an era in which the European powers found themselves exhausting their economic and military resources in order to stave off colonial rebellion and discontent. In contrast, having overcome its own rebellion in the shape of the Civil War of 1861–5, America's inland empire began to expand economically on an unprecedented scale. Given the advantage of a single continuous mass of territory, economic coalescence began through the building of railroads, which helped bind the east to the west physically, and then allowing settlers and commerce to also bind the east to the west economically and culturally.

The railroads provided the matrix of exchange for an industrial economy to thrive in the last third of the nineteenth century – whereas for Great Britain the industrial revolution spanned a century, America's took only a third of that time. Between 1860 and 1900 industrial production increased in value from under $2,000 million a year to over $13,000 million, and the amount of capital invested in manufacturing soared from $1,000 million to almost $10,000 million. This was achieved through a combination of several factors. First, its advances in heavy industry, notably iron and steel production, provided modern America, among many things, with its engines, locomotives and skyscrapers. Second, productive possibilities were compounded by radical technological innovation, with the typewriter, the telephone and Thomas Edison's electric light counting as the major inventions of the era. Finally, a thirst for big business consolidated American industry with the creation of several major holding companies that began to dominate production markets. Employing radical methods of efficient production and aggressive competition, industrialists such as Andrew Carnegie (steel), John D. Rockefeller (oil) and later Henry Ford (motor cars) helped to America as the world's leading industrial nation by the turn of the century (M. A. Jones 1995: 295).

If these mega-industrialists were the visionaries of America's industrial empire, its engine was provided by the millions of immigrants who came to its shores over the latter nineteenth century. Even in an age of embryonic globalization and mass social movement, America's was a unique story: 'the country not only received far and away more immigrants than any other country, it received more kinds of immigrants from a wider variety of countries' (Rauchway 2006: 27). Whereas earlier migrations in American history were largely Europeans seeking religious freedom and 'a place on an American homestead', the late nineteenth century was dominated by 'proletarian mass migration' as millions of low-skilled workers sought a better-paying part of the global market (*ibid.*: 25).

Although this suggests that travelling to the United States was something of a rational choice for aspiring migrants, the decision also carried substantial ideological weight. Owing to the historical intertwining of Enlightenment philosophy, Protestant ethics of productive religious duty and the virtues of freedom and equality captured in the Declaration of Independence, the historian James Truslow Adams (1931) saw this as representing a fresh and attainable 'American dream' for migrants, one that went unrivalled by other nations:

> The American Dream is that dream of a land in which life should be better and richer and fuller for everyone, with opportunity for each according to ability or achievement...It is not a dream of motor cars and high wages merely, but a dream of social order in which each man and each woman shall be able to attain to the fullest stature of which they are innately capable, and be recognized by others for what they are, regardless of the fortuitous circumstances of birth or position. (1931: 404)

The belief in hard work, freedom and opportunity among new Americans further strengthened and distinguished America's political philosophy from other nation-states. Having already established a carefully layered system of government designed to minimize political and personal interference, the multicultural nature of its immigrant population only underlined such divisions further. As Rauchway argues, 'workers who spoke different languages and worshipped at different altars were more sensitive to the cultural divisions among them and less attuned to their shared economic interests', thus making support for any kind of socialist movement unlikely. What did unite this diverse multitude, however, were the universal American values embedded in its Constitution and the 'American dream' as envisioned by its burgeoning immigrant population. One might surmise that the inland empire building of the United States at this time resembled something of a local 'rehearsal' for global American imperialism that would take place in the next century.

4.4   The beginnings of American empire

By the twentieth century, the combination of cultural and religious factors, which had driven its internal expansion, inspired American eyes to look outwards. Robertson quotes one US senator arguing in 1903 that 'God...has made us the master organizers of the world to establish system where chaos reigns' (R. T. Robertson 2003: 135). If Americanization on a global scale was not always expressed in such overt terms, it was at least strongly implied in how it foresaw capital market expansion. Rapid industrialization had already placed America in a more prosperous position, having produced nearly 13 per cent of world trade in manufacturing by 1913 (*ibid*.: 134). The early twentieth century also saw America emerge as an attractive money-making opportunity to overseas investors, which helped build up sufficient financial capacity to become a major world lender (having already been a substantial borrower). This position and outlook would transform its fortunes into significant power during the First and Second world wars, where it would extend substantial credit to its belligerent allies (Rauchway 2006: 33).

But perhaps the biggest carrier of a comprehensive Americanization in the twentieth century was that of consumer culture. This is because it represented an economic rationality of opening up its economic market to the rest of the world so that it could attract new investors, consumers and above all, profit. This was certainly made clear by President William Taft, claiming that 'our surplus energy is beginning to look beyond our own borders to find the opportunity for the profitable use of our surplus capital and for markets for our manufacture' (R. T. Robertson 2003: 135).

Yet the rise of American consumerism also carried with it a missionary faith in American virtues of freedom, equality and opportunity, like those it had established in its inland empire – one that was seen to transcend class and tradition. In her study of American cultural imperialism, the historian Victoria de Grazia (2005) observes how Taft's successor, Woodrow Wilson, when addressing a convention of salesmen in 1916 called for America's 'democracy of business' to take the lead in 'the struggle for the peaceful conquest of the world'. This required studying 'the tastes and needs of the countries where the markets were being sought … [to] suit your goods to those tastes and needs'. This was the 'American way', and as if to dispel any question over the country's suitability for the task, he climaxed his speech with the following 'simple message':

> Let your thoughts and your imagination run abroad throughout the whole world, and with the inspiration of the thought that you are Americans and are meant to carry liberty and justice and the principles of humanity wherever you go, go out and sell goods that will make the world more comfortable and more happy, and convert them to the principles of America. (2005: 2)

For de Grazia, this was illustrative of the origins of America's quest for 'market empire' throughout the twentieth century, resulting in its replacing of Europe as the world's major cultural producer. This comprehensive, ideological exertion of 'soft power' (to use Joseph Nye's term) operated on a number of fronts. First, consumer companies sought to present consumption as liberation. This required the removal of determining forces such as tradition, social class and patriarchy in favour of 'freedom' and 'choice'. Its assault would be advanced through its marketing and selling of an exhaustible number of irresistible cultural commodities, from vacuum cleaners to Disney movies, all made easier by its labour-saving convenience mediums of the supermarket, the department store and the cinema. American consumer freedom sat in stark contrast to Europe's old bourgeois regime of 'aesthetic consumption', where distinctions of culture and taste had cultivated hierarchies of privilege over thousands of years. America, on the other hand, promoted a more even playing field, enabling the working classes their share of the 'good life'. As a result, when America's salesmen were extolling the virtues of the latest kitchen utensil, or Elvis Presley record, they were not just selling need or desire, they were selling *freedom*.

Second, if the surface level of cultural freedom and rampant commodity consumption appeared crass and superficial to the aesthetic consumers of Europe, this would be overcome by the marketing and selling of its rationale – in the form of the service ethic – in much the same way. De Grazia notes how American values were first sold in the establishing of its own Rotary clubs across Western Europe in the 1920s. These clubs, whose membership would consist largely of local business and professional leaders, embodied 'small town American virtues' including a pro-business mentality and the service ethic, but also fairness and communitarian acts. Moreover, the clubs attempted to break local and traditional hegemonies of class by being high-status and invitation-only, yet also potentially open to any member regard-less of race, political affiliation of religion. Of course, in their commitment to American business values Rotary clubs would attract a largely older and wealthy membership, but this was arguably the point: in appealing to those who upheld local and national peculiarities of class and tradition, America could legitimize its own practices to foreign markets and spread its message further.

4.5   The theory of cultural imperialism

The question of whether the marketing of American culture and values across the world was illustrative of American imperialism has been subject to much debate from the mid-twentieth century onwards. Fears about the spread of American popular culture and its perceived negative effects on indigenous cultures can be traced back at least to the 'mass culture' debates of the mid-twentieth century, and even beyond, to nineteenth-century cultural critics such as Matthew Arnold. Strinati (1995: 21–38) provides a useful survey of the contributions, from Arnold's quasi-elitist equating of Americanization with mass democracy, through F. R. Leavis's more overtly conservative fears that Americanized mass culture was threatening a distinctly British way of life, to left-wing contributions from the likes of George Orwell and Richard Hoggart, for whom this imported American culture was destroying the organic cultures of working-class communities. Hoggart (1958) spoke of a culturally vacuous 'shiny barbarism' taking over the lives of younger generations, and in particular was 'concerned about the manipulative and exploitative influence exercised over the work-ing-class community, most especially over its more vulnerable younger members, by the America of the Hollywood film, the cheap and brutal crime novel, 'milk bars' and juke-box music' (Strinati 1995: 28; following Hoggart 1958: 247).

There were, of course, those for whom this wave of Americanization in the immediate post-war era offered not homogeneity and cultural emptiness but diversity and the potential for resistance (Hebdige 1979). However, the vast majority of contributions to the 'Americanization of culture' debate focused critically on the extent to which the media industry was heavily dominated by, and supportive of the interests of, American capitalism. Two such contributions stand out here: Herbert Schiller's *Mass Communications and American Empire* was first published in 1969 and as its title suggests specifically makes the link between media technology and American power (1992); Jeremy Tunstall's *The Media are American* first appeared in 1977 and provides what for many still is the definitive account of the historical rise of American media influences world-wide, theoretically interrogated as 'media imperialism' (1994), although the author has recently come to reassess his position on this in the wake of US media decline and the relative prosperity of Asian media networks (Tunstall 2008).

Schiller's work, coming as it does from a more overtly Marxian perspective as an exercise in political economy rather than media studies, deals not so much with media forms as with media and communications technologies. Control over these technologies goes hand in hand with economic and political control. As American television extends worldwide, Schiller argues, the benefits for major corporations in respect of advertising are enormous. Writing at the beginning of an era of corporate transnationalism and global branding which our generation takes for granted, Schiller comments on how the 'big spenders', the corporations which spend most on television advertising in the United States, are the 'engines of commercialization in the West', who, 'long ago ... captured the radio spectrum in the United States. Now they are waging successful campaigns to extend their conquests to Europe, Africa and Asia' (Schiller 1992: 143). The relationship between the media and big business is historically contextualized in the light of the constitutional safeguards against government regulation of the media in the United States (*ibid.*: 191).

This is not to say, though, that the United States government has no control over its media – quite the opposite, in fact, as Schiller notes the close, interdependent relationship between major media corporations and elements within the government, not least the Department of Defense. In Schiller's bleak vision, it is only a short step from newspaper, radio and television, which are primarily media of advertising for the benefit of these 'big spenders', to developments in satellite technology:

> The American post-war imperial thrust is unblushingly evident in space communications. In this entirely new area of human capability and technical achievement, the ambitious commercial-political objectives of the American decision-making elite have been straight-forwardly elaborated. The space communications goals and the structures that have been established to achieve them reveal the bold mechanics of American power maneuvering for world position in a strategic sector. (*Ibid.*: 171).

As a Marxist, Schiller equates American media imperialism specifically to the project of global domination, the subjugation of the poorer nations and the suppression of class consciousness. Tunstall himself provides a neat summary of the political-economic agenda Schiller is predicting: 'False consciousness would be plugged via satellite into every human home' (Tunstall 1994: 39). Schiller's disciple Alan Wells then provided evidence of this hegemonic project by focusing on the power of United States corporations and interests over Latin American television (Wells 1972). Tunstall's own project, which appeared a few years after Schiller's, is in many respects a far more ambitious and wide-ranging one. Tracing the origins of the process to the late nineteenth century, the author defines his 'core argument' as:

> [T]hat the media are American in much the same way that spaghetti bolognese is Italian and cricket is British. In the media, economies of scale tend to take extreme forms; it costs little to make extra copies of a film, TV series, audio disc or video cassette. Given these economics, world media production was destined to be a winner-takes-all industry, and in most cases this winner was the US. Newspapers, movies and space satellites were not invented in the US, but it was the US which gave each of these the basic mass media format that the rest of the world then copied and adopted. (Tunstall 1994: 13)

However, Tunstall's reading of the situation is not as bleak as Schiller's. The 'media imperialism' thesis which he ascribes to Schiller and Wells is, for Tunstall, overly simplistic. Anglo-American imperialism, from the British Empire to the hegemony of American media post-1945, has always been subject to the rule that power dynamics, between producer and consumer, operate in both directions. While exploring in some detail the impact of US media on the rest of the world, he concludes that the outcome is uncertain:

> At least two contrary trends can be foreseen: First, there may be an increasing tendency for films and television and media generally around the world to be put into primarily American packages...In this view the Americanization of the world still has a long way to go. Such improbable sights as hot-dogs, American-style drum majorettes, blue jeans and T-shirts saying 'Ohio State University' will be found not only in small provincial towns but around the entire world...There is, however, another argument, that the world is splitting up into smaller units and ethnic identities. Other trends in the media...will encourage localism, separatism, taking back to, and switching off from, authority, the centre, the national and foreign media. (*Ibid.*: 273–4)

In these two paragraphs Tunstall cleverly juxtaposes Americanization with balkanization, which we discuss in Chapter 8. Both trends, he insists, are likely to continue – the *international* media will remain heavily Anglo-Americanized, but there will be a huge expansion of *local*, ethnic media, and the result is likely to be the emergence of a 'middle level', a hybridized middle ground operating largely at the *national* level (*ibid.*: 274). So Tunstall offers a *guarded* defence of the 'media imperialism' thesis, careful to acknowledge the power of American media, but reluctant to follow Schiller down the overtly Marxian route of equating this with subjugation and hegemony.

The complexities Tunstall identifies are further taken up by subsequent cultural commentators keen to interrogate the nature of this American cultural imperialism via the exporting of its most popular television series, *Dallas*, *Baywatch* and *Friends*, for example, all of which celebrate peculiarly American ways of life. Jonathan Friedman describes this cultural imperialism as 'the increasing hegemony of particular central cultures, the diffusion of American values, consumer goods and lifestyles' (1994: 195; cited in Tomlinson 1999: 79).

4.6 American military imperialism

If cultural imperialism via media conglomerates and the selling of consumer goods represented something of an Americanization 'from below', attempts to Americanize 'from above' have proven to be more problematic. Generally speaking, resistance to America's exertion of 'soft' power has been met with similarly 'soft' acts of protest such as the reassertion of local or traditional identities (see Castells 2004) or the appropriation of American consumerism to suit local interests and tastes. American *military* imperialism, however, inevitably entails a more direct and explicit exertion of power, thereby putting Americanization *as a whole* up to similarly direct and explicit acts of resistance.

Of course, one can reasonably argue that cultural imperialism and military imperialism are two sides of the same coin. Both operate on separate levels of domination yet both are linked by the same motives and interests, namely the upholding and consolidating of American interests and power. In public, however, accusations of self-interest have either been rejected or at least downplayed by the US government while promoting its commitment to developing global change for the collective good.

As we have already seen, the factors that defined the formation of its inland empire would provide similar impetus for America's outland empire expansion. By the early twentieth century, America was ideally placed to assume the role as the world's supreme nation. Britain – arguably its previous incumbent – had been exhausted by half a century of policing the globe as

well as its own empire, and had now been overtaken economically and industrially by America's rapidly expanding business empire.

At this stage, however, 'empire' was still generally understood in colonial
terms. Following victory in the Spanish–American War of 1898, the United
States had acquired an empire of its own including the Philippines, Puerto
Rico, Hawaii, Guam and Cuba. Although this represented progress in
terms of trade expansion in the Far East, for many, including the American
author Brooks Adams, this approach did not go far enough to guarantee the
protection of American values and interests. Adopting an 'internationalist'
approach, Adams believed that economic power and ideological persuasion
alone would not produce hegemonic power, and that the United States would
have to take an increasingly dominant role in global relations. This required
a significant ideological shift, both economically and politically: on the one
hand, Adams argued that American economic supremacy was best served by
an unlimited global market rather than a restricted national and colonial one;
on the other hand, economic and moral power would have to be translated
into military power, with the US effectively becoming the world's 'policeman'
(McCormick 1989: 19).

Economically, one can argue that Adams's ideas were underpinned
by what we might recognize as a neo-liberal economic logic, recalling
Arrighi (1994) and Harvey (2003) as well as images of a 'borderless
world' and a global free market discussed in Chapter 2. We have also seen
in this chapter that economic liberalization was certainly in the mind of
President Woodrow Wilson, who recognized consumerism to be an essential part of converting the rest of the world to the 'principles of America'.
Whether Wilson saw his 'new global order' in terms of liberalization or
Americanization, or even 'transnationalization', given his advocacy of the
League of Nations, is a moot point, although he plainly argued that the
'removal of...all economic barriers' and 'an equality of trade conditions
among all the nations' were in the interests of everybody, not just America
(*ibid.*: 22).

Such plans would, however, prove premature as he failed to win over his
own government, which still retained strong protectionist sentiments, resulting in a return to semi-interventionism in foreign affairs. The impact of the
1929 Wall Street Crash and ensuing Great Depression would initially dampen
internationalism, free-trade and open-door policies worldwide as nation-states
sought to recover their domestic economies. Domestic recovery did, however,
precipitate a new wave of external expansion by the late 1930s, as Germany
and Japan sought to boost their economies through militaristic intervention
and intimidation with the intention of redistributing wealth, resources and
power in their favour. These actions would ultimately provoke the outbreak
of the Second World War in 1939. Although not initially an active participant,
the United States nevertheless saw the ascendancy of Germany and Japan
as 'the nightmare of a closed world' coming to life, thus putting America's

own long-term economic interests at risk. This did not go unrecognized by American President Franklin D. Roosevelt, who unlike his interwar predecessors was more of an internationalist in the Wilsonian mould.

Following the bombing of Pearl Harbor in 1941, entering the Second World War represented – for American leaders at least – 'diplomacy by other means'. As the historian Thomas J. McCormick argues, the war was fought 'not simply to vanquish their enemies, but to create the geopolitical basis for a post-war world order that they could build and lead'. This would create no doubt over how America saw itself in relation to the rest of the world, with the war creating the means by which the United States could assert and assume global hegemony and become the world's 'global workshop and banker, umpire and policeman, preacher and teacher' (*ibid.*: 33). Although victory in 1945 could be understood as representing a victory for liberal democratic values shared by the allied forces, the United States would effectively close the war by making a very singular statement of its own: the atomic bombings of Hiroshima and Nagasaki, carried out under the executive order of new President Harry S. Truman, would count among many things as an absolute assertion of America's hegemonic power.

Having established its position of global supremacy, one can argue that finding ways to avert the 'nightmare of a closed world' has shaped much of America's foreign policy since the end of the Second World War. Ranging from the competition and antagonism of the Cold War with the Soviet Union, to the attack on the so-called 'axis of evil' in the post 9/11 'war on terror', US foreign policy has been centred on spreading and upholding American hegemonic power and, where necessary, engaging in acts of 'containment' against perceived threats and instabilities (Duffield 2007). But what makes Americanization a *theory of the global condition* is how it sees American values and interests silently underpinning many of what we might view as impartial transnational institutions. Although the part played by the US in the post-war establishing of NATO, the United Nations, the GATT, the ITO (later WTO), the IMF and the World Bank might be seen as representing a commitment to economic liberalization and transnational governance, these nevertheless retained a distinctly American flavour.

According to McCormick (1989), this deliberate conflation of global interest and self-interest was symptomatic of America's post-war sense of self-righteousness, believing that only they possessed both the vision and capability to reorder and manage the world-system into peace and economic prosperity. Although acknowledging that the new system would provide personal economic gain, this would be bullishly defended on the grounds that the rest of the world would gain from the 'trickle-down' effects of American hegemony, as per the neo-liberal economic model. In other words, nation states would receive "greater security and material rewards in exchange for diminished authority' (*ibid.*: 48).

The practice of promoting and maintaining hegemony can be seen in its foreign policy. For Walter L. Hixson (2008), US hegemony has been historically asserted through continuous campaigns of violence against external enemies, ranging from Native Americans to Islamic fundamentalists. This, he argues, derives from America's puritan beginnings of glorifying violence as an instrument of moral purification, which have been sustained into its modern national identity. As a result, faith in its own moral virtues has been disguised as 'American diplomacy', thus allowing itself to initiate and institutionalize violent and bloody warfare on the basis that America's cause 'is the cause of all mankind'.

Sylvan and Majeski (2009) take a more structural approach, arguing that US hegemony has involved setting up an 'empire of client states', a process dating back to its role in the Spanish–American War of 1898. In this model, they see America aiming to control and regulate the world through its 'client states', which are employed to uphold US interests in the face of 'enemy states' such as the Soviet Union, North Korea and Iran. For major powers, such as France and Great Britain, this involved general support for American interests and involvement or membership in US-led alliances such as NATO and the Marshall Plan. For smaller and poorer countries, its client status usually represents more regional and strategic uses. This will often involve the support for, or even installation of, regimes that appear opposed to the US model. Yet regardless of whether a client state is governed by a democracy, monarchy or dictatorship, what matters is to retain supremacy in the global power network, and to prevent enemy states from forming their own alliances.

America's varying and malleable definitions of what constitutes an 'acceptable regime' in its client states suggests that American foreign policy was not (at least initially) concerned with establishing global American homogeneity. More important was laying the foundations for a world capitalist market in the neo-liberal mould. One can recall how America had entered the Second World War with the intention of maintaining its economic supremacy and make the argument that entering a Cold War against the communist Soviet bloc was a clear continuation of this logic. Although the US was itself placed in a position of economic supremacy by 1945, the government was fully aware that the world capitalist *system* had been heavily depleted by the costs and debt repayments incurred by its allied nations. This was further hindered by the fact that many of the European nations could no longer expect bailout from its empires, with political independence movements causing the break-up of imperial blocs in Asia and the Far East. Although the rebuilding of European capitalism would be undertaken through the Marshall Plan, this nevertheless created a twin concern to American foreign policy towards the rest of the world: first, that the continued weakness of post-war global capitalism would severely impact on US economic interests; and second, that the emergence of multiple newly independent nations could severely weaken the monopoly of the world capitalist system should they adopt protectionist or even communist economic policies. The fear of the Soviet Union – which via its Marxist-Leninist doctrine had espoused imperial ambitions of its own – propounded US policies in 'containment', which in the words of government advisor George F. Kennan was 'designed to confront the Russians with unalterable counterforce at every point where they show signs of encroaching upon the interests of a peaceful and stable world' (quoted in McCormick 1989: 75).

American military attempts at 'containment' would act as strategic chess-moves throughout the Cold War, with the intention of creating client states in supposedly contested and unstable regions. An example of this would be the overthrowing of Guatemala's democratic system in favour of a US-backed military government in the 1950s. In 1944 the country had taken major steps towards reducing poverty when its long-time dictatorship was toppled by popular unrest. In its place, a democratically elected government was installed leading to the implementation of labour reforms and the redistribution of land to peasant farmers. In 1951, Guatemala elected Jacobo Arbenz, who sought to build on these reforms by broadening voting rights, establishing a minimum wage and promoting healthcare and literacy programmes (Hixson 2008: 218–19). For the United States, however, these developments were deemed to be wholly antagonistic to its own interests. First, it had already been monitoring Central America with some concern over the possible threat of communism. Arbenz's reforms, although democratic, were nevertheless perceived by the US government to be another example of a growing 'leftist penetration' in Latin American politics, which might escalate into Guatemalan support for similar political struggles taking place in Honduras and Costa Rica. Second, Arbenz's labour and land reforms were marginalizing America's economic interests via the US-headquartered United Fruit Company, which had vast Guatemalan holdings. Such was the scale of hostility that the introduction of further reforms by Arbenz in April 1952 would provoke one lobbyist for United Fruit to approach the CIA. Around this time, the US had also been lobbied by Nicaraguan dictator Somoza to back an invasion of Guatemala by a former military officer Carlos Castillo Armas.

The US government's response was to sanction a CIA special operation with the intention of overthrowing Arbenz: according to Sylvan and Majeski (2009) this involved training and equipping Armas's army, and creating and disseminating anti-Arbenz propaganda both domestically and in the US, as well as isolating Guatemala from other states in Latin America. Fearful of impending invasion, Arbenz sought military aid from Europe, but this was blocked by the United States (Chomsky 2005: 105). Seemingly with few options left, he chose to purchase arms from Soviet-occupied Czechoslovakia. This was deemed to be requisite evidence of Guatemala's association with communism, whereby the CIA gave Armas the 'permission' (along with substantial military support) to invade Guatemala in 1954. Sylvan and Majeski allege that the Guatemalan military refused to fight for fear that defeating Armas's rebels would only provoke the US into using its own armed forces to crush its small army, thus making victory for Armas something of a formality.

As Hixson (2008) observes, Armas's US-backed military government took back the redistributed land from half a million peasants and returned oligarchy to power. For the next 20 years, Guatemala operated under a 'reign of terror'. Hixson also noted that in 1999 a UN-sponsored 'truth commission' report was filed detailing 'two generations of ferocious and indiscriminate violence carried out by the US-backed Guatemalan regime'. The report condemned the United States for 'training, covert assistance, and overall complicity in the slaughters and "disappearing" of some two hundred thousand Guatemalans' (Hixson 2008: 219). Yet for all the bloodshed and maintaining of morally reprehensible regimes, Guatemala nevertheless represented a successful covert operation for US military imperialism and the establishing of a Central American 'client state' (McCormick 1989; Sylvan and Majeski 2009). Upon victory, President Dwight D. Eisenhower reportedly thanked his military officials for 'avert[ing] a Soviet beachhead in our hemisphere' (Chomsky 2005: 103).

If the case of Guatemala suggested a somewhat binary approach to good and evil, Cold War paranoia continued to fuel American military imperialism for the next 40 years. However, its efforts to covertly establish client states in key regions would not always be as successful. Arguably the largest and most vulnerable regions were Asia and Indochina, which effectively became the proxy-battlegrounds of the Cold War for much of the 1950s and 1960s. The United States first suffered a major strategic blow when US-supported Chinese nationalists were defeated by the Soviet-supported communists in 1949, establishing China as a communist republic. The following year saw a similar conflict occur in Soviet-occupied Korea, which drew US forces (and European allies) into armed conflict. The result was the dividing of Korea into two separate nations: a communist North Korea and a republican South Korea. Finally, in 1954, the ailing French colonial territory of Indochina was subjected to armed rebellion from the communist Viet Minh, culminating in the withdrawal of France from the region and the establishing of four separate nations: one communist state (North Vietnam), one republic (South Vietnam) and two constitutional monarchies (Laos and Cambodia).

The US had provided military support to the French, and President Eisenhower was fearful that the spread of communism throughout the Far East would have the 'domino effect' of inspiring similar uprisings throughout the territory, and potentially extending as far as Japan, the Philippines and Australia. This was true to the extent that communist factions existed throughout Indochina, and in order to stem this perceived 'red tide of communism', America first set out to stabilize the region by supporting Ngo

Dinh Diem's authoritarian regime in South Vietnam in its battle against the Viet Cong guerrilla army, which had links to communist North Vietnam. This proved unsuccessful, as Diem's anti-communist regime was electorally corrupt and violently repressive towards political opponents, as well as antagonistic in its promoting of Catholicism to Vietnam's largely Buddhist population. Despite being initially touted as 'the miracle man of Asia', Diem would eventually be deposed in a US-backed military coup in 1963, thereby inciting a long and violent war with the Viet Cong army. This would eventually culminate in defeat for the US military and the unification of Vietnam as a socialist republic in 1976.

According to Hixson, the Vietnam War – which led to the death of 58,000 US soldiers, 2 million Cambodians and an estimated 3 million Vietnamese – represented the lengths that America was prepared to go in order to assert its own imperial project, where 'flush with economic prosperity and drunk on its own totalizing discourse', it 'pummelled Vietnam for nearly a decade' (Hixson 2008: 241). Routine and relentless bombing campaigns, chemical defoliation via 20 million gallons of Agent Orange and unlimited applications of napalm were representative of a scientifically managed 'war of attrition' strategy. The moral ambiguity of this crusade ultimately represented a significant stumbling block to Americanization via US military imperialism, for it opened up to scrutiny the legitimacy of its role as the 'world's policeman'. This, too, was propounded by the increasing presence of global media, which, as we noted in Chapter 1, provided significant visibility to the stages, methods and protagonists of armed conflict. As a result, the Vietnam War provoked anti-American sentiments and anti-war protest movements throughout the world, not least in the US itself. America's claim to moral superiority, not to mention its destiny to triumph over so-called evil enemy-others, would not go unquestioned again.

Despite such opposition, however, America's imperial project of an empire of client states would continue throughout the 1980s and 1990s. The legacy of Vietnam at least signalled a return to more covert and 'proxy' battles against enemy states, notably in the indirect funding of anti-communist Contra rebels following the Nicaraguan revolution in 1979, and the financing and arming of *mujahideen* insurgents to fight the Soviet Union following its invasion of Afghanistan the same year. For the Soviet Union itself, however, the Afghan War, together with ailing economic performance throughout the 1980s would ultimately contribute to its dissolution in 1991, effectively ending the Cold War. For many commentators, including Fukuyama (1989, 1991), this signalled the triumph of world capitalism and liberal democracy over communist statehood as well as placing the United States in the position of 'the world's remaining super power' (see Chapter 2 for more detailed discussion on Fukuyama).

Despite its post-Cold War supremacy the US still had enemy states to contend with, as well as client states to protect. By the 1980s much of its attention had been shifted towards the Middle East, a region with which America historically has had a complex and often fraught relationship, not least due to its continued military support for Israel. Much of this can be understood in terms of America's dependency on oil. This has arguably fuelled the desire to open up the region's vast supply to global trade – with the US itself keen to take the role of chief auctioneer – and has at least been successful in its acquisition of Saudi Arabia as an occasionally prickly yet financially lucrative client state. Attracting the support of its regional neighbours, however, proved more problematic. Iraq under Saddam Hussein, despite finding itself tactically allied with the US against Iran during the 1980s, had never enjoyed the friendliest of relations with the US. The relationship further deteriorated in 1990 when Iraq's invasion of Kuwait was deemed to be a threat to its neighbouring oil-rich client. Although America's interests in the resulting Gulf War did not extend much beyond defending Saudi Arabia, Iraq would remain an enemy state for a further ten years, with military aid being given to oppositional groups so as to 'goad' the regime into war (Sylvan and Majeski 2009: 216).

Iran, despite its hostility towards Iraq, was also deemed an enemy state. This status, however, was partially a 'blowback' to its original status as a client state under the Shah Reza Pahlavi. The Shah's modernist and Westernized reforms, however, were perceived to challenge Islamic traditions, leading to the regime being toppled in the Iranian Revolution of 1979 by Shiite fundamentalists under Ayatollah Khomeini. Whereas Iraq represented a relatively isolated threat, the Iranian Revolution on the other hand symbolized an extreme ideological rejection of Americanization that would continue to grow throughout the region.

The rise of Islamic fundamentalism and rejection of Americanization would climax with the terrorist attacks on the US on 11 September 2001. Although conceived as a message to the entire Western[ized] world, Hixson argues that the provocations for the assaults were more specifically directed at US foreign policy and its attempts to 'Americanize' the Middle East. This included its unstinting support for Israel in its conflict with Palestine, its military intervention in the Gulf War and the Afghan War, the establishment of its military bases in the 'holy land' of Saudi Arabia, and its drive to control the region's oil supply (*ibid.*: 279). As perhaps a testament to America's entangled approach to maintaining its hegemonic power, the attacks were the work of al-Qaeda: a terrorist network of Islamic fundamentalists whose leader Osama bin Laden was a former member of the mujahideen that had been financed and armed by the US in the 1980s. If one can see a consistency of intent in American military imperialism, its inconsistency of *method* was beginning to spawn new and more extreme opponents.

An analysis of the events following 11 September 2001 – the global condemnation of al-Qaeda, America's invasion and occupation of Afghanistan and Iraq, the global anti-war movement and America's continued struggle to build and sustain a Middle East that adheres to its ideals – invites debate as to whether America's 'war on terror' is representative of American imperialism, or global transformations resembling more a 'clash of civilizations' (see Chapter 8). In analyzing America's intent, we can once again see a conscious attempt to emphatically assert its claims to moral fortitude and its superior liberal democratic values. This could be seen in President George W. Bush's post-9/11 rhetoric, arguing that its perpetrators 'hate our freedoms – our freedom of religion, our freedom of speech, our freedom to vote and assemble and disagree with each other' (*ibid.*). As was the case with American cultural imperialism, this inferred a very US-oriented definition of freedom, one which involved a subscription to neo-liberal economic values in which the US was already the imperial chairman. Moreover, its inference of *democratic* freedoms was more contentious still, considering that the US had not strictly adhered to these morals when undertaking military intervention in the examples cited earlier.

Whether the 'war on terror' symbolizes Americanization at its apex or at its point of decline is open to debate. Islamic extremism, no matter how marginal, has attracted popular support beyond the Middle East, which at the very least suggests that there are alternative discourses to globality that are significantly removed from the Western-centricity of Americanization. But perhaps more significantly, critical approaches to Americanization are by no means limited to the Islamic world, with many across the world also identifying a disparity between US military imperialism and a transnational public good, and as a result calling for a change in global relations.

4.7 Conclusion

How are we to read the Americanization debate? On the one hand, it does present a significant, and starkly coherent, model of the contemporary global condition. At its crudest it presents a world being remade in the American image through the interplay of cultural, economic, political and military processes. At its more subtle level it demonstrates how these processes actually work even in the face of sharp criticisms of the model for being too simplistic, too one-directional. These criticisms themselves, though, do need to be considered carefully. There are perhaps three main such criticisms:

1. that the Americanization model betrays a nation-statist bias which ignores the significance of transnational institutions
2. that it over-estimates American power
3. that it ignores the extent to which local cultures actively resist Americanizing processes.

On the issue of its nation-state bias, it is worth reiterating the fact that, while much of the Americanization literature is Marxian in orientation, not all Marxist-inspired theory in global studies adheres to this model. Classically, the Marxian paradigm in the social sciences is designed specifically to expose the unequal power dynamics at play and to champion the exploited against the exploiter. When Lenin extended Marxian theory into the realm of international relations via his theory of imperialism, he explicitly set the agenda for subsequent Marxian works in this area. Many of the writers discussed in this chapter have been committed to extending the Marxian model of relations between classes (within nation-states) to the international arena and the relations between *nation-states*. In the literature on American empire, the world's most powerful nation-state stands alone in the role of the core, or the global bourgeoisie, the imperial centre. There is little acknowledgement here of the role played by transnational institutions, corporations and agents in sustaining existing power relations within the global capitalist economy. Leslie Sklair, for instance, has made some sharp criticisms of the theory of American empire for over-playing the influence of the (American) nation-state and ignoring these other power-players.

This leads us to the second criticism – that it over-states American power. The current debate on American empire seems especially influential within the American academy, but has so far been less favourably received in Europe. While it may be the case that the focus of much of the American Left remain inward-looking, it seems questionable whether under contemporary global conditions any country, even the last-remaining superpower, is powerful enough to execute such a project of global imperialism as is described by the Americanization commentators. If anything, its critics suggest, American empire only stretches so far. The rise of alternatives – most noticeably within the Islamic world and in China – to American power and American lifestyles reveal the limitations of the Americanization model and take us down the alternative route towards balkanization, which we cover in Chapter 8. It might reasonably be argued that 'Americanization' is no more useful a term, or more accurate a way of describing the current state of the world, than is 'China-ization' or 'Islamicization', and that its inclusion as a chapter in this book says more about the state of academic debate than about the state of the world. Naturally, advocates of the model of American empire would very quickly beg to differ.

Even so – even if there is a dominant imperialist project being orchestrated by the world's most powerful country through cultural and military means – is it not too crudely simplistic to suggest that this project is irresistible? For some of its critics, Americanization is presented as if it is a tidal wave which mercilessly sweeps aside all before it, destroying local cultures, values and practices and imposing American ones in their place. The issue of *resistance* was first taken up in a significant way by the so-called 'Birmingham School' of cultural studies, which showed how working-class youths, rather than being passive dupes obedient to Americanized values, actively appropriated the symbols of the wider repressive system and imbued them with alternative meanings as part of their project of resistance. This is a theme we will take up in more detail in Chapter 6.

McDonaldization: A One-Dimensional World

5.1 Introduction

In this chapter, we will be exploring the tradition within global studies that focuses on how practices and institutions around the world are becoming increasingly similar. While we might choose to refer to this process as 'homogenization' or 'standardization', we have opted instead to use the term given to us by the American sociologist George Ritzer which has sparked a distinctive literature within contemporary social theory, particularly in the debates around global change. For us, 'homogenization' and 'standardization', while perfectly fine terms, cover issues which extend beyond the core debates within global studies. Indeed, historically, this literature goes back at least as far as the writings of Max Weber, with his emphasis on the 'rationalization' of the world, and grew to prominence in two distinct movements in the 1950s and 1960s, namely, the functionalist 'convergence theories', associated with Clark Kerr, Daniel Bell and others, and their neo-Marxist counterpart, Herbert Marcuse's 'one-dimensional society' theory. These antecedents will, of course, be discussed, but the focus of the chapter is on the latest revival of the Weberian position in the theory of McDonaldization developed by Ritzer.

Readers may very well ask at this point why this framework is not already covered under the auspices of the previous chapter, Americanization. For sure, the two processes are often discussed together and sometimes synonymously under a broader heading of 'Westernization', but for us, they are sufficiently distinct, and represent quite different theoretical traditions, for them to be discussed separately. Americanization suggests the remaking of the world in the American image. McDonaldization, however, describes a process by which the practices, values and institutional arrangements of nation-states are becoming increasingly the same. While the template for this may very well be American, the dynamics underpinning this are not necessarily reducible to American culture or politics. For one thing, Americanization at least implicitly suggests the building of an empire based on dependency, which necessarily weakens the autonomy of nation-states. By contrast, the McDonaldization model does not necessarily suggest any threat to, never mind the dissolution of, the nation-state system.

But before we address this model, we need to understand its heritage in debates around 'industrialization' and 'modernization' which preceded the current debates around 'globalization'. Although the ghost of Weber looms large in the background of both, it is interesting to note that interpretations of Weber's famous work on rationalization have inspired left-wing neo-Marxists and centre-right liberals alike.

5.2 The functionalist tradition: modernization and convergence

Let us start with the centre-right liberals. As we have already discussed, albeit briefly, in Chapter 1, in the 1950s, a distinctive branch of the structural-functionalist tradition in the social sciences rose to prominence as a theoretical approach within the emerging sociology of development, and within development policy more broadly. The approach became known as 'modernization theory' and its basic premise was that the process of social *evolution* (which for an earlier generation of social scientists was understood to be a largely organic process) equated to modernization; that is, that nation-state societies, regardless of their current stage of development, could effectively be steered on a journey to achieving the level of social and economic modernity enjoyed by the 'advanced' industrial Western societies. All it takes is the appropriate amount of investment required to revitalize a country's economy and stabilize its social infrastructure.

Modernization theory was heavily criticized for relying on the assumption that these 'modernized' Western societies somehow represented a template for the ideal society to which others should aspire. Crucial here was a belief that technological progress effectively shapes social, political and cultural life (Kerr *et al.* 1960; Huntington 1976). Accordingly, the institutions and practices of modern societies become standardized – in effect, the process of modernization becomes synonymous with a process of convergence, as nation-states become increasingly similar (Huntington 1976). In the language of convergence – which clearly pre-dated the current discourse of global studies – the world is essentially viewed as undergoing a process of unification organized along the lines of a generally consensual set of principles and practices.

Like modernization theory and the more general structural-functionalist tradition from which it hatched, convergence theory in its definitive form proved to be a short-lived perspective, very much a creature of its time which suffered heavily with the re-emergence of more radical approaches. Faced with charges of technological determinism, and perhaps more significantly of over-emphasizing the extent to which Western industrial societies represented some idealized modernity (and thus of being merely another form of Westernization and an apology for capitalism), the approach faded away in the 1970s. However, its central idea has proven to be surprisingly resolute and adaptable. Indeed, within the broader global studies discourse, it has laid the foundations for a distinctive school of thought in which 'globalization' is defined as the standardization of cultural and political practices at the nation-state level due to an underlying shared global culture. Convergence can occur because it is 'functional' (in the language of the earlier modernization theorists operating largely within their neo-evolutionist framework) or because it is 'rational', but in either case the 'convergence' model visualizes a world of nation-states operating according to relatively standardized procedures. From this uniformity of practices emerges a coalition of mutual interests and 'complex interdependence' (Keohane and Nye 1989), thus presenting a largely liberal-democratic version of world order opposed to both the anarchic world-view of the 'balkanization' theorists we will turn to in Chapter 8 and the borderless world of those in the 'liberalization' camp we discussed back in Chapter 2. From this neo-convergence approach comes the 'world polity theory' of Meyer and his colleagues, to which we will return later.

5.3   The neo-Marxist tradition: one-dimensional society

If convergence theory represented the structural-functionalist strand of post-Weberian theory, then a more radical tradition emerged from the contributions of the members of the so-called Frankfurt School of Critical Theory, and in particular Herbert Marcuse (1964), in the form of the theory of one-dimensional society. This theory is, effectively, a blending of Weber's theory of rationalization with a Marxian commitment to social change and human freedom. Marcuse's analysis is not strictly speaking Marxist because, like other members of the Frankfurt School, he identified the central problem in contemporary society not as capitalism *per se* but as the increasing dehumanization and negation of freedom brought about by instrumental rationalization, of which capitalism is one manifestation alongside Soviet-style communism and European fascism. Although superficially distinct, each political system is identifiable, Marcuse suggests, by its reliance upon instrumental rationality, the kind of means–end, problem-solving logic derived from scientific analysis, which has spread like a cancer across all the social spheres. The *standardization* that is at play here is a standardization of a particular form of rationality which reduces the world to measurable objects, which, while perhaps fine when limited solely to the laboratory experiment (now is not an appropriate place to explore Marcuse's theory in depth, including his belief in the inherently ideological character of scientific analysis), should have no place in the worlds of culture and society, and which is exemplified by the spread of *positivism* in the social sciences. It is a wholly oppressive system of rationality because by presenting itself in scientific terms (as 'truth') it automatically closes down the alternatives.

As illustrations of this process, Marcuse looks specifically at the realms of philosophy, politics and culture. In philosophy, 'one-dimensional thought' comes to dominate when instrumental rationality starts to drive every area of intellectual pursuit, promoting the idea of knowledge as scientific truth rather than a means of liberation. In politics, states are becoming increasingly similar be they East or West, Left or Right, and within 'democratic' societies choices between rival candidates are in truth rarely ever a choice, as it is the nature of 'mainstream' politics to converge around a comfortable centre ground, anything outside of which is unelectable, thus reinforcing the consensus politics of the status quo. Oppositional and revolutionary potential is quickly negated within such systems, as threatening groups in society (not least the working class in which Marx had held such faith) become integrated into the mainstream (through, for example, pro-welfare social policies, trade unions and citizenship programmes). Similarly, in culture, a myth of choice (what Marcuse's colleague Theodor Adorno called 'pseudo-individualization') is perpetuated when in fact choice and freedom are being closed down through what amounts to the commodification of culture. So, as great cultural forms are reproduced as images on a postcard, music in an elevator, or paperbacks in supermarkets, their revolutionary value – which derives from their ability to give 'power to the imagination' and inspire the idea that 'another world is possible'[1] – is negated (through what Marcuse dubs 'repressive desublimation').

Thus, for Marcuse, in philosophy, politics or culture, all that exists on the margins, and which is therefore politically dangerous, is brought into the mainstream and thus stripped of its revolutionary potential. 'One-dimensional' society is a society without alternatives, populated by uncritical conformists. However, unlike the pessimist Weber from whom the theory of rationalization derives, Marcuse and the Frankfurt School more generally did believe that it was possible for those on these margins to exercise 'negative thinking', to *refuse* the oppressive offer of un-freedom disguised as choice, and replace the working class as the new agents of historical change. It is noticeable that, writing in the 1960s, Marcuse himself felt that students were sufficiently untainted by the bureaucratic system to take the lead in this new revolutionary moment. Nearly half a century later, and in the United Kingdom at least, the rebranding of higher education in business and economic terms, and the commodification of the student experience, have almost certainly killed off those ideals, but perhaps therein lies the 'proof of the pudding' of Marcuse's theory: that which is sublime is made mundane, that which is outside the dominant order and potentially threatening to it is dragged into the mainstream, its radicalism negated.

---

1. We present these two famous slogans, one associated with the students of 1968, the other with the contemporary anti-global capitalism movement, in relation to one another like this without apology.

More so than anyone Marcuse makes the link between standardization and political repression. One-dimensional society is a society in which the shared values and aspirations celebrated by the structural-functionalists are revealed as masking an inherent lack of freedom. The working class comes to believe in the ideology of capitalism, bought off by the false promises of welfare-state social democracy. Students become consumers who see higher education as a platform for getting a job and making money. Rap music and other cultural forms screaming politically from the margins are targeted by the culture industry, and thus become popular, commercial, mainstream and inherently depoliticized. The choice one gets in such a society is akin to the choice between, say, a Big Mac and a Whopper, which, in the great scheme of all things culinary, is really no choice at all. Therein, then, lie the (sesame) seeds of George Ritzer's theory of McDonaldization.

5.4   The theory of McDonaldization

In an influential book first published in 1993, Ritzer followed in this tradition of Max Weber and the Frankfurt School with his introduction of the term 'McDonaldization' to refer to the current phase of bureaucratization and homogenization taking shape across America and around the world. Indeed, Ritzer clearly identifies this as the *latest form* of a specific historical process which has its roots in at least three significant turn-of-the-century ideas, namely, Weber's concept of 'formal rationality', Frederick Taylor's 'scientific management' and the assembly line mass production techniques associated with Henry Ford. In each case, the instrumentalist drive towards increased efficiency and simplicity is accompanied by ever-decreasing levels of human engagement and creativity and, ultimately, by dehumanization.

According to Ritzer, McDonaldization shares with these notable precursors four underlying bureaucratic principles: *efficiency, calculability, predictability* and *control*. Efficiency refers to the search for the best means of achieving a specific end, but in a McDonaldized society, Ritzer argues, this becomes an institutional rather than an individualized calculation, because, as the author states, 'it would be inefficient for people to be required to continually rediscover the optimum means to ends' (Ritzer 1993: 35). Maximum efficiency in a McDonaldized world is achieved with minimum fuss and effort. Service is of the Fordist assembly line variety, devoid of character, creativity or individuality, which would be wholly inefficient qualities! At the same time, calculability equates to quantification, to the extent to which the consumer experience becomes commodified (to use a Marxian expression), and quality becomes subordinate to quantity. Predictability, meanwhile, appeals (in theory) to the perceived consumer dislike of surprises – it is famously claimed that the success of the McDonald's chain rests with its uniformity, which pro-vides reassurance to the customer regardless of its location. While Ritzer him-self extends his discussion of predictability into the realm of popular cinema, clearly there are parallels with Adorno's concept of pseudo-individualization in respect of music. The desire for this parochial reassurance is nicely summa-rized by the anthropologist Ulf Hannerz in reference to the central character of Anne Tyler's book *The Accidental Tourist*, who:

> makes his living by churning out travel books for anti-cosmopolitans, people (mostly business travellers) who would rather not have left home; people who are locals at heart. These are travel guides for Americans who would want to know what restaurants in Tokyo offer Sweet'n'Low, which hotel in Madrid has king-size Beauty-rest mattresses, and whether there is a Taco Bell in Mexico City. (Hannerz 1990: 241)

The fourth feature of McDonaldization, according to Ritzer, is control, which is intrinsically linked to the utilization of new technologies. It has ever been a feature of industrialization (and post-industrialization) that technologies have gone hand-in-hand with the drive towards maximum efficiency. There is, of course, a considerable sociological literature on the extent to which technology in the workplace results in the deskilling and ultimately the alienation of the worker (Blauner 1964). Under conditions of McDonaldization, this simply becomes the norm – the counter attendant whose job could equally as effectively be done by a robot in fact *becomes* a robot (Ritzer 1993: 106–7). Fast-food restaurants are typical, Ritzer says, of the way in which social spaces from shopping malls to workplaces have become like factories, slaves to technology perhaps, but at the same time that technology effectively imprisons those within the spaces, subjecting them to spatialized forms of social control. This not only applies to the worker (as it may have done in the early factory), it also applies to the consumer. Weber himself has described the process of rationalization as an 'iron cage' of bureaucracy, and many of us are quick to imagine this in the form of cus-tomer help-lines 'staffed' by computerized voices directing the caller through an increasingly frustrating labyrinth of options, or of the waiting area at some or another service providers, in which the consumer pulls a number and takes her or his place in the queue. Thus, McDonaldization amounts not only to deskilling but to dehumanization.

Indeed, common to all bureaucracies as a consequence of the inevitable dehumanization that they facilitate is that they suffer from what Ritzer refers to as the *irrationality of rationality*. As an example of this, Ritzer points out that in an increasingly McDonaldized society, defined by the ideology of bureaucracy and a reliance upon technology, subtle but signifi-cant changes occur within the division of labour which are ultimately ben-eficial to the profit-generating interests of capitalism. There are numerous examples of how the consumer is required to serve as an unpaid employee – in the fast-food restaurant, she or he is often presented with only the basics of the meal, cooked in a standardized way, and it is up to them to add condiments and the like; similarly, the petrol station is no longer serviced by an attendant, so the consumer has to take on that role; equally, the consumer does her or his own packing at the supermarket (*ibid.*: 42–5). These may seem like trivial examples, says Ritzer, but they are representative of a trend that is far from trivial. Late capitalism benefits not only from the exploitation of the worker, but also of the consumer. What is entirely 'rational' and 'efficient' from the point of view of the fast-food restaurant or its equivalent is entirely *irrational* and *inefficient* from the perspective of the consumer.

Ritzer's debt to critical theory is evident here. The Frankfurt School were describing the inherent irrationality of a system that purports to be rational, and so is Ritzer – in both cases, the irrationality is located within the restrictions placed upon individual freedoms. The practices described by Ritzer, driven by the logic of scientific 'predictability' (for which, read marketing) and 'efficiency' (read profit), have become standardized, taken for granted, in institutions ranging from fast-food restaurants to universities, resulting in docile employees and customers (Ritzer 1993, 1996). Equally, in postmodern vein, these standardizing processes are superficial, based no longer on materiality or universalizing claims; economic exchange in a McDonaldized world is effectively devoid of content (Ritzer 1996, 2004). Indeed, it is this 'nothingness' which takes on material form in such a world of commodification, in which reality surrenders to simulation (Baudrillard 1983, 1988b).

Clearly, this framework presents a radically different interpretation of standardizing and homogenizing processes to the 'convergence' framework celebrated by the structural-functionalists and technological determinists of the 1950s. Indeed, just as the earlier generation of one-dimensional society theorists were consciously set against the theorists of modernization and the end of ideology as rival frameworks for understanding the dynamics of social change, much the same can be said of their successor models. While the convergence model emphasizes democratization, the McDonaldization framework – while acknowledging the potentially unifying aspects of the process – views it as wholly anti-democratic, in so far as its accountability is to consumers not citizens, and its driving logic is capitalist accumulation not emancipation (Barber 2003).

To summarize, the McDonaldization framework focuses on the apparent standardization of cultural, political and economic *practices*. Although Ritzer initially used the term to refer to a process occurring within American society, it has become intertwined with the global studies literature to define a dystopian model of global transformation as homogenization and the destruction of local diversities. Thus, what commentators refer to as 'globalization' refers more accurately to the remaking of local values and practices in the image of Western culture and in the interests of transnational capitalism. McDonaldization represents cultural, technological and political uniformity and homogeneity, reproduced through global finance, communications, popular culture and the mass media (Barber 2003). This homogeneity derives from an American template, but the process itself transcends a simple Americanization (*ibid*.), just as its major symbols – McDonald's, Coca-Cola, Nike, Gap – have transcended their American origins and become 'global brands'.

Biography Box 11: George Ritzer

George Ritzer (1940–) is Distinguished University Professor of Sociology at the University of Maryland. A New Yorker by birth, he is well known as the author of textbooks on sociological theory but is most famous for introducing the idea of McDonaldization in his 1993 book *The McDonaldization of Society*, which became an international best-seller.

5.5   A history of McDonald's

Before we explain the practice of McDonaldization, we must firstly reiterate that Ritzer's theory of McDonaldization does not intend to present McDonald's' restaurants or the fast-food industry as the principal 'driving force' of global convergence. Rather, the worldwide rise of McDonald's restaurants acts (somewhat ironically) as a simple, recognizable symbol of standardized, one-dimensional practices, capturing their essential appeal to both institutions and consumers. As our references to Weber and the Frankfurt School already indicate, McDonaldization should be recognized as a process that pre-dates and transcends the history of McDonald's restaurants themselves. The history of McDonald's therefore operates as an effective case study, capturing the motives, strategies and resulting consumer conventions of a wider homogenizing and standardization process.

As already noted, the history of standardized labour is founded on three significant concepts in early twentieth-century modern thought: formal rationality, Taylorism and Fordism. Formal rationality was seen by Max Weber (1978) to be the principal motor of industrial modernity: an amoral, means-obsessed logic of control, efficiency and calculability that would become irresistible to businesses and organizations worldwide. By the early twentieth century, formal rationality had become a powerful organizational force, aided especially by the rise of the modern bureaucracy which according to Weber represented formal rationality's most essential and powerful institutional expression. Its capacity to maximize efficiency through the breaking down of tasks into simple, specialized tasks resulted not only in high productive output, but also a new means of human coercion: with each job defined and 'owned' by the organization rather than the incumbent, the organization can assert a certain degree of 'pattern maintenance' among its employees, with the organizational culture providing the values that govern individual action.

From this summary, we can observe that the productive potential of bureaucratic labour has more to do with the power of the wider organizational schema than the individual skills and motivations of the workers themselves. This emphasis was certainly recognized by the American engineer F. W. Taylor, who pioneered 'scientific management systems' in the late nineteenth and early twentieth centuries. In his model, Taylor extended the division of labour to the extent that each task was broken down into its smallest constituent units, which could be timed and measured. From this, management could construct and control the labour process by eliminating all irrational and inefficient behaviour and thus maximize productive output. Much of this perceived 'irrationality' stemmed from the workers themselves, who might customize their labour through employing their own preferred methods and styles, elucidate their own personal wisdom or labour philosophies, and be motivated (or demotivated) by a variety of disparate, personal and unpredictable factors. As a result, Taylor saw that jobs should be deskilled so as to restrict individual workers from making themselves indispensable to the labour process: with knowledge being power, it was important to ensure that it resided firmly within the hands of the organization, not the labourer. This would also facilitate the employment of cheaper labour, though motivation would be increased through the introduction of a piece-rate incentive scheme which would raise productivity through the individual competition for rewards. This heavily individualized work ethic would also have the effect of discouraging collective action and trade unions, thus maintaining the absolute controlling powers of the organization.

All in all, Taylor's scientific management system played a significant part in the growing use of, and justification for, 'non-human technology' and the minimization of individual autonomy and innovation. The emphasis placed on efficient, uniform and calculable labour processes would invariably mean increased profits for those enterprises that adopted them. Although the *direct* influence of Taylor on standardized labour practices is questionable (see Nelson 1974; Ozanne 1979; Goldman and Van Houten 1980), Taylor*ism* nevertheless embodied key organizational and productive trends that characterized much of the twentieth century, and would attract followers and imitators across the world. Taylorism certainly played a major part in shaping the motor car industry, Taylor's method laying the foundations for industrial modernity's second great innovation, the assembly line of the Ford Motor Company. Ritzer (2008) notes that Henry Ford was initially inspired by an overhead trolley system used by Chicago meatpackers, where time would be saved by assembling a line of specialized butchers to perform specific tasks on each steer as it was propelled along the carousel. This system echoed the scientific management principles of Taylorism, as it would save time and energy through specialized task-making and was efficient in that it would reduce the skill requirement for each employee. Ford took this model and applied it to his own Ford automobile plant, which he set up in 1913. Here, he developed a set of principles to guide assembly line technology later known as 'Fordism':

1. Workers are not to take any unnecessary steps; work-related movements are reduced to an absolute minimum.
2. Parts needed in the assembly process are to travel the least possible distance.
3. Mechanical (rather than human) means are to be used to move the car (and parts) from one step in the assembly process to the next.
4. Complex sets of movements are eliminated, and the worker does 'as nearly as possible only one thing with one movement'. (Ford 1922; quoted in Ritzer 2008: 32)

Although successful in terms of productive and efficient output (not to mention sales), the unintended consequence of high employee turnover meant that Fordism as a 'pure' method was short-lived as firms sought greater organizational flexibility as market competitors grew (giving rise to post-Fordism, which we will discuss later; see also Grint 2005: 299–301). Nevertheless, Fordism and Taylorism played a significant part in laying the foundations for modern capitalist production in the twentieth century. The consumer boom of 1920s America, which soon expanded across the world, owed much to Ford and Taylor's productive ethic of maximizing output and profit through managing and controlling every stage of the production process, thus giving priority to the virtues of efficiency, calculability and predictability. The fact that such techniques were pioneered predominantly by US companies appeared initially to give the consumer boom something of an American flavour, thus inciting opposition to perceived hegemonic 'Americanization' among European nations (see de Grazia 2005; Sandbrook 2005). This may have been true in terms of the American-style products being sold, and the desire for US companies to create a global market to reign supreme, yet no secret was made of their commitment to scientific management techniques and assembly line production systems. As a result, it was felt that anyone who possessed the required business instincts would be able to adopt the same productive model to a section of the consumer market and make healthy profits (de Grazia 2005).

Thus, McDonaldization theory argues that while Fordism and Taylorism complemented in particular America's own social and economic outlook, their universality and multi-applicability to other markets, not to mention their productivity, suggested more of a *global* transformation towards evolutionary consensus in manufacturing and service techniques rather than American economic imperialism. As a result, from the 1920s onwards the production and selling of commodities converged towards efficient and effective uniform models which would appear in varying degrees across the world – to the extent that Fordism and Taylorism would even become the bedrock of Stalin's plan to industrialize and modernize the Soviet Union in the 1920s and 1930s (see Hughes 2004).

Among its American advocates were two brothers, Mac and Dick McDonald, who opened a restaurant in Pasadena, California, in 1937. As Ritzer (2008) notes, they based their restaurant on the principles of 'high speed, large volume and low price', using assembly line procedures for cooking and serving food. Like Ford's plant, the brothers' limited menu 'allowed them to break down food preparation into simple, repetitive tasks that could be learned quickly', thus creating specialist roles such as 'grill men', 'shake men' and 'fry men' who followed clear instructions in order to create products that were standardized and homogeneous yet ultimately reliable. Assembly line techniques also extended to service (including a 'drive-in' facility) and presentation so as to maximize its customer turnover.

The McDonald brothers' restaurant soon became a local sensation, and was one of many so-called 'fast-food' outlets that emerged during the period. As their popularity continued to grow, certain restaurants such as Big Boy, Burger King and Kentucky Fried Chicken started their own franchises in an attempt to build from its solid, profitable manufacturing model to establish a network of duplicate restaurants across the country. Although the McDonald brothers themselves had little interest in managing a franchise, and were satisfied with $100,000 annual earnings from their original restaurant, the wider business potential was recognized by a local businessman named Ray Kroc. Impressed by its efficiency, Kroc saw opportunities for extending McDonald's as a national (and even international) business. Having become their franchising agent in 1954, Kroc soon after bought out the brothers to build and control his own empire of McDonald's restaurant franchises. Unlike other franchisers at that time, however, Kroc maximized central control by maintaining uniformity throughout the system by using the McDonald brothers' restaurant as his template. He also granted franchises one at a time and rarely granted more than one franchise to a specific individual. Despite this seemingly conservative approach to franchising, Kroc created a unique system of interdependence for its budding franchisees:

> [Kroc] set the fee for the franchise at a rock-bottom $950. Other franchisers had set very high initial fees and made most of their money from the initial setup. As a result, they tended to lose interest in the continued viability of

the franchisees. At McDonald's, profits did not come from the high initial fees but from the 1.9% of store sales that headquarters demanded of its franchisees. This mutual interest was Kroc's greatest contribution to the franchise business and a key factor in the success of McDonald's and its franchisees, many of whom became millionaires in their own right. (Ritzer 2008: 38)

Kroc effectively took the bureaucratic rationality that drove the productive output of the original McDonald's restaurant and applied it to the wider fast-food *market*, both regionally and nationally. By having a franchised outlet in every region, he would be controlling a much bigger and more lucrative bureaucracy: a rational system of rational subsystems, each geared towards upholding the company's brand values by dominating its own local market. Moreover, this would be achieved through the uniform adoption of the same practices which, as illustrated in its 1958 operations manual, echoes Taylorism in its mathematical precision:

It told operators *exactly* how to draw milk shakes, grill hamburgers, and fry potatoes. It specified *precise* cooking times for all products and temperature settings for all equipment. It fixed *standard* portions on every food item, down to the *quarter ounce* of onions placed on each hamburger patty and the *thirty-two slices per pound* of cheese. It specified that French fries be cut at *nine thirty-seconds of an inch* thick. And it defined quality *controls* that were unique to food service, including the disposal of meat and potato products that were held more than *ten minutes* in a serving bin. (Love 1986; quoted in Ritzer 2008: 39)

The simple and predictable appeal of McDonald's restaurants quickly expanded throughout America, and soon to the rest of the world. The success of McDonald's today is apparent: in 2006, its revenues were $21.6 billion, with 31,667 restaurants operating throughout the world by the beginning of 2007 (Ritzer 2008: 2). The success of this simple yet effective business model has resulted in it being extended not only to other fast-food franchises (such as Burger King, Wendy's, Pizza Hut and Kentucky Fried Chicken) but also other areas of the commercial sector, with Wal-Mart supermarkets, Barnes & Noble bookshops, IKEA furniture stores and Fitness First gyms each drawing their success from the virtues of uniformity, efficiency and predictability.

5.6   McDonaldization and post-Fordism

It can, of course, be observed that images of an over-regulated, bureaucratized, one-dimensional society is more likely to recall a modernist, industrialist past than a picture of today. Certainly, our *experience* of production and consumption has changed significantly since the mass production era: if we consider the plurality of different career paths and identities now open to us, not to mention the seemingly endless choice of consumer products available in the 'global supermarket', we might in fact struggle to recognize global homogenizing processes taking place at all. So how might this apparent era of freedom and choice equate to a McDonaldization of society?

In terms of our experience of work, there is plenty of evidence to suggest that Fordism and Taylorism no longer drive global production. The increasingly global interconnectedness of markets, fuelled by the neo-liberal logic of freedom and competition (see Chapter 2), as well as the growth of a more reflexive and 'individualized' generation of autonomous consumers (Giddens 1990; Beck 1992; Pakulski and Waters 1996) has arguably redefined production and consumption practices. For companies, global competition has heightened the need for flexibility, adaptability and the short-term production of goods to suit the volatile and fluctuating tastes of the consumer market. As a result, individual workers are now less likely to remain tied to one particular job or career path, as greater emphasis is placed upon mobility (depending on where the jobs are) and skill flexibility (depending on which jobs are available). For contemporary firms and companies, the standardized predictive output of Fordism has been replaced by the flexible, unique output of 'post-Fordism'. Similarly, the totalitarian and impersonal modern bureaucracy has been replaced by the trans-territorial networked and democratic 'post-bureaucratic' system (Heckscher 1994).

At a surface level at least, post-Fordism and post-bureaucracies can be seen as having a liberating effect on individuals. Such transformations were characterized by Aronowitz and Cutler as indicative of a 'post-work society' where lifestyle is no longer arbitrarily conditioned by the oppressive demands of the modernist work ethic (Aronowitz and Cutler 1998). Of course, more free time and greater economic prosperity open up greater opportunities for reflexive identity construction through promiscuous consumption. Indeed, processes of consumption are even being seen as analogous to Bakhtin's 'carnival' and the postmodern bricolage (Lash and Urry 1994; Lash 1999) where the customer is king and has the freedom to shop from a seemingly endless array of seductive and desirable consumer products. Choice and diversity, it seems, are the buzz-words of modern shopping: even the purveyors of standardized commodities, McDonald's' restaurants, have also had to adapt its menu to include special 'limited edition' choices, as well as the introduction of salad bars and 'McCafés'.

All in all, this image of flexible production and consumer choice might appear to discredit McDonaldization as a theory of global society. However theorists of global convergence would contend that rather than accept freedom and consumer choice at face value, rather, one should consider the *structural preconditions* of flexible labour practices and the 'consumer society'.

In terms of labour and production, flexible, market-driven production can still be interpreted within a critical theory framework of disenchantment and dehumanization. First, as Stephen Wood (1993) notes post-Fordism represents more of an *evolution* within Fordism than a transformation of it. As a result, for all its prioritization of flexibility, post-Fordism nevertheless rests on the 'fundamental bedrock of Fordism work study, assembly lines, and mass production and marketing' (Wood 1993: 535). Second, many organizational sociologists have argued that companies' applications of 'post-bureaucratic' methods have in fact been implemented with the intention of exerting *greater* control over its workforce in the pursuit of profit, especially when considering the calculative and auditing capabilities of contemporary project management schemes and e-network systems (see Metcalfe 1997; Hodgson 2004; Räisänen and Linde 2004).

This does not suggest a particularly liberating picture for individuals: rather than being married to the firm, workers today are now married to an entire *labour value system*. Richard Sennett (1998) argues that post-Fordism increases demand for flexible and spatially mobile workers on temporary contracts, which in many cases require few skills beyond computer data entry or till operation. For those outside of the global elite, this has dire consequences: on the one hand, Sennett argues that an emerging work culture founded on short-term thinking runs the risk of seeping into a wider behavioural phenomenon, where notions of loyalty, commitment and trust in social and cultural relationships are discouraged, resulting in an individualized 'corrosion of character' (1998: 26–7). On the other, the overarching power of the system means that adherence to individualism and flexibility is emphatically non-negotiable: notions of flexibility, adaptability and short-termism might seem to be the new dominant conditions of employment, but they are not presented as such. Instead, Sennett argues that they are now seen as 'moral virtues'.

In this sense, we seem to be returning to the dehumanizing and alienating conditions of labour originally characterized by Weber and Marx as workers drift from one job to another. This phenomenon was memorably captured by Douglas Coupland in his 1991 novel *Generation X*, describing 'low-pay, low-prestige, low-dignity, low-benefit, no-future' work roles as 'McJobs', which are 'frequently considered a satisfying career choice by people who have never held one' (Coupland 1991: 5). The irony of the McDonald's' reference is notable: such is the notoriety of the term in popular culture today that it has entered the Merriam-Webster dictionary in 2003, with McDonald's campaigning unsuccessfully for its removal.

If work remains standardized and alienating, one might see consumerism as providing a much-needed source of freedom and choice. According to Bauman (2000), however, the apparent freedom of consumer choice arguably masks a more oppressive reality: consumption is an exhilarating yet anxiety-making experience because ultimately, 'there is no end to the shopping list' and no matter how long the list, 'the way to opt out of shopping is not on it' (2000: 74). In other words, 'consumer freedom' in fact represents a very narrow definition of freedom: a freedom to choose from a prescribed set of commodities which have been lifted from their original cultural context and standardized for public consumption. Freedom, in this sense, is illusory and potentially more damaging than the age of mass production in that it masks an increasingly standardized reality, where 'things which inhabited different worlds and value systems...now occupy a single cultural space' (Slater 1997: 196).

So for all the consumer choice and career flexibility available in contemporary global society, McDonaldization theory contends that opportunities for greater individuality and self-autonomy have proven to be illusory. In fact, by marketing a consumer-defined freedom 'aesthetic', we are perhaps surrendering more of our personal autonomy than we realize. As a result, McDonaldization offers a pessimistic account of standardization and homogenization processes taking place beneath the surface. What makes this process innately global is its reach is that the basic McDonald's' model has effectively become the essential template for all commercial businesses. In other words, we are witnessing a global standardization of capitalist models of 'best practice', where successful design, production and marketing techniques are exchanged and adapted by businesses across the world.

The result of ongoing global exchange of successful business models is a world that is becoming more and more familiar to us: whether you are travelling to Buenos Aries, Moscow or Cape Town, a tourist's navigation and acclimatization is made easier by a familiarity with certain rules, behaviours and institutions. Almost regardless of where you visit, the chances are that you will arrive on a Boeing 747 aeroplane, go through standardized procedures at passport-control, reclaim your luggage from a revolving baggage-claim carousel, pick up cash from an ATM or currency exchange booth, travel to your hotel via bus, taxi or car rental, get issued an electronic key-card from hotel check-in, contact friends via Skype, Facebook or Twitter (all through hotel-provided internet services), phone for room service (vegetarian option available) and then sit down in your hotel room to watch CNN and BBC World on television, or national channels showing licensed versions of global franchises such as *Pop Idol*, *Big Brother* and *Who Wants to Be a Millionaire*. The town, city or country appears near-irrelevant; such is the extent that practices and procedures are universally recognizable and predictable.

These universal 'non-places' (after all, most airports, hotels, banks and shopping centres ultimately look the same) have multiplied across the world, either suffocating local diversities or commoditizing them to suit the tastes of the homogeneous global consumer – causing, in Ritzer's words, a process of 'grobalization': essentially the 'globalization of nothing' (Ritzer 2004). This also infers the argument that our interaction with such institutions has become increasingly standardized too, to the extent that we expect a McDonald's-style uniform service in all of society's institutions. This is a suggestion well worth interrogating – to what extent can we see a 'McDonaldization' going on in our public institutions? As a case study, let us consider the realm of politics.

5.7 The McDonaldization of politics

One can argue that a theory of the McDonaldization of politics entails two distinct yet interlinking processes. On the one hand, the content of politics is becoming increasingly homogeneous across the world, with nation-states more often reaching consensus on which political principles are most important, and which political systems are most successful in maintaining the smooth running of society. On the other hand, the practice and delivery of politics has been subject to standardization, with politicians, parties and campaign groups echoing the rational logic of McDonaldization by using what have now become the most efficient and effective methods of gaining public support.

Like fast food, the standardization of political delivery can be seen as representing a prioritization of means over ends, where political discourse relies more on image, style and sound bites than the validity of its content. The latter, too, has become more standardized and predictable with the political spectrum becoming narrowed through the global convergence of ideas. This makes it harder to differentiate between opposing leaders and parties in terms of content, leaving the media debate of style and delivery more accessible and easier to grasp for the general public. Moreover, the dialectical relationship between these two processes can be seen as creating a downward spiral which only serves to rationalize and homogenize modern politics further.

We can begin by exploring arguments that purport a narrowing of the political spectrum. In this view, it is seen that a basic global consensus is being reached on what constitutes legitimate philosophical values, efficient systems of governance. An analysis of political convergence addresses a broad field of literature including both evolutionary and critical theories, yet these different approaches nevertheless recognize similar trends in the structure and conduct of contemporary political life. Arguably the bedrock of a homogeneous global politics is the liberal democratic system. Recalling Chapter 2, liberalism operates according to universal values therefore making a transition into an inclusive, homogeneous 'global philosophy' relatively easily. At a structural level, the inclusivity of free trade between countries is seen as reducing the possibilities for disagreement on the assumption that everyone understands the rules of the game. This is seen to be a civilizing process as the sharing of philosophical values eliminates more violent means of attaining power, not least as the 'fairness' of free trade is seen to generate legitimate wealth creation to the benefit of all via trickle-down processes. At the level of agency, liberal democracies can be seen as actively promoting a rights discourse predicated on inclusivity and universality: one that advocates an individual equality of opportunity and rights against collectivizing and divisive forces such as racism, sexism and classism. Liberalism also transcends the divisiveness of nation-state politics in that individuals must be free from unnecessary state intervention, and that the role of the state must be to serve the people. Having established the existence of a global stage, freedom and fluidity are important requisites to being able to enjoy its opportunities for cultural exploration and wealth creation.

Earlier on in this chapter we traced the heritage of the McDonaldization framework to the debates around convergence and 'one-dimensionality' in the 1950s. While Ritzer's work is clearly indebted more to the latter, we suggested that a tradition does exist which is more in keeping with the ideas of the former. The most significant representative of this school of thought is the 'world polity theory' associated with John Meyer and his colleagues at Stanford University in the United States, who locate their perspective largely within a framework inspired by the theory of 'institutionalism', in which the focus is on how organizational practice is steered by its institutional *culture*. Crucial here for our analysis of political practices is its focus on the historical development of universal (or globalized) cultural values which compose 'rationalized modernity' (Meyer *et al.* 1979). Such values influence the development and direction of nation-states worldwide. Accordingly, the contemporary world can be described as 'bifurcated' (Rosenau 1990) in so far as it operates on two distinct but interconnected levels – the level of the nation-state system, or 'world polity', and beyond that the level of a set of globalized values and strategies, or 'global culture', which frames the institutional dynamics of nation-states (Meyer *et al.* 1979). In other words, these values influence the development and direction of nation-states worldwide. Within the context of such a globalized culture, all new and emerging nation-states are likely to develop in accordance with such values, so as to gain recognition, acceptance and entry into the nation-state system (Meyer *et al.* 1979; see also Meyer 1980; Meyer and Hannan 1979). Thus, in so far as democracy and human rights are among these global values, they become institutionalized in the strategies of nation-states – democratization at the nation-state level, then, is a natural reflection of the globalization of democracy as a universal value (Diamond 1993; Meyer *et al.* 1979). These values are promoted at the transnational level by campaigning organizations who thus exert more influence upon nation-states than is sometimes recognized (Boli and Thomas 1997). One consequence of this is that instances of 'unacceptable behaviour' – for example, torture, which is largely condemned by the world community – are made public, precisely because they contradict the globalized value system. Transnational institutions such as the United Nations can be seen as the articulators, perhaps even the custodians, of these values at the supra-national level.

There is, of course, a historical as well as theoretical precedent to the idea of a liberal democratic convergence. Fukuyama (1991) chronicles the remarkable rise in number of liberal democracies since the eighteenth century, as it has usurped alternative, exclusivist political systems such as monarchism, fascism and communism to become the sole uncontested ideology at the 'end of history'. Again recalling Chapter 2, we can infer Fukuyama's analysis of the rationality of liberal democracy, and its capacity to override any internal conflicts and contradictions through its core values: liberalism which promotes individual rights and protects individuals from state tyranny; democracy which incorporates citizens in the decision-making process; and capitalism, which ensures economic stability and the opportunity for individual wealth creation. Depending on one's argument, the liberal democratic model can be seen to represent either Durkheim's model of society, via its shared norms and values and ethic of societal evolution, or Weber's bureaucracy through its system of rationalized organizations which consumes individuals' everyday lives while minimizing opportunities for alternative, holistic discourses to prosper.

Either way, the triumph of liberal democracy can be understood in how it has smoothed the rough edges of the political spectrum. In this respect there has historically been a significant difference between British and US politics – the former always having been more ideological and partisan. The idea of 'consensus' politics emerged in the post-Second World War era as Butler's Conservatives and Gaitskill's Labour Party coalesced into a 'Butskillite' middle ground. After this, consensus politics was largely eschewed in favour of ideological distinction, and the epitome of this came with the move rightwards of the Conservatives in the 1970s. However, ironically, this also laid the foundations for the new political consensus politics of the 1990s and into the new millennium, the 'Third Way' which briefly dominated American as well as British politics. The neo-liberal governments of Thatcher and Reagan in the 1980s dutifully dismantled Keynesian welfare politics in favour of economic liberalization and in doing so established a new order of economic efficiency and flexibility, as well as a market-defined ideology of individualism. Although a more detailed analysis into the 'irresistible appeal' of neo-liberalism has already been undertaken in Chapter 2, we should at least point here to the seeming 'irreversibility' of its economic project, ranging from the cutbacks in welfare spending and multimillion-pound privatization deals (Evans 1997; Adonis and Pollard 1997) to the perceived 'death of class' via the new demands for flexibility and mobility in the labour market (Lash and Urry 1987; Beck 1992; Beck, Giddens and Lash 1994; Beck and Beck-Gernsheim 2002). From this emerged what became known as the 'Third Way', the new political agenda 'beyond Left and Right' which quickly took hold in the UK, the US, Germany, Brazil and elsewhere. As Anthony Giddens (1994) points out, the ideological conjecture between the 'radical' Left and the 'conservative' Right gave way to a new politics of pragmatism, in which the Right had become increasingly radical in its advocacy of the market and the Left had shifted to the centre in its commitment to social justice within a conservative framework of individual responsibility, resulting in a peculiar blend of communitarianism and neo-liberalism. The new consensus politics, then, is perhaps more accurately described as *combining* rather than *transcending* Left and Right (Driver and Martell 1998).

Is this an example of the 'McDonaldization of politics'? Perhaps the jury is still out on that one, but while awaiting the verdict we should consider, by way of evidence of the growing homogeneity of liberal democracies, Thomas Friedman's (1999) 'Golden Arches Theory of Conflict Prevention':

> Every once in a while when I am travelling abroad, I need to indulge in a burger and a bag of McDonald's French fries. For all I know, I have eaten McDonald's burgers and fries in more countries in the world than anyone, and I can testify that they all really do taste the same. But as I Quarter-Poundered my way through the world in recent years, I began to notice something intriguing ... And it was this: *no two countries that both had McDonald's had fought a war against each other since each got its McDonald's* ... 'The Golden Arches Theory of Conflict Prevention' ... stipulates that when a country reaches a level of economic development where it has a middle class big enough to support a McDonald's network, it becomes a McDonald's country. And people in McDonald's countries don't like to fight wars anymore, they prefer to wait in line for burgers. (Friedman 1999: 195–6; emphasis added)

Although Friedman's theory is somewhat tongue-in-cheek (as well as contestable if one were to question what constitutes modern warfare), his point remains an interesting one. With economic liberalization creating networks of liberal-democratic states, one can argue that individual countries have little to gain and much to lose by initiating armed conflict against a fellow liberal democracy. As a result, in becoming a neo-liberal capitalist democracy – of which opening a McDonald's restaurant perhaps represents its symbolic coronation – a country is entering a global network of political consensus: one in which market capitalism and representative democracy are systems come to define our understanding of politics and economics and as a result go largely unquestioned.

So, at the level of political ideology, it would appear that widespread consensus over the primacy of liberal democracies has created a narrowing of the political spectrum as parties vie for the centre ground, thereby providing a limit to the range and diversity of political issues and policies at stake during general elections. At the same time, media demands and conventions help to shape a widely accepted model of political *presentation* which is carefully tailored to public demand. In a media-dominated world, style and presentation take precedence over substance, and political spin doctors and media consultants become genuinely important political players. Like all public figures, politicians recognize the need to be seen as possessing personality as well as intellect, character as well as content (Corner and Pels 2003: 7). While media visibility benefits them in that it allows them to reach a wider audience, at the same time it exposes their mistakes and their shortcomings (Thompson 1995). As an example of this, Ritzer (2008) notes how political speeches are increasingly written with television audiences in mind, which in turn affects structure, delivery and impact. During the 1984 US presidential campaign, he observes, only about 15 seconds of a speech would likely find its way onto national news programmes; by 1988, this had shrunk further to nine seconds. As a result, political speechwriters would have to concentrate on creating short but memorable 'sound-bites' that were likely to be picked up by television networks. The sound-bite device can be understood as less of a simple message than a standardized 'gimmick' created with the intention of coercing voters through style rather than content: the BBC journalist Nicholas Jones laments how 'in the pursuit of publicity even the humblest and most obscure MPs have had to become slaves to the sound-bite, capable of encapsulating their arguments in a few short, sharp sentences' (N. Jones 1995: 12). Ritzer, too, argues that this emphasis on shortness and immediacy 'has clearly reduced the quality of public political speeches and, therefore, the quality of public discourse on important political issues' (Ritzer 2008: 92). This stands in stark contrast with political speech-making in the pre-television age, such as the Lincoln–Douglas debates of 1858 in the US in which 'candidates spoke for ninety minutes each on a single topic' and even the 1930s, where political speeches on radio would often last an hour (*ibid.*).

So, with the media setting the agenda, political discourse becomes something of a reality television programme, driven by the logic of increased audience and profitability rather than the commitment to genuine public debate. Indeed, as John Street points out, it actually blocks any such commitment to full political participation and debate (2001: 197). This, in turn, transforms the general public into similarly homogeneous 'McCitizens' who are 'consumers of politics' (Turner 1999; Street 2001). The Frankfurt School theorist Theodor Adorno, whose work on homogenization and cultural commodification was taken up by both Marcuse and Ritzer, had foreseen much of this when he bemoaned the extent to which the culture industry was impeding 'the development of autonomous, independent individuals who...would be the precondition for a democratic society' (Adorno 2001: 92).

5.8 Conclusion

What are we to make of the McDonaldization approach? Perhaps it is too easy, in the context of this volume, to highlight its weaknesses and, taking the role of critic, attack it from both sides. For some, it has to be said, McDonaldization does not go far enough to identify the political and ideological dynamics which underpin this particular form of rationalization. Such dynamics might lead a critic more in the direction of Americanization, for example. For others, though, it suffers from the same weaknesses as does Americanization, namely, its overly simplistic, one-directional approach to global social change, which duly ignores those acts of resistance to any dominant ideology, or of appropriation and indigenization, which make global culture a far more heterogeneous and complex beast. Such critics are likely to favour the creolization model which we turn to in the next chapter.

But it is worth pointing out that Ritzer never intended to present McDonaldization as a form of globalization, but rather as an updated version of Weber's classic rationalization thesis suitably applied to particular organizations in society. That it has become intertwined with the literature on globalization is cause for its inclusion here, but in truth it stands in as a useful way of describing a process of global standardization which actually pre-dates the current interest in globalization quite comfortably. By referring to this process as McDonaldization rather than standardization or homogenization, are we perhaps guilty of presenting it in a biased way? Perhaps so, but, in any case, we should all remember that for many people there is much to be praised about McDonald's restaurants, and much to be applauded in they way they are run.

The issue at stake is largely a moral and a political one – to return to Marcuse, does such a process of standardization, if it exists, really represent a negation of freedom? Given that Marcuse put his faith in the potential of students to shatter the closed walls of one-dimensional society, perhaps it is appropriate to end with the impact of McDonaldization on higher education, as an example of how it can be applied to a given institution. Following Ritzer's lead there has been much talk of how universities have been undergoing such a process, of how we might be seeing the onset of the neo-Fordist university, or 'McUniversity' (Parker and Jary 1995; Ritzer 1996). What might be the characteristics of such an establishment? It would be entirely committed to simplification, and to 'downsizing', although not in respect of student numbers. Short-term, junior, non-tenured staff would be employed; distance learning would be encouraged; strategies for the efficient use of information technology and virtual learning via cyberspace would be developed; satellite schools and campuses would be opened up; while campuses themselves would become more like shopping malls... Ritzer (1996) provides a neat summary of hypothetical characteristics. Academic staff might see themselves as becoming increasingly enslaved by technology in a drive for increasing efficiency, just as the job description of the university lecturer has been transformed substantially by the technological revolution of the last 30 years, taking on much more responsibility for administration than had hitherto been the case. The emphasis upon calculability comes into the equation as well: Ritzer (1993: 77) cites the former President of Stanford University, Donald Kennedy, who expressed concerns about the perceived emphasis on quantity rather than quality in assessing research output. But, what role might the student play in such an organization? She or he appears to occupy a dual position, as both consumer and product. While, on the one hand, the 'student-as-consumer' model suggests the empowerment of the student who is then able to maximize their best interests in the political semiotics of the curriculum, on the other, the 'student-as-product' is largely disempowered, processed in large numbers and lacking in individuality and the distinctiveness to survive out in the marketplace.

Academics and students reading this book, we leave it to you to decide whether any of this sounds even remotely familiar, and thus to judge for yourselves whether the logic of the fast-food industry has at all crept into such other areas of our lives.

Creolization: Hybrid Societies

6

6.1 Introduction

Drawing on the work of Benedict Anderson, the cultural anthropologist Arjun Appadurai asks us to think of the constitution of the world in terms of 'imagined communities', or as he calls them, 'imagined worlds', and to develop a new theory which appreciates the constructed nature of the multiple cultural flows which form the 'building blocks' of these imagined worlds (Appadurai 1996: 33). Appadurai lists five such flows, which can be summarized in tabular form for the sake of convenience (see Table 6.1).

According to Appadurai, the world is not easily reducible to any singular process of transformation, but is rather the arena in which these flows are contested. Following Appadurai and others, the 'creolization' framework focuses on these flows and exchanges of products, practices, ethics, aesthetics and people, between cultures, and interrogates an imagined world in which global interconnectedness results in the constant redefining of these flows in respect of localized meanings (Appadurai 1990, 1996; Houlihan 1994). Contrary to alternative perspectives, these flows are not one-way (although at the same time they are not fully reciprocal). Localized meanings given to them require a constant renegotiation of 'local' or 'national' cultures in the light of these influences. The creolization framework thus views cultures as hybridized, rather than static and homogeneous (Nederveen Pieterse 1995; Hannerz 1996). For example, dispersed peoples may have no fixed sense of 'identity', because they belong simultaneously to several 'homes', dwell at the intersection of various cultures and histories (Hall 1992a, 1992b).

This framework is complementary to the literature on colonialism and imperialism, in so far as creolization and hybridization are treated as products of these processes – modernity is inherently 'dislocating' (Gilroy 1993). However, it rejects the simplicity of cultural imperialism or Americanization (which we discussed in Chapter 4) and homogenization or McDonaldization (see Chapter 5) in favour of a concern with the reception and indigenization of cultural forms – an active interplay between core and periphery (Hannerz

Table 6.1 Types of cultural flow

Ethnoscapes	'the landscape of persons who constitute the shifting world in which we live: tourists, immigrants, refugees, exiles, guest workers ...'
Mediascapes	'the distribution of the electronic capabilities to produce and disseminate information ... throughout the world, and to the images of the world created by these media'
Technoscapes	'the global configuration ... of technology ... (which) now moves at high speeds across various kinds of previously impervious borders'
Financescapes	'the disposition of global capital ... [by which] currency markets, national stock exchanges, and commodity speculations move megamonies through national turnstiles at blinding speed'
Ideoscapes	'concatenations of images ... to do with the ideologies of states and the counter-ideologies of movements ... oriented to capturing state power ... including freedom, welfare rights, sovereignty, representation, and ... democracy'

Source: Appadurai (1996: 33–6).

Biography Box 12:   Arjun Appadurai

Arjun Appadurai (1949–) is John Dewey Professor in the Social Sciences and also Senior Advisor for Global Initiatives at the New School, New York City. He was born in India and has been one of the leading analysts of global processes within the discipline of social anthropology. His publications include *Modernity at Large* (1996).

1996). The framework thus provides a significant alternative to these models in terms of describing global transformations at the cultural level. The following table, comparing the two approaches, is taken from Nederveen Pieterse (1995: 62):

Creolization thus stands in stark opposition to homogenization, whether of the Americanizing or McDonaldizing kind. Whereas proponents of homogenization bemoan a world increasingly losing its richness of diversity and local culture, the creolization thesis describes a world of flows, of resistance and of perpetual change.

A good example of this distinction is the case of Coca-Cola. While the McDonaldization framework might see Coca-Cola as exemplary of the standardizing processes it describes, an alternative reading would focus on the meanings attributed to the drink in different local settings, such as

Table 6.2   Homogenizing and diversifying forms of global change

Globalization/homogenization	Globalization/diversification
Cultural imperialism	Cultural planetarization
Cultural dependence	Cultural interdependence
Cultural hegemony	Cultural interpenetration
Autonomy	Syncretism, synthesis, hybridity
Modernization	Modernizations
Westernization	Global mélange
Cultural synchronization	Creolization, crossover
World civilization	Global ecumene

its indigenization through being blended with other drinks, or the peculiar qualities attributed to it by various audiences. Howes (1996) puts it succinctly:

> No imported object, Coca-Cola included, is completely immune from creolization. Indeed, one finds that Coke is often attributed with meanings and uses within particular cultures that are different from those imagined by the manufacturer. These include that it can smooth wrinkles (Russia), that it can revive a person from the dead (Haiti), and that it can turn copper into silver (Barbados)…Coke is also indigenised through being mixed with other drinks, such as rum in the Caribbean to make *Cuba Libre* or *aguadiente* in Bolivia to produce *Poncho Negro*. Finally, it seems that Coke is perceived as a 'native product' in many different places – that is you will often find people who believe the drink originated in their country not in the United States. (Howes 1996: 6)

In this chapter we will look in detail at the 'creolization' framework, drawing on some of the excellent case studies presented by its key advocates (such as Hannerz 1996). To better understand it, though, we need to trace its history prior to its application to the field of global studies, from its development within the neo-Gramscian tradition in cultural studies, through its association with theories of 'postmodernism' and 'postmodernity' (Featherstone 1991), and 'post-colonial hybridity' (Bhabha 1994).

6.2   Cultural studies and the theory of resistance

The creolization framework is closely allied to a development within the study of culture that emerged most famously from the Birmingham University Centre for Contemporary Cultural Studies in the 1970s. Researchers at this famous Centre drew on a number of existing traditions in socio-cultural theory – most prominently the neo-Marxism of Antonio Gramsci – to develop a theory of culture which treats its subject matter as the site of permanent struggle between competing groups. While schooled in the theory of power and domination presented by Marx and later Marxists, the Birmingham School drew attention to the dynamics of resistance undertaken by subordinate groups within power relationships, and in particular to resistance through appropriation of the symbols of subordination. In later years this emphasis on resistance, largely divorced from its original political-economic context, was taken up by more populist and postmodernist theorists of culture.

The starting point for this theory within cultural studies was the concept of 'hegemony', as introduced into Marxian theory by Gramsci to refer to the process through which the dominant class achieves the consent of the people and thus maintains its position. According to Gramsci, such consent is manufactured through culture-ideology. This was later taken up by the French structuralist Marxist philosopher Louis Althusser, in his work on how 'dominant ideologies' were systematically reproduced through the 'ideological state apparatuses' such as the education system, religion and the media. However, while Althusserian Marxism seems resigned to the inevitability of successful systemic reproduction, and can be viewed as a form of determinism which ignores the actors involved in such a process, the Birmingham School's neo-Gramscian approach treats hegemony as a complex process which involves the participation of the subordinate group, requiring as it does negotiations and concessions between it and the dominant group. For sure, according to the Birmingham scholars and others sympathetic to their approach, bourgeois values *do* constitute a dominant ideology in society, and the project of this ideology *is* to reshape alternative, potentially revolutionary cultures in its own image, as such alternative or revolutionary cultures – working-class cultures, youth subcultures, the cultures of ethnic minorities and so on – *do* represent a threat to this dominance. A good example of this is how the 'moral panic' around the crime of mugging was constructed through the ideological state apparatuses to direct the gaze of an angry public away from the problems of the state and towards the alleged criminality of young black males, in order to provide public legitimacy for the mobilization of the *repressive* state apparatuses, such as the police, prevent widespread dissent and strengthen social control (Hall *et al.* 1978).

However, many such subordinate groups emerge in part as a response to the frustrations existing within suppressed communities. For example, important work was carried out on how certain youth subcultures, such as mods, rockers, teddy boys and punks, came into being in this way (Cohen 1972). Such 'subcultures' are often expressed in terms of 'imaginary relations' such as 'symbols' and 'styles' (*ibid.*), exercising what Stuart Hall and Tony Jefferson (1976) famously referred to as 'resistance through rituals'. This resistance to the dominant ideology is often expressed through the appropriation of particular cultural forms, symbols, clothing, and so on otherwise associated with the dominant bourgeois culture, and infusing them with new meanings, 'oppositional meanings' not intended by the producer (Hebdige 1979). Meaning thus results from what Stuart Hall calls 'articulation', and has to be understood in its context. Musical styles, fashion, even language which might otherwise have been used for the purpose of subordination, have been duly appropriated by subordinate groups and reproduced as positive symbols of identification. Some have argued, for example, that in direct contrast to the fears held by the 'mass culture' theorists about Americanization, which we have already discussed at length in Chapter 4, popular Hollywood cinema provides working-class youths with positive symbols of identity and resistance (White 1986), while the content of girls' magazines, which might at one level appear to serve the interests of a patriarchal society, is often redefined and even confronted by the readers themselves (McRobbie 1991).

Within the field of cultural studies, the neo-Gramscian power-resistance paradigm developed by the Birmingham School became so influential it was almost synonymous with the subject itself. Parallels were drawn with the work of Michel Foucault, and also with that of Pierre Bourdieu in sociology. Latterly, though, the approach has been somewhat watered down through the influence of 'postmodernist' theory, which is less concerned with broader, structural dynamics of power (we will discuss 'postmodernism' in greater detail below). For such 'cultural populists' (a term not favourably received by many to whom it is applied), the everyday experience of cultural forms is as or more significant than their ideological 'structures', and people are not 'cultural dopes' but agents actively involved in interpreting and appropriating cultural forms to suit their own experiences. Accordingly, people are seen as 'consumers' busily 'reading' cultural forms, making sense of them and using them as a form of localized resistance to such broader ideologies (Fiske 1987, 1989a, 1989b). Consumption is thus a highly creative act which actually *produces* culture (Willis *et al.* 1990). The 'cultural field' is duly separated from the economic field, and it exists as a site of struggles between competing interpretations, thus challenging any possible claim that a single dominant ideology can even exist (Fiske 1989b).

In its earlier form, then, the theory of resistance, inspired largely by Gramsci and Althusser, was located firmly in the radical, neo-Marxist camp, committed as it was to the idea that a dominant ideology exists but equally committed to the belief that local resistance to this domination *matters*. In its later form, despite its claim that consumption operates as a form of resistance and empowerment, it comes across as less critical, more inclined towards social pluralism, prioritizing as it seems to do the individual over the wider social structure and legitimizing, as some have suggested it does, liberal democracy and free market capitalism. In the field of global studies, and in particular within the framework of creolization, parallels exist with each 'wing'. Some of the more 'postmodernist' work on creolization concentrates its efforts largely at the level of consumption, emphasizing the extent to which 'cultures' are fluid constructs, constantly being negotiated and renegotiated, while a lot of the more Marxian-influenced work looks at how creolization operates as a form of resistance to dominant global structures (*contra* Americanization), and has its roots in post-colonial theory – a good example of which being Arjun Appadurai's sophisticated account of the 'Indianization' of cricket (Appadurai 1996: 95). It is worth turning our attention now to the contested terrain of colonialism and post-colonialism.

6.3   Post-colonialism and the theory of Orientalism

'Post-colonialism' is the name given to a broad movement across the humanities and social sciences that is concerned with how colonized peoples 'write' their own histories, tell their own stories, in response to the impact of imperialism and colonialism. It seeks to identify the legacies of colonialism in the contemporary world and to open up spaces for the multiple voices of the subordinate party, or 'subaltern', to be heard. This *construction of identity* is presented as a form of resistance to the colonizer, but one which is firmly embedded *within* the power dynamic, rather than outside it. It often draws heavily upon the language, styles and cultural forms of the colonial oppressor.

Probably the most significant text in post-colonial theory is Palestinian writer Edward Said's *Orientalism*. Originally published in 1978, Said shows in eloquent fashion how those from the West who study the East have done so from within the comfort of their own Western power structures, thus silencing the voices of those they study.

Biography Box 13:   Edward Said

Edward Said (1935–2003) was a Palestinian-American cultural commentator and literary theorist and one of the most famous intellectuals of the late twentieth century. His 1978 publication *Orientalism* sparked off a major and heated debate on the issue of how Asia and the Middle East have been portrayed in Western culture, and is considered to be the archetypal example of post-colonial theory. He was University Professor of English and Comparative Literature at Columbia University until his premature death at the age of 67.

Said's work is heavily indebted to structuralist theory. Structuralism in this sense should not be confused with the approach to political economy discussed in Chapter 3. Rather, it is a broad intellectual movement originating in linguistics, which, during the latter half of the twentieth century, exerted considerable influence in the disciplines of anthropology, sociology, psychology, cultural studies and literary theory. The crux of the structuralist argument is that in language a distinction should be made between the arbitrary and culturally relative performance of communication, including words, and the universally applicable rules of language construction, which constitute a deep structure capable of scientific analysis. In the social world, such a distinction can be made between the rich variety of cultural *practices* exhibited across the many diverse societies, and the universal needs of human society (including kinship, worship and so on) they represent. Crucially, though, these are constructed within the inescapable framework of language itself, which not only defines things according to what they are not and thus relies upon *binary opposites*, but also contains an inherent power dynamic, in so far as these binary opposites become representative of ideological distinctions between 'good' and 'bad', 'right' and 'wrong'.

In Said's writings, 'East' and 'West', or more precisely 'Orient' and 'Occident', are themselves presented as binary opposites, constructed in relation to one another, and thus containing their own inherent power relationship; the 'Orient' is reproduced through representation as the negative counterpart to the 'Occident'. For Said, 'Orientalism' is far more than a field of study, the pursuit of academic knowledge about the Orient. Rather, it 'is a style of thought based upon an ontological and epistemological distinction between "the Orient" and... "the Occident"' (2003: 2), which produces a certain way for the West to approach the East: 'dealing with it by making statements about it, authorizing views of it, describing it, by teaching it, settling it, ruling over it: in short, Orientalism as a Western style for dominating, restructuring, and having authority over the Orient' (*ibid.*: 3). In the view of another significant post-colonial theorist, Gayatri Chakravorty Spivak, in her *A Critique of Postcolonial Reason* (1999), this amounts to the exclusion of the subaltern from the category of the human subject. Thus, for Said, 'the Orient that appears in Orientalism... is a system of representations framed by a whole set of forces that brought the Orient into Western learning, Western consciousness, and later, Western empire' (Said 2003: 202–3). Accordingly:

> A new dialectic emerges out of this project. What is required of the Oriental expert is no longer simply 'understanding': now the Orient must be made to perform, its power must be enlisted on the side of 'our' values, civilization, interests, goals. Knowledge of the Orient is directly translated into activity, and the results give rise to new currents of thought and action in the Orient... The Orientalist has now become a figure of Oriental history... its shaper, a characteristic *sign* from the West. (*Ibid.*: 238)

Said's theory, from its origins in the study of post-colonial and comparative literature, has developed into an indispensable framework across the humanities and social sciences generally, and it is clearly of particular relevance to the field of global studies. After all, it is about the perception and construction of the non-Western world through the perspective of the West (Said 2003). While it clearly understands contemporary global dynamics as part of a broader set of issues inseparable from imperialism and colonialism (Said 1993), significantly it does not treat these current dynamics as being in themselves the simple inheritors of this imperialism. Rather, in a way that predates Hardt and Negri's revision of the idea (Hardt and Negri 2000), if it can be argued that today's world constitutes an empire, defined by a dialectic of oppression and subordination, then it is an empire with no discernible core, a decentred empire rather than a crude American empire or a set of core–periphery relations. Said's work, while it has clear affinities with the subject matter of Chapter 4, takes us down rather more sophisticated terrain than does much of the Americanization literature. If there is a hegemony at work, then it is a 'scattered' hegemony, not reducible to a single core or direction (Grewal and Kaplan 1994).

While not disagreeing with Said's central argument, the Indian cultural theorist Homi K. Bhabha, in *The Location of Culture* (1994), is quick to point to the danger of over-emphasizing difference which emerges from Said's grounding in structuralism. If the dominant and subaltern voices in the post-colonial world are treated as binary opposites then the consequence is the reproduction of a dominant ideology. Far better, advises Bhabha, to combat this power relationship by recognizing, and emphasizing, the *hybridity* of these two worlds. Others influenced by Said have raised similar concerns. Spivak has sought to overcome the apparent contradiction between political activism and intellectual essentialism by introducing the concept of 'strategic essentialism' as a politicized response to Orientalism, while Paul Gilroy (1993) has substantially rethought the suggestion that black communities in the West are somehow 'dislocated' from their roots, which is grounded in an ethnic essentialism, by emphasizing the growth of a fluid, hybrid and transnational 'Black Atlantic' culture. However, Said has responded to such concerns in a later book, *Culture and Imperialism* (1993), and in a revised edition of *Orientaism* (2003), by insisting on the interrelatedness and interdependence of cultures, and laying down a direct challenge to those academics who see 'diversity' as leading inevitably to conflict, not least Samuel Huntingdon, who we will discuss in Chapter 8:

> How can one today speak of 'Western civilization' except as in large measure an ideological fiction, implying a sort of detached superiority for a handful of values and ideas, none of which has much meaning outside the history of conquest, immigration, travel and the mingling of peoples that gave the Western nations their present mixed identities? ... And this was one of the implied messages of *Orientalism*, that any attempt to force cultures and peoples into separate and distinct breeds or essences exposes ... the way

in which understanding is complicit with the power to produce such things as the 'Orient' or the 'West'. (Said 2003: 349)

One of the most significant developments to have emerged as a result of the influence of Said and post-colonial theory in general has been the interest among social theorists in 'new ethnicities' or 'new cultural identities', largely within the major metropolitan centres of the former colonial countries. Homi Bhabha (1994), Stuart Hall (1991b, 1992a, 1992b), Paul Gilroy (1993), Arjun Appadurai (1990, 1996) and John Eade (1997) are among those who have contributed to this literature. According to such writers, post-colonial diasporas in global cities exhibit a blend of tradition and modernity, globality and locality, opening up a multiplicity of identities available to them. Arjun Appadurai (1990), for example, claims that global processes have broken down the once-dominant paradigm of nationalism, constructing new identities which, rather than detracting from the local, actually encourage it. John Eade's work among young Bengalis in London's Tower Hamlets reveals how such individuals strategically select from a range of identities, including Bengali, Bangladeshi, English, Muslim, Londoner and so on (Eade 1997). In such an ever-changing, creolized world, individual identity formations are necessarily fluid and dispersed – subject to a process that Homi Bhabha (1990), Kevin Robins (1991) and Stuart Hall (1992b) all refer to as 'translation':

> This describes those identity formations which cut across and intersect natural frontiers, and which are composed of people who have been dispersed forever from their homelands. Such people retain strong links with their places of origin and their traditions, but they are without the illusion of a return to the past. They are obliged to come to terms with the new cultures they inhabit, without simply assimilating to them and losing their identities completely. They bear upon them the traces of particular cultures, traditions, languages and histories by which they were shaped. The difference is that they are not and will never be unified in the old sense, because they are irrevocably the product of several interlocking histories and cultures, belong at one and the same time to several 'homes' (and to no one particular 'home'). People belonging to such cultures of hybridity have had to renounce the dream or ambition of rediscovering any kind of 'lost' cultural purity... They are irrevocably 'translated'. (Hall 1992b: 310)

The idea of 'translation' thus opens up a new space in which to interrogate the idea of cultural identity, between that which speaks of dislocation from some (imagined) homeland, and that which bemoans its decline in the face of homogenizing forces. With this in mind, we should now turn to the related idea, which is central to much of the creolization debate as articulated by Hall and others – the idea of 'postmodernity'.

Biography Box 14:   Stuart Hall

Stuart Hall (1932–) was born in Jamaica but has been based mostly in the United Kingdom since 1951. He took over from Richard Hoggart as the Director of the Centre for Contemporary Cultural Studies at the University of Birmingham in 1968 and under his guidance it produced some of the most ground-breaking cultural commentaries of the 1970s, including the co-authored *Policing the Crisis* (1978). In 1979 he took up the post of Professor of Sociology at the Open University, and is now Emeritus Professor at that institution. A highly regarded public intellectual in the United Kingdom, he has written extensively on social theory generally and on the theory of modernity specifically, as well as on racism, youth culture, criminality, the changing face of the political Left and the politics of Thatcherism.

6.4   Creolization and postmodernity

As Hall and others insist, culture is the product of a complex series of historical social exchanges and relationships which raises the question as whether it is possible for cultural identities to retain any sort of 'purity' or permanence. Historically, social groups have often constructed and ascribed unfamiliar cultures as 'foreign' and discreditable, while at the same time doing everything they can to symbolically affirm their own. Yet through the legacy of colonialism and migration cultural meanings and associations become more complex which today means that attempts to make arbitrarily distinctions between cultures is an increasingly meaningless activity. Instead, the subjectivities and fluidities of culture have come to the fore – particularly their positive, creative capacities – to create a world of growing hybridity and difference, or what Hannerz usefully refers to as a 'global ecumene'. He explains further:

> What is at the core of the concept of creole culture, I think, is a combination of diversity, interconnectedness, and innovation, in the context of global center–periphery relationships. The diversity in question involves a mostly rather recent confluence of separate and quite different traditions... The interconnectedness typically takes the shape of a relatively continuous spectrum of interacting meanings and meaningful forms... The cultural processes of creolization are not merely a matter of constant pressure from the center toward the periphery, but a more active interplay. (Hannerz 1996: 67–8)

Tomlinson defines creole culture in a similar fashion:

> [T]he increasing traffic between cultures that the globalization process brings suggests that the dissolution of the link between culture and place is

accompanied by an intermingling of these disembedded cultural practices producing new complex hybrid forms of culture. (Tomlinson 1999: 141)

Both of the above quotations can be seen as implying a dynamic role for the actor-as-consumer who is capable of actively constructing new cultural meanings out of a wide range of commodities from across the globe. This role is also open and democratic in the sense that, in a capitalist society, everyone is a consumer regardless of their class or ethnic background. Hannerz and Tomlinson also infer that cultural commodities are mostly subservient to the consumer's interpretation and use for them: as objects they are might be free-flowing and flexible, but as *texts* they are not necessarily capable of inducing a fixed meaning from its reader. In a nutshell, all cultural objects today are commodities, or at least able to be turned into commodities, and cultural exchange is now synonymous with capitalist exchange. Culture is therefore no longer an ideological field as its objects have no fixed social meaning or context once they become commodities. This means that their previous structural capacity to reproduce dominant power relations in society have been diluted by the free-flowing and consumer-empowering 'spirit' of global capitalist consumption.

This disordered and unpredictable view of global culture owes much to theories of postmodernity, notably in the works of Lyotard (1984), Baudrillard (1988b) and Bauman (1992, 2001). Indeed, some writers make the link between creolization and postmodernity explicit. For example, Jan Nederveen Pieterse (1995) insists the globalizing process he calls, following Bhabha, 'hybridization' does not derive from modernity or modernization *per se*. Rather like the globalization theorist Martin Albrow, who we discussed in Chapter 1, Nederveen Pieterse equates modernity with the nation-state. The hybridization process, he insists, begins in the 1960s, with the onset of *post*modernity. A similar claim is made by Mike Featherstone, for whom creolization is an aspect of the postmodernization of the world (1991), while Stuart Hall (1991a: 32, 1992b: 302–3) speaks of the 'global post-modern' which arises out of the modernist project of globalization.

Although its validity as a stand-alone theory has been much contested by critics (see Giddens 1990; Sardar 1998), the theory of postmodernity does at least help us to identify some of the key presuppositions of creolization as an autonomous, creative activity. We can firstly consider Lyotard's (1984) proclamation that postmodernity has initiated 'the end of meta-narratives' (such as Enlightenment science, nationalism or Marxism) in contemporary society. Historically, meta-narratives have claimed to provide a stable and holistic account of society's past, present and future, but in a postmodern society the proliferation of knowledge via global media communications technologies has produced a conflation of different knowledge discourses. Consequently, Lyotard argues that there is no longer any certainty to knowledge, only a plurality of smaller narratives that compete with each other.

The end of meta-narratives effectively entails the end of the idea of an objective truth: all that is left are better or worse ways to interpret things. For the culture industry, this means that the previously unquestioned objects of 'mass culture' are now able to be deconstructed and reinterpreted by consumers, giving rise to exercises in eclecticism, bricolage, pastiche and parody. In broader terms, this causes the flattening of modern, materialist cultural distinctions such as high culture/mass culture, truth/fiction, mind/body, science/art and dominant culture/subculture. In its place is a free-flowing, infinitely changing 'political economy of signs' for consumers to choose from. Therefore, in postmodern consumerism it is increasingly difficult to distinguish 'reality' from 'hyper-reality', or present culture from past culture as postmodernity essentially produces culture that is without a sense of historical narrative, where consumption is locked into the 'discontinuous flow of a perpetual present' (Storey 2003: 65).

Underpinning all of this, of course, is the growing dominance of consumer capitalism, which allows creolization to be practised on a global scale. As we have observed before, capitalism initiates a continuous search for new markets and consumers, resulting in the exchange of a wide range of cultural commodities across the globe. Significantly, Harvey (1989) observes that late capitalist production has caused a *time–space compression*, meaning that in order for cultural objects to become global commodities they must become separated from their original culture-specific context. For example, a piece of indigenous music recorded in Africa in the 1960s takes on a whole new meaning once it is selected as part of a CD compilation of 'World Music' and sold to middle-class Western consumers via Amazon.com or Virgin Megastore. Traditional or local meanings are therefore lost in transit once they become commodities, for in the global supermarket, 'things which inhabited different worlds and value systems, and were consumed by different audiences, now occupy a single cultural space' (Slater 1997: 196).

To make such transactions possible, capitalism requires a form of production that complements the increasing diversity of cultural products demanded by consumers worldwide. For this we can recall the rise of post-Fordist production methods. We noted in the last chapter that post-Fordism represents more of an evolution within Fordism than a transformation of it, meaning that its greater flexibilities in work and production are nevertheless underpinned by traditional Fordist notions of organizational control and the pursuit of profit. Yet the reason for an evolution of its productive methods represents partially a turnaround on the assumption that consumer taste and buying power could be mapped out fairly predictably along traditional dimensions of social structure. Instead, post-Fordist production and marketing disaggregates markets and consumption into different 'lifestyles' and 'niche markets' which are not defined by broad social demographic structures such as class, gender or ethnicity, but rather by cultural meanings that link a range of goods and activities into a coherent image (*ibid*.: 191). Not only does this process reflect acts of creolization *already* taking place, it also succeeds in structurally *reproducing* it as a legitimate form of cultural production and consumption, and one that can be transferred and reproduced throughout the world.

Of course, cultural hybridization can only take place if its participants are themselves sufficiently open-minded to deconstruct the meanings of objects and shop for something outside of their immediate cultural environment. Implicit within creolization is the decline of tradition as the basis of authoritative knowledge in society. Traditional knowledge incorporates the fetishism of values and practices from the past which are justified on the basis that they 'contain and perpetuate the experience of generations' (Giddens 1990: 37). As a result, traditional knowledge is somewhat static, leaving little room for meaningful generational change or reflection outside of a society's dominant social values. According to Giddens (1990, 1991), however, traditional authority in modern society has now been held to public scrutiny through education and the spread of media and communications technologies which has helped uncover individuals' capacity to think *reflexively*, enabling the critical reflection of, and ultimately the dissolution of, traditional ways of life. We will expand on this theory in more detail in the next chapter.

There are clear social consequences to the decline of tradition: with the reflexive reordering of culture through consumerism and the decompression of time and space, not to mention the greater mobility demands of the global labour market, individuals are now left feeling 'disembedded' from secure, authentic society. This marks the disappearance of the 'narrative temporality' of individuals' cultural identity. The solution according to Giddens is for individuals to place identity as a new and creative 'reflexive project of the self' (Giddens 1991: 9). Thus, 'the more tradition loses its hold, and the more daily life is reconstituted in terms of the dialectical interplay of the local and the global, the more individuals are forced to negotiate lifestyle choices among a diversity of options' (*ibid.*: 5). Giddens's view is also shared by Bauman (2000, 2001), who sees the dissolution of tradition as transforming human identity from a 'given' into a 'task'. This opens up many possibilities:

> Unpredictability breeds anxiety and fear...But the unsteadiness, softness and pliability of things may also trigger ambition and resolve: one can make things better than they are, and need not settle for what there is since no verdict of nature is final, no resistance of reality is unbreakable. One can dream of a different life – more decent, bearable or enjoyable. (Bauman 2001: 141)

This theory positions consumer culture as the principal site of identity construction. Performance in this field invokes Bakhtin's notion of 'carnival' where consumerist revellers are free to try on a set of masks or identities. As Lash and Urry argue, the range and variety of masks performs the dual role of weakening the old social structure while imposing a new, postmodern system of floating identifications. Moreover, questions of 'authenticity' are rendered obsolete by the fact that *nobody* or indeed *nothing* in consumer culture is capable of sustaining any degree of cultural purity: as Bauman notes, a claim to authenticity is no longer even desirable for it sets an artificial limit to the self-empowering 'flexibility of the self' (Bauman and Tester 2001: 121).

6.5   The creolization of food

So, we can see creolization today as the product of two interlinking processes: one, the effects of imperialism and colonialism causing the cultural interplay of different traditions and national identities; and, two, the postmodern commercialization of culture. At a purely aesthetic level, creolization involves a fusion of different cultural meanings to create new expressive forms, as its constituent parts become dislocated from their original historical narrative. But creolization is not simply an exercise in postmodern bricolage: it also symbolizes the tearing up, dislocation and juxtaposition of a series of different cultural *identities*, *histories* and *livelihoods*. Therefore, a hybridized commodity can be seen to both reflect and help reproduce a wider, socio-cultural creolization process that has transformed people's lives across the globe. Massey (1994) gives us an illustration:

> Take, for instance, a walk down Kilburn High Road, my local shopping centre. It is a pretty ordinary place, north-West of the centre of London. Under the railway bridge the newspaper stand sells papers from every county of what my neighbours, many of whom come from there, still often call the Irish Free State...At the local theatre Eamon Morrisey has a one-man show; the National Club has the Wolfe Tones on, and at the Black Lion there's Finnegan's Wake. In two shops I notice this week's lottery ticket winners: in one the name is Teresa Gleeson, in the other, Chouman Hassan.
>
> Thread your way through the often almost stationary traffic diagonally across the road from the newsstand and there's a shop which as long as I can remember has displayed saris in the window. Four life-sized models of Indian women, and reams of cloth...On another ad, for the end of the month, is written, 'All Hindus are cordially invited'. In another newsagents I chat with the man who keeps it, a Muslim unutterably depressed by events in the Gulf...Overhead there is at least one aeroplane – we seem to be on a flight-path to Heathrow and by the time they're over Kilburn you can see them clearly enough to tell the airline and wonder as you struggle with your shopping where they're coming from. (Massey 1994: 152–3)

Ulf Hannerz gives us another colourful illustration of creolization at work:

> There is indeed a sense of the global ecumene here, of the simultaneous presence within one's field of experience of ancestral gods, Western philosophy, and the jazz of black America; and it is all being worked on right

there, in the township. Distinctive cultural currents are coming together, having been separated by oceans and continents, working their way into one another over time, developing new ways of shaping human beings. (Hannerz 1996: 167)

In each case there is a clear vibrancy to the respective locale, made possible by creolizing processes. Yet the locales in question are hemispheres apart. The former example concerns Kilburn, an inner suburb of London historically associated with the Irish diaspora. The latter concerns Sophiatown, a suburb of Johannesburg, South Africa. Naturally, such illustrations present us, as academics from a wide range of disciplines, with a pressing agenda for research. As Nederveen Pieterse (1995: 53) asks:

How do we come to terms with phenomena such as Thai boxing by Moroccan girls in Amsterdam, Asian rap in London, Irish bagels, Chinese tacos and Mardi Gras Indians in the United States...?

In other words, the *lived reality* of creolization raises important questions as to how we should conceptualize global hybrid cultures. As this book has shown, global economic exchange remains a topic of much critical conjecture. Implicit to theories of Americanization, McDonaldization and polarization is the understanding that global flows are overwhelmingly one-sided, inferring the reproduction of specific power relations. Applied to culture, one might observe that the proliferation of, say, McDonald's restaurants across the world can be interpreted as either representing global cultural standardization, hegemonic relations through capitalist dependencies or American cultural imperialism. For theorists of creolization, however, these views are one-dimensional in that they all see cultural exchange as an autonomous and deterministic process with little room for negotiation. Studies in postcolonialism have shown us already that culture should be understood at least as a field of active struggle and resistance against dominant interests, with Nederveen Pieterse observing that 'cultural experiences, past and present, have not been simply moving in the direction of cultural uniformity and standardization' (*ibid.*: 53). To ignore this 'overlooks the counter-currents – the impact non-Western cultures have been making on the West'. Culture is therefore opened up as a global field of exchange which does not necessarily reproduce any particular power relation, as 'the mixing of Asian, African, American, European cultures...is the making of global culture as global melange' (*ibid.*: 60). It is thus necessarily *intercultural*, emphasizing 'the mixing of cultures, and not their separateness' (*ibid.*: 62).

To explain how cultural exchange can be seen to circumvent deterministic power relations one must consider the actual *practice* of exchange itself. The 'global supermarket' might exist as an abstract conceptualization of market consumerism that reflects the vast array of culturally dislocated commodities on offer, yet once such an object is sold across the world it soon becomes localized by those who consume it. Global consumption is thus a very physical practice, as it takes place not in a cultural vacuum but in the multitude of malls, mini-marts and shopping centres across the world. Each locale, too, has its own codes and schemas of meaning and interpretation, making the synthesis between the global and the local ever more creative and unpredictable. This somewhat tempered, of course, by the corporate apparatus of global business, which seeks to control its audiences through segmented marketing strategies. Through a process known generally as 'glocalization', 'thinking globally' and 'acting locally' requires multinational businesses to customize global commodities for specific local audiences, which helps to build local roots and loyalties. For theorists of creolization, however, this depiction of cultural exchange is mostly one-sided, undervaluing the actual reflexive *experience* of cultural consumption. For Appadurai (1990), the term 'indigenization' provides a more accurate description of the everyday appropriation of global commodities. He sees that the production of the 'local' is itself an active and continuous creative process, making creole culture a significant part of everyday consumption as ahistorical, free-floating global commodities are adapted and reinterpreted for new culture-specific locales.

To illustrate the practice of creolization we may consider the theme of food and cuisine. Traditionally, food has been a key expression of local identity, with differences in practices of cooking and eating often reflecting particular social hierarchies. This traditionalized picture has been complicated by the effects of modern capitalist production, however, which has initiated a 'recasting' of traditional notions of time, work and leisure. With food consumption becoming increasingly professionalized and individualized through wholesale production and consumption, Mintz (1984) observes how this had helped to desocialize eating cultures, with individuals becoming 'disembedded' from the familiarity and intimacy of family cooking traditions. This recalls our discussion of McDonaldization in Chapter 5 and, while it is true that traditional practices of food culture have been increasingly dominated by the rationalities of consumer capitalism, creolization theorists are keen to stress that increased standardization does not necessarily mean the end of culture as a creative activity. Far from it, in fact, if one is to consider the greater range of food types made available through the global supermarket: not only has this helped inspire a more reflexive approach to cooking styles from around the world, it has also helped to provide new expressions of creolization.

To illustrate this, we can use as an example the appropriation of Indian cuisine in the UK, which incorporates both the post-colonial legacy of Asian migration and the creolization of traditional culinary styles to satisfy the tastes and requirements of its new audience. Today, there are around 8,300 curry houses in the UK, where Britons are said to spend at least £2 billion per year, and the post-colonial origins of this fixation has led many, including in 2001 then-Foreign Minister Robin Cook, to name curry as Britain's national dish. For Cook, the particular curry in question is the chicken tikka masala, arguably the best-known example of post-colonial culinary creolization in the UK. The dish contains Indian spices and is made using tandoori cooking styles associated with Indian food, but was actually invented in Britain's Indian restaurants in the early 1970s. Although enormously popular in the UK it has nevertheless attracted a somewhat contentious cultural image that arguably exemplifies some of creolization's perceived shortcomings. According to the historian Lizzie Collingham, the dish's most heinous crime, according to its critics, is that it is a 'fabricated dish' that nakedly rejects the importance of cultural authenticity:

> Chicken tikka masala, they sneered, was not a shining example of British multiculturalism but a demonstration of the British facility for reducing all foreign foods to their most unappetising and inedible form. Rather than the inspired invention of an enterprising Indian chef, this offensive dish was dismissed as the result of an ignorant customer's complaint that his chicken tikka was too dry. When the chef whipped together a can of Campbell's Tomato Soup, some cream and a few spices to provide a gravy for the offending chicken, he produced a mongrel dish of which, to their shame, Britons now eat at least eighteen tonnes a week. (Collingham 2005: 2–3)

Cultural hybrids therefore do not always infer connotations of creativity or innovation. In fact, some see creolization as serving to obfuscate more nefarious cultural power dynamics in which an intrinsically meaningful indigenous culture is arbitrarily raided to suit the needs of mass consumption. The dubious cultural value of a 'mongrel' creation such as the chicken tikka masala comes from its generalized association as an 'Indian dish', despite it being virtually unknown in India. Yet Collingham observes that the very label of 'Indian food' is something of a myth as the range of culinary styles within India means that notions of authenticity are tied to specific regions. Moreover, the history of Indian food also reflects the major cultural impact of its own migrant populations. The first such group of significance were the Mughals, who came from Persia to rule much of northern India between the early sixteenth and mid-nineteenth centuries. The Mughals brought their own culinary practices to India, many of which clashed with the more ascetic eating habits of the locals. Nevertheless, the Persian dish of aromatic pilau rice would soon synthesize with the traditional conventions of Indian cooking to produce a number of the favourite Indian dishes of today.

In the south of India, the influence of Portuguese spice traders also helped to significantly transform indigenous cuisine. In 1530 Portugal established a trading capital at Goa with the intention of using it as a base to develop its own spice trade. Perhaps their most significant import was the chilli pepper, which today is arguably the spice most associated with Indian food. Collingham notes that chillies quickly became an essential part of the south Indian diet as it provided a cheap and easy way to give taste to simple rice dishes that the country's poor depended on.

The power of both the Portuguese colonialists and the Mughal Empire would eventually be supplanted by British imperialism, first through the spread of the East India Trading Company, and then more formally as India was swallowed up into the British Empire in 1858. It is perhaps the impact of British rule – known as the Raj – that would have the strongest impact on synthesizing the country's plurality of regionalized food cultures into a single discourse of 'Indian food'. The establishing of independently ruled provinces linked together through networks of trade, communication and transport would provoke a creolization of regionalized cooking practices. This involved applying some of the appealing aspects of particular regional dishes to meals across the country: the fish dish kedgeree and the 'Madras' curry were products of this process. In doing this, Collingham claims that Anglo-Indian food was to become the first truly pan-Indian cuisine as the British 'adopted recipes, ingredients, techniques and garnishes from all over the subcontinent and combined them into a coherent repertoire of dishes' (*ibid*.: 118). Yet these creations could never be described as a truly national cuisine, as Anglo-Indian hybrid curries were only consumed by the British in India. Moreover, labelling all Indian food as 'curry' is also a foreign (and misappropriated) taxonomy, as no Indian would have referred to his or her food as such.

The popularity of Anglo-Indian food with British diplomats in India would soon result in curries spreading to Britain and by the 1840s a number of Indian products, including hot sauces, chutneys and a homogenized blend of basic spices known as 'curry powder', would appear in British markets and stores. By the early twentieth century, the human traffic generated by trade from the East India Company had resulted in a small community of Syhletis (modern-day Bangladeshis) living in the East End of London who set up cafés and boarding houses to cater for Indian seamen and deserters. By the 1940s, the Syhletis expanded their enterprises by reopening cafés that had been left derelict in the aftermath of the Second World War and serving fish and chips and curry and rice. Curries soon became popular among British working-class locals and many of the cafés were transformed into inexpensive Indian restaurants and takeaways (though many retaining the surprisingly popular combination of curry and chips, arguably another creole creation). The food served was a combination of Anglo-Indian, Punjabi and Mughlai cuisine which would soon become part of the standardized 'Indian' menu in the UK.

The Asian population in the UK had grown exponentially in the late 1950s with the relaxation of British immigration laws as Indians, Pakistanis and Bangladeshis living in the UK brought their families over to join them, resulting in the creation of dense ethnic communities in major cities. This meant that for a generation of Asians growing up outside of the Indian subcontinent, Anglo-Indian restaurant food was as authentically 'Indian' as the food they ate at home. By the 1960s this post-colonial legacy would combine with the effects of reflexive modernization – where Britons sampled different styles and tastes outside their own traditional cultural paradigm – to make Indian cuisine a key part of British food culture.

The fact that the chicken tikka masala has been dubbed the national dish of modern Britain makes Indian food something of an effective symbol for the synthesis of post-colonial and postmodern creolization. Yet interpretations of this story do not necessarily see it as such, Collingham noting that many argue that 'the prevalence of curry in the British diet is not a sign of a new multicultural sensitivity but rather is symptomatic of British insularity' (*ibid.*: 236). Questions over the 'authenticity' of Indian food in Britain are often invoked here, but as Collingham argues, this 'fails to acknowledge that the mixture of different culinary styles is the prime characteristic of Indian cookery and that this fusion has produced a plethora of versions of Indian food from Mughlai to Anglo-Indian, from Goan to British Indian' (*ibid.*: 237). So in many ways, questions over the authenticity of Anglo-Indian food are undermined by the rich cultural legacy of post-colonialism and the significant intersection of British Asians who possess their own cultural history and identity in the UK. Nevertheless, the indigenization of Indian cuisine in the UK opens up questions over the flows, directions and power relations in creolization processes, in other words, who is performing creolization, and why. We shall expand on these themes in our second case study.

6.6 The creolization of music

In many ways, the production and consumption of music – especially popular music – is inseparable from processes of creolization. As an aesthetic form, music 'frees us from the everyday routines and expectations that encumber our social identities' (Frith 1987: 144). The detaching of music from its original cultural context is also perhaps an easier process than other cultural forms: whereas to make a foreign dish might have to rely on the importing of foreign ingredients, music on the other hand is increasingly a post-materialist cultural form. Via online trading companies one can download a piece of music onto a computer within a matter of seconds. Music, too, forms an integral part of our everyday soundscape, featuring in a diverse array of social contexts, from shopping malls, airport departure lounges and cafés, to bars, designated clubs and music venues. Its fluidity and omnipresence makes music a significant part of Appadurai's 'ethnoscape', for it acts as both a reflection of, and a tool of expression for, the 'landscape of persons who constitute the shifting world in which we live' (Appadurai 1996: 33).

Although the technologies of global cultural exchange appear to complement processes of creolization, the making of hybrid sounds through the mixing up of styles, sounds and techniques has long been a practice of musicians and composers worldwide. Modern-day technologies and industries, however, have both transformed and intensified flows of global cultural exchange which has, of course, helped to facilitate greater participation in acts of musical hybridization. But this has also resulted in creolization becoming a more *political* process than before, as global music ultimately represents the juxtaposition of cultural traditions and identities with a global business incorporating markets, profits and power relations. The extent to which creolization can continue to exist as a 'pure' act of cultural creativity within this rationalized context is open to debate.

In Western societies, musical creolization is perhaps more representative of postmodern processes. This exists at an aesthetic level, with postmodern artists inspiring 'avant-garde' composers such as John Cage and Karl-Heinz Stockhausen to deconstruct the rules, conventions and expectations of musical performance. Moreover, the flexibilities of post-Fordist production methods twinned with the individualizing effects of reflexive modernization have laid the foundations for forms of music, identity and subculture to be more freely played around with outside of traditional intellectual circles. Western pop music, which the musicologist Timothy D. Taylor (1997: 1) notes has 'travelled far more widely than any other western idiom' is a particularly interesting example of creolization. On the one hand, this may seem something of an erroneous statement as with its long-standing emphasis on catering to teen-oriented mass markets, pop music has long been cited by critical theorists as the epitome of the homogenizing power of Adorno's 'culture industry' (Adorno 2001). Yet, at the same time, popular music has also incorporated the dynamic interplay of different youth cultures and ethnic identities, with popular music even as a homogeneous category incorporating a mix of Afro-American blues, soul, jazz and gospel along with the folk ballad traditions prevalent in music of white origin. Creolization can be seen in the latter records of The Beatles, who blended into their music references to American blues and rock 'n' roll, European avant-garde, Eastern philosophies, Indian classical music and British music hall (MacDonald 1994; Moore 2000), but also in the sample-heavy conventions of modern rap and hip-hop music where acts such as Public Enemy, Kanye West, Jay-Z, Mos Def and De La Soul take a rhythm, sound or melody from a wide range of musical styles and work it into a new form of musical expression (Schloss 2004).

The UK band Gorillaz perhaps exemplifies musical creolization and post-modernism at its most self-aware. On the one hand, their music has been described as 'hip hop-based cut-and-paste of poppy melodies, old horror movie themes and any sonic style available' (Gaiman 2005), utilizing the rhythms of Reggae and Latin music and juxtaposing them with classical Chinese and Lebanese orchestras. On the other hand, Gorillaz is a 'virtual' band made up of cartoon characters which feature on album covers, music videos and are even 'interviewed' in the music press. Masterminded by British musician Damon Albarn and illustrator Jamie Hewlett, the cartoon aesthetic represents a deliberate attempt to separate the music from any preconception an audience might have of its creators, thus enabling the group to be more musically adventurous without being weighed down by demands for artistic 'authenticity'.

These practices in creolization are global in the sense that non-Western musical styles are often incorporated into the bricolage of sounds seen in Western pop music or hip-hop. Musical creolization is not, of course, a process exclusive to the West, but the construction of non-Western music in the global consumer market arguably belies some of the more nefarious power relations within the creolization-as-consumerism paradigm. Taylor (1997) notes that most of the music produced from outside of Western societies has been labelled by record companies and stores as 'world music'. This, of course, represents something of a 'meaninglessly wide literal field of reference' (*ibid.*: 5) and exemplifies the determining powers of mass capitalist production and its traditional tendency to establish standard, homogeneous categories that in practice are neither stable nor homogeneous at all. At an aesthetic level, 'world music' serves as a more useful category in terms of explaining what sort of music it is *not* – that is, music 'untouched' by Western influences.

This arguably sets up a structural binary between 'the West' and 'the rest' that is in many ways self-fulfilling. Taylor argues that the category of world music is very limiting for the musicians and performers themselves as its very taxonomy immediately implies a Western audience. This plays a significant part in determining how world music is produced and marketed, Taylor identifying three major discourses used by record companies. First, he notes the selling of world music as 'sonic tourism', which uses an image of its performers not far removed from that of a 'happy native'. This strategy is directed at Western listeners tired with the standardized, shopping-centre range of mass culture and who are therefore 'looking for something out of the mainstream'. This implies something of a novelty to world music, a mass-produced declaration of individuality. For more self-conscious consumers, Taylor invokes the discourse of music as an expression of 'authenticity'. We may have already noted Bauman's dispelling of such a notion, yet it exists at least in consumer definitions of a 'sincerity to a true self' representing a 'commitment to one's art' (Taylor 1997: 21). More explicit still, authenticity might come to represent an expectation that its musicians and performers be 'natural ... premodern, untainted, and thus musically the same as they ever were' (*ibid.*: 21). This also infers the selling of 'emotion' and 'spirituality' where music is created not to make money, but to express 'selfless wisdom' in order to 'set the human race and planet free' (*ibid.*: 24). For Western consumers, engagement with the 'authentic' arguably represents a conscious effort to 're-embed' with meaningful culture, albeit through capitalist channels of global consumerism. Whether this sort of authenticity is tainted by acts of creolization within the subaltern itself is seen to be of less importance: what matters is that it shows no signs of a 'modern', Westernized influence. Third, and finally, Taylor notes that a discourse of authenticity and spirituality often 'distances the makers of musics so far that to bring them back for consumption by westerners an intermediary is required' (*ibid.*: 28). This infers narratives of the Westerner-as-explorer and cultural vanguard, one which also receives the most amount of recognition for music.

Such discourses are, of course, extremely limiting to 'world music' artists, and arguably perpetuate the superiority of Western artists in their freedom to engage in acts of postmodern creativity, or be celebrated as creative van-guards and facilitators for their 'discovery' of world music forms. By contrast, the actual 'world music' artists are expected to conform to preconceived, Westernized notions of creole culture, one that is ultimately weighed down by expectations of a premodern 'authenticity'. This suggests that there are structural contradictions endemic to capitalist creolization processes and Taylor uses the example of American singer Paul Simon, whose 1986 album *Graceland* juxtaposed the songwriting craft of his own Western background with the music and rhythms of black South Africa, showcasing in particular the vocal ensemble Ladysmith Black Mambazo. He explains:

> Capitalist structures that protect western subjects, with the most visible of these being stars, allow western culture to emerge as simultaneously always mongrel and always pure. 'Culture flows like water', says Simon, defending his work with black South African musicians. 'It isn't something that can just be cut off'. Note yet another natural metaphor. Simon means, though, the 'natural' culture of 'natives'; his 'culture' isn't culture in this anthropological sense at all: it is civilization, intellectual property. So *his* culture *can* be cut off: he has copyrights, agents, lawyers, publishers, record company executives at his disposal. And Simon's hybrids, appro-priations, syncretisms – supported by these capitalist music-industrial structures – are conceived as nothing other than his individual creations, meaning they are only thought of as his original works. Western culture is neither pure or impure because it is owned. It is constructed as outside the purview of such ideas as authenticity. But other cultures' forms are avail-able to be constructed as pure or impure when they are not owned, and even, sometimes, when they are. (Taylor 1997: 22)

This does not deny the existence of creolization as a global activity, but it does suggest that its processes are supported, and to some extent shaped by, world hegemonic power relations. For middle-class consumers in the West, creolization becomes an attractive part of the consumer market as they have the time, education, money and cultural capital to enter Bakhtin's carnival and play with foreign identities, sounds and cultures. The same applies to middle-class musicians and artists in the West. By contrast, musicians from the margins of the global economy are constrained by demands of authentic-ity made of them by Western listeners, even if these Third World musicians grew up listening to Western popular music. Taylor cites the example of the Senegalese singer Youssou N'Dour, who has been accused by modern music critics of becoming 'too Western'. His defence is clear: 'In Dakar, we hear many different recordings. We are open to these sounds. When people say my music is too Western, they must remember that we, too, hear this music over here' (*ibid*.: 201). Again, this example does not deny that genuine, creative cultural hybrids are being produced across the world; indeed, it suggests that creolization is more prevalent and far-reaching than ever, but it would appear that there are underlying power structures that dictate who is involved in making of creole commodities, and how they are distributed. While it might be too simplistic to infer Wallerstein's core–periphery model as outlined in Chapter 3, we can at least ask the question: creolization exists, but in whose interest?

6.7 Conclusion

Theorists of creolization are best located within a debate with those who emphasize alternative models, particularly Americanization, McDonaldization and balkanization. While they overtly reject the explicitly homogenizing processes described by proponents of Americanization and McDonaldization, they stand equally in opposition to those whose vision of global heterogeneity is of separation and ultimately conflict. Instead, they draw attention to the blend of cultures found in contemporary societies: as Stuart Hall says, 'modern nations are all cultural hybrids' (1992b: 297). Nor is this blending necessarily a recent historical phenomenon – while there is a clear appreciation of the extent to which a heightened creolization is a feature of the *post-colonial* world, implicit in the literature is a nod to the wisdom of Benedict Anderson, for whom *all* communities are 'imagined'.

It may be easy, then, to dismiss this framework of global change for being overly descriptive of the *way things are*, and insufficiently engaged with the underlying power dynamics..To many of us, the former seems obvious and undeniable, and need not detract us from interrogating the latter. But as we have seen, few theorists of creolization are so naive. After all, an appreciation for the reality of cultural diversity and pluralism does not demand an ignorance towards the perpetuation of hierarchies, inequalities and conflicts. Moreover, its advocates would tell us that the creolization framework presents us with a far more sophisticated study of these contemporary power dynamics than does, say, the Americanization framework, which is unduly one-dimensional.

In this sense, processes of global cultural exchange depicted in the theory of creolization may not be wholly dissimilar to those exemplified as examples of Americanization or McDonaldization. Creolization does not deny the powerful productive capacities of multinational corporations, but instead recognizes that it is not an exorable process, as no process of cultural exchange can take place without some degree of personalized consumer interpretation and appropriation. We can tackle this complexity directly by considering Melissa Caldwell's (2004) case study of the indigenization of McDonald's food in Russia: having witnessed the proliferation of multinational eateries appearing in post-communist Moscow, Caldwell identified processes of McDonaldization at work – particularly in the spread of American-style cafés where Muscovite consumers had visibly adapted their traditional eating habits to conform to the largely individualized conventions of Westernized service and etiquette.

Yet this only told part of the story. Far from being passive recipients of Western rationalization, she instead saw Muscovites as reflexive and autonomous social agents, even if their choices were somewhat constrained by the effects of McDonaldization. To illustrate this she draws attention to how McDonald's restaurants have become, somewhat ironically, an 'intrinsically and authentically local space' for Muscovites. To some extent, this has been facilitated by deliberate 'glocalization' marketing strategies, with McDonald's making concerted efforts to provide local community investment schemes and also to promote the local origins of their produce. Yet this move 'enabled McDonald's to position itself within the parameters of the imagined – and, more importantly, *trusted* – collectivity to which its Muscovite customers' (Caldwell 2004: 244), causing Muscovites to take the significant step of incorporating McDonald's into their 'home cooking', a domain considered to be uniquely Russian. This has produced hybrid dishes that are 'authentically indigenous and personally meaningful', reflecting an embracement of creolization practices and the blurring of 'national' and 'foreign' distinctions (*ibid.*: 246). All in all, Caldwell argues that Moscow's consumers are far more autonomous than discourses of McDonaldization would suggest, as not only have they set the indigenous standards that McDonald's have had to satisfy, they have 'accepted McDonald's as a local and personally meaningful experience', one which they have 'privileged...over other, more visibly foreign and uncomfortable, experiences' (*ibid.*: 249).

This story might be interpreted as purporting a case for either creolization or McDonaldization. On the one hand, the former argues that no multinational corporation can ever have it their own way as cultural exchange is inextricably bound up in subjective processes of consumer interpretation and appropriation. This means, in effect, that all cultural exchange incorporates some degree of creolization. On the other hand, McDonaldization theorists might accept the existence of creolization but question its wider significance – so what if corporations have to customize their marketing to satisfy different audiences? Ultimately, consumer power does little to stand in the way of broader structural power dynamics.

Theorists of creolization do not necessarily dismiss the latter argument – they accept that creolization is a 'weak' phenomena, but one that is interesting precisely *because* it is an ordinary, everyday experience. Recalling Anderson, this view infers a critique of the prevalence of 'boundary fetishism' within the social sciences, where arbitrarily constructed categories of class, nation, ethnicity and culture are perceived as determining social behaviour. By failing to examine the more subjective *reality* of such categories, exponents of 'methodological nationalism' are themselves guilty of perpetuating the very existence of these imagined boundaries. As Nederveen Pieterse (2001) argues, we should view global culture as a creative, dynamic process and one that is not necessarily determined by such fixed categorizations. Therefore, 'as some boundaries wane others remain or are introduced' and 'as national borders and government authority erode, ethnic or religious boundaries, or boundaries of consumption patterns and brand names emerge in their place' (2001: 239).

The questioning of such fixed categorizations does at least highlight the crisis of the modern nation-state – the ultimate 'imagined community'. Creolization invokes the *separation* of nation and state and the delinking of cultural from political identity, and what results is the emergence of what Hall and others call *new* cultural identities, in which nationalism co-exists with, but does not assert authority over, 'race', gender, sexuality, religion, *and* citizenship; in Appadurai's terms, thinking 'ourselves beyond the nation' (1996: 158). Such a position has been taken by Marxists, feminists, post-modernists as well as 'mainstream' sociologists, though the actual *extent* to which the nation-state has been truly superseded as an institution of authority remains hotly contested. We will explore this theme in more detail in our final two chapters.

Transnationalization: A Space beyond Place

7

7.1 Introduction

One of the challenges of this book has been to show how the language of 'globalization' has been used to refer to a variety of processes which may or may not be occurring concurrently, thus highlighting the complexity of contemporary global dynamics. In some cases, the processes described are often explicitly used as *alternatives* to the idea of 'globalization' (such as Americanization). In others (such as liberalization) we are describing processes which their chief advocates often consciously refer to *as* globalization. This is not always a straightforward project to comprehend.

The matter is about to be complicated even further. In this chapter, we discuss a process we refer to as 'transnationalization'. Clearly, we present it as a different model of global change – otherwise it would not warrant its separate inclusion here – yet few if any of its chief theoreticians actually use this term. Most are happy to present their accounts as theories of *globalization*. Our argument is that the framework they propose presents a radically different model of the contemporary global condition than does the one described back in Chapter 1, which we called 'globalization'.

It is, though, a model which has had enormous influence in sociology and in international relations, among neo-Marxists, liberals and social democrats alike. It is, in short, the model which understands contemporary global change as a shift in the organization of power and decision-making, of production and administration, *from* the nation-state, *to* a level *above it* which cuts across and impacts upon nation-states and their boundaries. Yet at the same time, it does not imagine *the globe* as a single place in the way that the globalization framework does. Rather, it recognizes the perceived *reality* of a world in which nation-state sovereignty, in law and politics, is relativized and potentially undermined by the 'higher' demands of international law and institutions of transnational governance, the principal agents of what Rosenau (1990) calls 'post-international politics', such as the United Nations, a world in which corporate practices transcend nation-state limitations, and a world

151

in which major cities become hubs of cosmopolitan identities and activities existing regardless of their locations within nation-state borders. Rosenau provides a useful description of what he calls the 'multi-centric world' being described here as comprising transnational *organizations* (NGOs and crime syndicates as much as corporations), transnational *problems*, transnational *events*, transnational *communities*, and transnational *structures* (Rosenau 1990; summarized in McGrew 1992: 82–3).

Many of the writers included in this section are among the most eminent and important contributors to the field of global studies. In most cases, they do not consciously identify with one another in terms of shared influences or traditions, yet they address many of the same issues. In very different ways, Andre Gorz (1982), Claus Offe (1985), Jürgen Habermas (1976), Scott Lash and John Urry (1987), David Harvey (1989), Frederic Jameson (1991), Manuel Castells (1989, 1999, 2000, 2004), Bill Robinson (2004) and Leslie Sklair (1991, 2002) have all written at length about a *new* kind of capitalism, a capitalism derived but distinct from that which so fascinated Marx in the nineteenth century, a capitalism which employs *post*-industrial or *post*-Fordist production techniques including flexible accumulation and an *international* division of labour, is *disaggregated* or *disorganized*, emphasizes *knowledge-based economies*, drives forward a new global *consumerism* through global branding techniques, and is the playground of *transnational* corporations run by *transnational* capitalists. Some go so far as to suggest the presence of a transnational capitalist *class* (Robinson 2004; Robinson and Harris 2000; Sklair 2001, 2002; Van der Pijl 1984, 1998), although others have preferred to speak of a new 'informational elite' (Castells 1989). At the same time, the likes of Habermas, Richard Falk, Ulrich Beck and David Held focus on the shift of influence from nation-state governments to the United Nations and similar institutions, in many cases presenting a normative cosmopolitanism including a commitment to the potential for international law to overcome problems of social injustice, human rights violations, warfare and so on. Castells, Saskia Sassen (1991, 1998), Doreen Massey (1994) and others have highlighted the extent to which cities such as London, New York and Tokyo have become centres for the transnational flow of capital and information, powerful financial hubs operating within this transnational 'grid', thus identifying a new politics of space and place. Harvey, Sklair, Beck, Lash and Anthony Giddens are among those who have sought to theorize these transformations within a framework of *late* capitalism or *late* modernity, developing such concepts as 'reflexivity' and 'risk', the 'disembedding' of social practices and the changing relationship of time and space. And for many of these writers, including Giddens, Harvey, and James Rosenau (1990), one of the key factors driving the transition from an earlier nation-statist model to a contemporary transnational one is technology. Much of this we have actually discussed already in this book, but now we need to bring them together as part of what we feel is a distinctive approach within global studies.

To do this, we are going to look in sequence at some of the principal *forms* of transnational activity identified by the various writers listed above. As a useful starting-point – a guide, if you like – we are going to draw on the model proposed by one of the most important of the transnationalist writers, Leslie Sklair. In his book *Globalization: Capitalism and Its Alternatives* (2002), which was a development of his earlier work, *Sociology of the Global System* (1991), Sklair presents us with one of the most sophisticated yet refreshingly clear and understandable accounts of the dynamics of capitalism today, as distinct from its previous form. According to Sklair, capitalism today is defined primarily by its 'transnational practices'. Three such practices, he suggests, are paramount: transnational *corporations*, a transnational *capitalist class* and the transnational cultural-ideological project of *consumerism*. In this chapter we are going to follow a slightly amended, and extended, version of this model. First, we are going to discuss the development and current role of transnational corporations. Second, we are going to address the controversial question of whether we can speak of transnational classes. Third, we are going to look at what we will call transnational practices, specifically the practices employed by corporations in respect of production and consumption. Following this, we will summarize some of the major work on global cities as transnational *spaces*. We are then going to look beyond transnational *capitalism* per se to discuss the emergence of transnational *political* institutions. To conclude, we will look at how the emergence of this transnational dimension has been theorized in the literature on 'reflexive modernization'.

Biography Box 15:   Leslie Sklair

Leslie Sklair (1940–) is Emeritus Professor of Sociology at the London School of Economics, where he has taught for many years. Initially a sociologist of development, he moved into the area of globalization with his 1991 book *Sociology of the Global System*. Although initially intended to be a critical contribution to the study of development, this book became a major work in the emerging sociology of globalization such that in 2002 he substantially revised it to more directly address the challenges of transnational capitalism. The result was *Globalization: Capitalism and Its Alternatives*.

It is worth bearing in mind that, whether Marxian or 'bourgeois' in their theoretical influences, the writers discussed herein share an absolute commitment to the idea that *something new* is happening in the world, and so to the belief that a discussion of contemporary global change is far more than just empty rhetoric. Significant neo-Marxists such as Harvey (at least in his work mentioned here; some of his more recent work has been in a different tradition) and Sklair part company quite dramatically from others mentioned in this book who adhere in some form or another to the broader Marxian tradition, such as Frank, Wallerstein and those others mentioned in Chapter 3 on 'polarization', or Panitch (and the more recent work of Harvey) mentioned in Chapter 4 on 'Americanization'. They take issue, for example, with the former, for maintaining a commitment to seeing the nation-state (and by extension the international system of nation-states) as the principal unit of analysis, insisting instead that capitalism today is not bound up within such a state-centred system. Their critique of the latter is an extension of this – suggesting that it naively over-emphasizes the role of one powerful nation-state in directing the course of a capitalism which they argue transcends even it. This emphasis on the *novelty* of late capitalism is significant. Harvey's earlier writings, and also the contributions of Urry and Massey, are often associated with the 'New Times' school of neo-Marxism, the commitment by various left-oriented scholars to 'update' Marxism in the light of what they saw to be 'postmodern' cultural conditions (see Hall and Jacques 1989; incidentally, much of the work on creolization and hybridization discussed in Chapter 6 originated within this movement as well). Others such as Habermas, Held and Beck, and in a different vein Lash, draw more explicitly on Frankfurt School critical theory, as discussed at length in Chapter 5, either by developing Adorno's theory of late capitalist commodification and the role of the 'culture industry' or by studying capitalism in terms of its tendencies to crisis. Giddens draws on a variety of sources, and, for a 'bourgeois' sociologist at least, has in the past been broadly sympathetic to the Marxist-Weberian project of critical theory. Sklair identifies directly with the influence of the Italian Marxist Antonio Gramsci, whose humanistic Marxism is appreciated by subsequent critical theorists at the same time as his concept of hegemony became the single most important influence upon the 'Euro-communism' of the New Times school. So, despite its diversity, there is *some* kind of identifiable heritage uniting these important figures.

7.2   Transnational corporations

The prominence, and significance, of transnational corporations is rightly considered by almost all commentators to be a key factor in the contemporary global condition. Such corporations are associated with the production and in some cases retail of all the 'big businesses' – oil, cars, computer hardware and software, film and television media, communications, electronics, pharmaceuticals, food, tobacco, tourism and so on. These 'mighty transnational corporations' constitute what Sklair calls the 'vehicle' for global capitalism (2002: 63). Held and McGrew (2007: 111; following UNCTAD 2006) suggest that in 2005 'there were 77,000 TNCs worldwide with 770,000 foreign subsidiaries selling $22.17 trillion of goods and services within every continent, equivalent to some 50 per cent of the world GDP, and employing 62 million workers'. Such figures sound impressive, although as we will see, statistics do not always give us a meaningful picture.

The term 'transnational corporation' (or, for brevity, TNC) has replaced the somewhat misleading earlier term, 'multinational corporation', in most quarters. In presenting a history of TNCs, Sklair acknowledges the significant body of research that has been carried out in this field from across the social sciences (Barnet and Muller 1974; Bartlett and Goshall 1989; Fieldhouse 1986; Jenkins 1987; Stopford and Strange 1991). However, it is difficult to provide any comparative literature review on this as the emphasis of the research is so diverse: for example, some define TNCs purely in terms of economic efficiency, some distinguish according to size or type of industry, some are presented as anti-corporate polemics and so on (Sklair 2002: 64; see below for two ways of measuring TNCs). Early examples of such corporations (dating back to the late nineteenth and early twentieth centuries) were primarily European, although the first actual reference to the term 'multinational corporation' is generally credited to the head of the Tennessee Valley Authority, David Lilienthal, in 1960 (Sklair 2002: 63, following Fieldhouse 1986).

One significant factor is the extent to which these corporations exercise some form of monopoly in their respective sectors, due in no small part to 'unprecedented levels' of mergers and acquisitions, often resulting in new forms of cross-sector activity (Sklair 2002: 65). For example:

> Since the 1990s the world of media has been dominated by a small group of globalizing conglomerates with interests in a variety of business sectors. For example, in 2000 AOL (an Internet company) and Time-Warner (an entertainment company) merged, thus creating the first global mass media content and delivery conglomerate. (*Ibid.*)

The relevance of this for Sklair's work, and for this book as well, is evident: 'TNCs are loosening their ties with their countries of origin and seeking alliances all over the world with other companies for commercial advantages' (*ibid.*). Attached to this, clearly, is the question of accountability. Democratic governments are, at least in theory, accountable to their citizens. Corporations are accountable to their shareholders. Governments are actors within the political sphere, driven by the desire to preserve power. Non-governmental organizations (NGOs) are actors within the sphere of civil society, their motivations being driven by whichever set of ethics is championed by the NGO in question. Corporations, though, operate within the economic sphere, their motivation and the measure of their success being reducible to financial achievements. The literature and discourse on corporate citizenship, business ethics and corporate social responsibility notwithstanding, questions remain about the appropriateness of corporations driven by economic motivations exercising more political power worldwide than many governments and not in most cases accountable to or subject to sanctions by even the more powerful nation-state political authorities. The involvement of TNCs in 'exploiting' (according to critics of such practices) the resources of oil-rich countries like

Nigeria provides a good case study (see Sklair 2002: 79–81). Of course, as Sklair rightly points out, the issue of whether, under current global capitalist conditions, governments are entirely powerless to kerb the perceived excesses of such corporations is a contentious one. Sklair draws attention to the work of Cioffi (2000) who, in distinguishing between 'neo-liberal', 'neo-corporate' and 'statist' forms of government, seeks to show that the extent of government resistance depends on the political culture of the state in question. Even so, the *transnational* project of global capitalism is not so easily quashed, and any such resistance is effective solely at the level of the nation-state in question, and in practice does little to actually undermine the broader influence or practices of the TNCs.

All of which is well and good, but who, actually, *are* the TNCs? How comparatively wealthy and powerful *are* these corporations? Let us now consider the 'facts and figures' related to some of the world's largest and most prominent companies? As we have already said, following Sklair, there is no absolute way of ranking the world's largest TNCs. The familiar names are usually included in any list: General Motors, Ford, Honda, Mitsubishi from the world of car manufacturing; Exxon-Mobil, Royal Dutch Shell and BP from petroleum; Wal-Mart from retail; Philips, IBM and General Electric from the various electronic industries. One system is the Fortune Global 500, which ranks corporations according to revenue. Historically, oil and automobile companies dominate this list. In 2009, the top ten looked as shown in Table 7.1.

A comparison of the leading TNCs according to sales and a selection of nation-states according to gross domestic product is a standard feature of most commentaries on the global economy. However, as Held and McGrew (2007: 104–5) show, a comparison of such economies reveals that the highest ranking TNC comes in only 44th, well below the richest nation-states. Table 7.2 compares the five leading corporations in this index compared to certain nation-states.

Table 7.1 Fortune Global 500 top ten 2009

Rank	TNC	Country	Industry
1	Royal Dutch Shell	Netherlands / UK	Oil
2	Exxon-Mobil	USA	Oil
3	Wal-Mart	USA	Retail
4	BP	UK	Oil
5	Chevron	USA	Oil
6	Total SA	France	Oil
7	Conoco-Phillips	USA	Oil
8	ING	Netherlands	Banking
9	Sinopec	China	Oil
10	Toyota	Japan	Automobiles

Source: CNN(http://money.cnn.com/magazines/fortune/global500/2009/).

Table 7.2 Countries and TNCs ranked as economies

Rank	TNC	Sales $ bn	Rank	Country	GDP $ bn
44	Wal-Mart	67.7	43	Chile	70.5
48	Exxon-Mobil	52.6	45	Pakistan	61.6
53	General Motors	46.2	49	Czech Republic	50.8
55	Ford	45.1	54	Hungary	45.6
56	Mitsubishi	44.3	58	Nigeria	41.1

Source: Held and McGrew (2007: 105), based on Wolf (2002a: 7).

Table 7.3 Transnationality index

Rank	TNC	Country	Industry	Index %
1	Thomson	Canada	Publishing	95.4
2	Nestlé	Switzerland	Food and beverages	95.2
3	ABB	Switzerland	Electronics	94.1
4	Electrolux	Sweden	Electronics	93.2
5	Holcim	Switzerland	Construction	91.8
6	Roche Group	Switzerland	Pharmaceuticals	91.5
7	BAT	UK	Food and tobacco	90.7
8	Unilever	UK/Netherlands	Food and beverages	89.3
9	Seagram	Canada	Beverages and media	88.6
10	Akzo Nobel	Netherlands	Chemicals	82.6
Selected others				
22	Exxon-Mobil	USA	Oil	68.0
24	McDonald's	USA	Restaurants	67.1
26	Coca-Cola	USA	Beverages	65.2
27	Honda	Japan	Automobiles	64.7
35	Philips	Netherlands	Electronics	59.9
43	Royal Dutch Shell	Netherlands/UK	Oil	56.3
45	Volkswagen	Germany	Automobiles	55.7
50	IBM	USA	Computers	53.7
75	General Electric	USA	Electronics	36.7
82	Toyota	Japan	Automobiles	30.9
83	General Motors	USA	Automobiles	30.7
90	Wal-Mart	USA	Retail	25.8

Source: Dicken (2003: 222–4); calculated from UNCTAD (2001: Table III.1).

So, according to this evidence at least, concerns over the comparative economic power of TNCs compared to states are somewhat overstated. Peter Dicken (2003) is equally sceptical. Dicken takes issue with the claim that the largest corporations are inherently 'placeless', disembedded from their national contexts. By contrast, Dicken shows that the companies which top his comparative index of 'transnationality', namely those with the highest percentage averages of foreign assets, sales and employment to total assets, sales and employment, come from 'smaller' countries (in economic terms), while the major corporate giants rank relatively poorly. Dicken's table shows that the 'the largest TNC (in terms of foreign assets), General Electric, ranks 75th on the index of transnationality; GM (4th in terms of foreign assets) ranks 83rd; IBM ranks 50th; VW ranks 45th; Toyota, the 6th-ranking TNC in foreign assets ranks 82nd on the broader index' (*ibid.*: 221–4). The top of the table and significant others are worth looking at in table form (see Table 7.3).

We present these tables not because they show us anything more 'accurate' than any other set of tables we could produce, but because they give us reason to be a little cautious when discussing the claim the 'corporations rule the world' (Held and McGrew 2007: 104). But that should not detract us from interrogating the growing power of these TNCs within a transnationalizing world.

7.3   Transnational classes

For Sklair, one of the reasons why Cioffi's argument, namely that countries adopting more 'statist' systems of government have been successful in taking on and limiting the influence of TNCs in their territories, is unconvincing is that it fails to acknowledge the motivations and interests of those *in power*. Central to Sklair's theory is that, if TNCs constitute the *vehicle* for global capitalism, then a transnational capitalist class is its driver (Sklair 2002: 63). The transnational capitalist class is not composed solely of the chief executives of TNCs (although these do constitute a distinct and significant group), but includes those who benefit from the exploitation of labour and resources worldwide, including political decision-makers. Thus, it is perfectly feasible to suggest that where states have actively blocked TNC involvement, it is because to do so is to best protect the specific interests of the local transnational capitalist class at that point.

It is fair to say that, of the factors Sklair associates with the current phase of global capitalism, the idea of the transnational capitalist class, although it has its defenders and has been intelligently theorized (see also Robinson 2004; Robinson and Harris 2000; Sklair 2001), has met with the most hostility, even among otherwise like-minded intellectuals. The reason for this, of course, is to do with the meaning of the word 'class'. In the traditional Marxist sense, classes are relatively straightforward things, because they are *objectively* defined by clear criteria, namely, one's relationship to the means of production. One either *owns* it, and thus benefits through exploiting the labour of others, or one *works* it, selling one's body and time for a fixed sum and alienated from one's product and its commodification: *bourgeoisie*, or ruling class, and *proletariat*, or working class, respectively. Sklair rather upsets this straightforward Marxist distinction by making it clear that 'the transnational capitalist class is not made up of capitalists in the traditional Marxist sense. Direct ownership or control of the means of production is no longer the exclusive criterion for serving the interests of capital, particularly not the global interests of capital' (Sklair 2002: 98). Certainly, as Beck (2007) has argued, the rampant consumerism of transnational capitalism and its associated process of 'individualization' has effectively eroded the traditional class structures of modern societies, at least in terms of class as an objective category (we will say more on this below). So, who does constitute this new 'class'? Sklair divides it up into four 'fractions': the *corporate* fraction, including the executives of the TNCs and their local affiliates; the *state* fraction, including the politicians and bureaucrats at state and interstate levels; the *technical* fraction, or 'globalizing professionals'; and the *consumerist* fraction, comprised of 'merchants and media' (Sklair 2002: 99). Its role is clear: 'organizing the conditions under which its interests and the interests of the global system...can be furthered within the transnational, inter-state, national, and local contexts' (*ibid.*).

One does not have to be a certified conspiracy theorist to acknowledge that such people *exist* or that they exercise considerable influence on world affairs. The name of someone like Rupert Murdoch is well known to us, as is that of Bill Gates, but in truth the vast majority of these individuals are relatively anonymous. For sure, they form part of an undeniable global *elite*. Indeed to some extent Sklair's four fractions reads rather like an update of C. Wright Mills's famous 'power elite' in the classic book of the same name (Mills 1956). Mills saw American society as governed by a coalition of three elite interest groups, the political, economic and military elites, exchanging favours for their benefit of their respective interests. The global network of 'mates' (to use John Pilger's term: Pilger 1992) comprising politicians, media barons, business tycoons and the like is well documented. Whether they constitute a *class*, and thus whether one can accurately speak of a transnational class structure, is another matter. Manuel Castells (1989), in his wide-ranging Marxian-influenced survey of the dynamics of the 'network society' defined by its 'informational mode of production', prefers to speak of an 'informational elite' behind the metaphorical wheel. Beck also feels that class culture has been 'uncoupled' from class position, leaving capitalism in its current phase without classes *for themselves* (Beck 2007: 686). But at the same time, it is difficult to ignore the reality of a 'super class' (Adonis and Pollard 1997), a small group of individuals who embody the opportunities of a transnational society, for whom money is ever fluid, moving rapidly as they do from opportunity to opportunity, committed to no use value, loyal to no community or rules (Slater and Tonkiss 2001: 14), possessive of sufficient economic *and cultural* capital to travel freely across borders and exploit opportunities for greater economic and cultural wealth acquisition (Weiß 2005), capable of utilizing their money and their knowledge to avoid the many risks created by an unpredictable capitalism whether by emigrating to 'safer' countries, purchasing more expensive healthcare, or perhaps just installing more security cameras outside their safely guarded homes (Beck 2007).

Inevitably, if the unrestricted, fluid and extra-territorial nature of private capital made possible by the global capitalist system has raised the capacity for wealth acquisition so dramatically as to create a socio-economic elite, or transnational capitalist class, more advantaged in absolute terms than ever before, then at the same time it has had the effect of increasing relations of *inequality* across the globe (Adonis and Pollard 1997: 82–4). Those *without* access to capital necessarily become more vulnerable to 'transnational currents, forces and powers' (Beck 2007: 691). Scott Lash makes similar observations in relation to the increasing disparity between class groups within the informational mode of production, which he associates with 'reflexive modernity' (Beck, Giddens and Lash 1994). He identifies not only a new middle class – which due to the nature of informational capitalism is no longer a 'service class' but rather a crucial and powerful group exploiting the needs of the information society – and a new, 'upgraded' and reflexive working class, both of which are 'winners' in the system (*ibid.*: 129–30), but also a sizeable 'information underclass' which is wholly excluded from the mode of information, from the structures of information and communications technology (*ibid.*: 130–4).

Given the close relationship between information, media and consumerism and their centrality within global capitalism, Sklair is unlikely to disagree. Perhaps, then, whether one can reasonably speak of a transnational class culture per se is not as important as recognizing the new forms of social inequality generated by contemporary capitalism. So far we have discussed this new capitalism in terms of its constitution, namely, corporations and classes. We now need to look more closely at its operations and practices.

7.4 Transnational practices

The core defining feature of transnational corporate activity and a new form of global capitalism appears to be the employment of certain transnational practices which distinguish the current capitalist moment from its precursor. This is not an entirely new revelation, and is at the heart of a series of major intellectual contributions from the 1980s on the new face of capitalism, namely, the shift from Fordist to post-Fordist production methods. Among these contributions are those from Claus Offe (1985), a neo-Marxist schooled in the tradition of critical theory, urban sociologist Ray Pahl (1988) and Scott Lash and John Urry, sociologists influenced by Marx, Weber and postmodern theory (articulated in their definitive book on this, *The End of Organised Capitalism*; Lash and Urry 1987), on 'disorganized' or 'disaggregated' capitalism, feminist Ruth Pearson (1986) on the exploitation of women in the 'First' and 'Third' Worlds by the TNCs, and David Harvey, a neo-Marxist geographer in his skilful attempt to explain the 'postmodern phenomenon' (which we discussed in Chapter 6) within a relatively orthodox Marxian framework (in his book *The Condition of Postmodernity*; Harvey 1989).

Of these, Harvey's is arguably the most significant. The task he sets himself is straightforward enough: to take issue with the claim made by the likes of Jean-Francois Lyotard (1984) that we have entered into a new phase of history defined not by the 'old rules' but by the 'postmodern condition'. But Harvey wants neither to add his applause to Lyotard's celebration of the perceived 'liberating effects' of this transformation, nor to dismiss the post-modern argument out of hand. Rather, he critically accepts the emergence of a postmodern 'style' but seeks to understand it firmly within a modernist, Marxist theoretical paradigm, specifically, as the cultural 'form' of a new kind of capitalism. Marxism has traditionally treated culture as super-struc-tural – that is, as an ideological reflection of the economic base which serves to reproduce capitalism. Earlier capitalism was defined by Fordist production techniques, discussed previously in this volume. Fordism required a certain degree of simplicity and structure, and was mirrored in the cultural field by modernism, a movement defined by its emphasis on structure. However, *late* capitalism, Harvey suggests, is defined instead by disorganization, disaggre-gation, an international division of labour and the post-Fordist practice of 'flexible accumulation'. Postmodernism as an artistic style, characterized by its breakdown of binary opposites (think, if you like, of the Pompidou Centre in Paris as an example of postmodern architecture, or, post-Harvey, the films of Quentin Tarantino which deliberately break down traditional binary opposites such as good/bad, beginning/end) merely reflects this new form of capitalist production.

Biography Box 16:   David Harvey

David Harvey (1935–) is a British-born social geographer and one of the world's leading Marxist intellectuals. Already famous for his work on urban geography, the publication of *The Condition of Postmodernity* in 1989 established him also as one of the most important theorists of his generation. In that and other texts he described the dynamics of a new form of transnational capitalism, although in his more recent works, particularly *The New Imperialism* (2003), he has turned his attentions to the problem of American empire. He is presently Distinguished Professor at the Department of Anthropology, City University of New York.

What, then, are these new transnational, post-Fordist practices? Harvey (1989: 174–9) does us the favour of summarizing three earlier attempts to sign-post the key aspects of the transition: one by Halal (1986), which is rela-tively pro-capitalist, the one by Lash and Urry (1987) already mentioned above and a third by Swyngedouw (1986), which is closer to a traditional Marxist account. In fact the tables he produces to present these three accounts are too long to be included directly here, so we will attempt a summary of two of these frameworks. Halal's account distinguishes between the 'industrial' and 'post-industrial' paradigms. The transition from industrial to post-industrial society has been richly theorized within sociology (especially by Bell 1973, who was primarily interested in the shift to an economy based on services, knowledge and information) and international relations (e.g., Rosenau 1990, whose work we will discuss below). For Halal, its impact upon capitalism is to replace a mechanistic and authoritarian structure with one defined by market networks and participatory leadership, financial goals with multiple goals, operational management with strategic management, profit-centred 'big business' with 'democratic free enterprise', and the dichotomy of capitalism versus socialism with a blend of the two. Swyngedouw's (1986) account is more wide-ranging because it is concerned with the shift from one mode of production to another, but in respect of the actual production practices (which concern us here), he emphasizes, among others, the change from mass to small-batch production, standardization to flexibility, large stocks to no stocks, post-production testing to quality control and resource-driven to demand-driven priorities.

Lash and Urry's version, though, is best reproduced in full (see Table 7.4).

Biography Box 17:   Scott Lash and John Urry

Scott Lash and John Urry are both widely respected as sociological theorists in their own right, although it is as a writing pair that they have made arguably their biggest contributions to global studies: first with the publication of *The End of Organized Capitalism* (1987), which became a central text in the study of the new 'disaggregated' capitalist economy, and then with *Economies of Signs and Space* (1994), both blending insight from a wide variety of intellectual traditions, including Weber, Marx and Foucault. They came together at Lancaster University, where Urry still holds a position as Professor of Sociology. American-born Lash, who has also co-authored *Reflexive Modernization* (1994) with Ulrich Beck and Anthony Giddens, is Professor of Sociology at Goldsmith's, University of London.

Harvey's explanation for the transition from the old capitalism to the new, from Fordism to flexible accumulation, involves a return to Marx, and, in particular, to Marx's claim that capitalism is inherently contradictory and thus crisis-prone (Harvey 1989: 180–1). The result of such crisis tendencies, invariably, is *over-accumulation*. In the early part of the twentieth century, Fordism was ill equipped to do anything substantial to counter this problem, but post-war planning produced more sophisticated means of containing

Table 7.4 The differences between 'organized' and 'disorganized' capitalism

Organized capitalism	Disorganized capitalism
Concentration and centralization of industrial banking, and commercial capital in regulated national markets	Deconcentration of … corporate power away from national markets; increasing internationalization of capital and … separation of industrial from bank capital
Increasing separation of ownership from control and emergence of complex managerial hierarchies	Continued expansion of managerial strata articulating their own … agendas … distinct from class politics
Growth of new sectors of managerial, scientific, technological intelligentsia and of middle-class bureaucracy	Relative/absolute decline in blue-collar working class
Growth of collective organizations and bargaining within regions and nation-states	Decline in effectiveness of national collective bargaining
Close articulation of state and large monopoly capital interests and rise of class-based welfare system	Increasing independence of large monopolies from state regulation and diverse challenges to centralized state bureaucracy and power
Expansion of economic empires and control of overseas production and markets	Industrialization of Third World and competitive deindustrialization of core countries which turn to specialization in services
Incorporation of diverse class interests within a national agenda set through negotiated compromises and bureaucratic regulation	Outright decline of class-based politics and institutions
Hegemony of technical-scientific rationality	Cultural fragmentation and pluralism coupled with undermining of traditional class or national identities
Concentration of capitalist relations within relatively few industries and regions	Dispersal of capitalist relations across many sectors and regions
Extractive-manufacturing industries dominant sources of employment	Decline of (these) industries and rise of organizational and service industries
Strong regional concentration and specialization in extractive-manufacturing sector	Dispersal-diversification of the territorial-spatial division of labour
Search for economies of scale through increasing plant (workforce) size	Decline in plant size through geographical dispersal, increased by subcontracting, global production systems
Growth of large industrial cities dominating regions through provision of centralized services …	Decline of industrial cities and deconcentration from city centres into peripheral or semi-rural areas resulting in acute inner-city problems
Cultural-ideological configuration of 'modernism'	Cultural-ideological configurations of 'postmodernism'

Source: Lash and Urry (1987), as summarized by Harvey (1989: 175–6).

the problem. The transition can thus be explained in terms of the 'crisis of Fordism' (*ibid.*: 185), namely, when its options for dealing with the crisis of accumulation 'ran out'. During the last third of the century, the crisis required capitalism to effectively reinvent itself, and so the system of flexible accumulation emerged. In Harvey's words: 'there has ... been a sea-change in the surface appearance of capitalism since 1973, even though the underlying logic of capitalist accumulation and its crisis-tendencies remain the same' (*ibid.*: 189).

Pahl (1988) provides a succinct account of the impact of this new capitalism worldwide:

> Cash crops take the place of subsistence production, men migrate to find work, women carry excessive burdens of household production and survival, the multinational companies seek out and create green labour, and new technology affects manufacturing production from Silicon Valley to Taiwan and from Liverpool to Mexico City. There is a global domino effect that is not checked by national boundaries. (1988: 602)

Ultimately, late capitalism orchestrates, and relies upon, the reproduction of a transnational consumer culture; what Lash and Urry (1994) call an 'economy of signs and space'. The transnationalization of consumer culture is crucial to Sklair's argument. Indeed, for him the theory of the culture-ideology of consumerism as the basis for cultural imperialism not only challenges but actively displaces the 'easily disproved' theory of Americanization, which we discussed in Chapter 4. According to Sklair:

> This phase of capitalism is eroding the nation-state, and the transnationalization of communications that it produces is necessary for the creation of phenomena like the global supermarket and the global village. In this phase, the means of communication tend to become the dominant ideological apparatus. (Sklair 2002: 172–3)

Somewhat inevitably, the transition from national to transnational consumption practices has been mirrored in how cultural goods are produced and marketed. Whereas Fordism assumed that different patterns of consumer taste and buying power were generally mapped out along the stable dimensions of the social structure, post-Fordism, with the domination of information, media and signs, prefers to disaggregate society into 'lifestyles', 'niche markets' and 'target consumer groups' and the associated new designs and techniques (Lash and Urry 1994: 122; Slater 1997: 191). In this way, one can see consumer culture as being generated by a constant dialogue between producers and customers across the globe, with the reflexive, and flexible, production and commodification of the culture industries increasing the scope for the further reflexive consumption of individuals, and vice-versa. This is discussed in depth by Ulrich Beck in his theory of 'individualization', which we shall return to below.

7.5 Transnational spaces

For Manuel Castells, the practices described above form part of what can best be referred to as the 'network society'. The logic of the new, transnational capitalism is far more than simply a shift from 'industrial' to 'post-industrial', 'Fordist' to 'post-Fordist' production, but rather involves a significant culture shift and a shift in the dynamics of power. The network society is a transnational grid (Sassen 1991) of networks, what Castells calls the 'space of flows', which is detached from locality. Networks meet at particular 'hubs', the major financial, political and cultural centres which are 'global cities'. These cities are therefore lifted out of their fixity in place and become 'transnational spaces'.

Biography Box 18:   Manuel Castells

Manuel Castells (1942–) is a Spanish social theoretician who first established himself as a major Marxist urban sociologist, but who came to global prominence as a leading theorist through his three-volume series, *The Information Age,* incorporating *The Rise of the Network Society* (1999), *The End of Millennium* (2000) and *The Power of Identity* (2004). He is now considered by some to be the pre-eminent theorist of our contemporary, technology-dominated world. He is Emeritus Professor of Sociology and of City and Regional Planning at the University of California, Berkeley.

Global cities share a number of characteristics: they are likely to be centres of global financial activity, bases for major banks and economic institutions, but they are also likely to be spaces in which major political decision-making takes place, whether national, regional or transnational, magnets for global tourism, host venues for global mega-events and residential addresses for members of the global elite, or transnational capitalist class. However, they are also likely to be spaces that are home to high populations of migrants, many of whom constitute the transnational proletariat or underclass. They are, therefore, heavily contested spaces. In the definitive study of global cities, Saskia Sassen (1991) focuses on New York, London and Tokyo, which is a fairly conventional approach, and essentially based on economic power. Tokyo is clearly included for this reason but remains, culturally, distinctly Japanese – Melbourne, by contrast, might be one of the world's most multicultural cities but lacks economic or political power. Because there are so many categories including in the definition of a 'global city', there is no clear ranking system, although in 2008 a useful list was produced by the journal *Foreign Policy* for which Sassen served as a consultant. Taking a variety of

Table 7.5   Ranking of 'global cities'

Rank	City
1	New York
2	London
3	Paris
4	Tokyo
5	Hong Kong
6	Los Angeles
7	Singapore
8	Chicago
9	Seoul
10	Toronto

Source: *Foreign Policy* (2008).

factors – business activity, human capital, information exchange, cultural experience and political engagement – Table 7.5 shows which cities made it into the top ten.

Sassen argues that the global city is a specific site of new types of transnational social forms, and clearly not defined solely by the economic power concentrated therein. She describes this eloquently in a published interview:

It endogenizes global dynamics that transform existing social alignments. And it enables even the disadvantaged to develop transnational strategies and subjectivities... Transnational immigrant households, and even communities, are perhaps emblematic of this. (Sassen, in Gane 2004: 130)

It is for this reason that discussion of the research on 'global cities' is included in this chapter. The city as a microcosm of the 'global village' would be the subject matter of Chapter 1 – the globalization of the city. But the work on global cities actually concerns itself with the role major cities play in political and economic decision-making, forming part of a level of activity, a transnational grid, which operates above the nation-state. Global cities are not just centres of national activity and neither are they just manifestations of the world in one place. They are the capitals of the transnational world. In fairness, Castells would not agree with this assertion – for him, the networks rather than the cities are the actual sites of power. In any case, they are transnational spaces. Perhaps, though, this is a difficult concept for the reader, who lives in such a place, to understand, given that the theorization of global cities often renders them rather abstract concepts. Perhaps the best analogy is to say that the global city is to the transnational grid of economic and political power what an airport is to the ordinary traveller: when you are in it, you get the sense that you have left the nation-state, and while it is fair to say that you don't feel like you exist 'in the world' as one place, you do get the sense of existing *outside* of place. Such is the transnational.

Biography Box 19:   Saskia Sassen

Saskia Sassen (1949–) is Robert S. Lynd Professor of Sociology at Columbia University and Centennial Visiting Professor at the London School of Economics. Born in the Netherlands, she is most famous for her work on *The Global City* (1991).

7.6   Transnational institutions

So far we have used Sklair and Harvey as our guides through the labyrinth of transnationalism. This is because we have concentrated on the transnationalization of capitalism, which is the focus of both authors' work. But, of course, the transnationalization framework is not limited to economic analyses. Indeed, the vast majority of work in this tradition has concentrated instead on the emergence of transnational *political* institutions, and in particular the role of the United Nations. In previous chapters the role of the UN has perhaps been implicitly acknowledged; now it is time to address it explicitly and show how its existence contributes to a distinct model in global studies, namely transnationalization.

We should begin by summarizing the structure and history of the United Nations. As this has, rather conveniently, been done elsewhere, what follows is liberally taken from that other source, albeit in abbreviated form (O'Byrne 2002: 79–87). Although the UN was formed in 1945, immediately after the end of the Second World War, it grew out of the defunct League of Nations, which had been formed in 1919 after the First World War by France, Italy, Japan, the United Kingdom and the United States, the five principal allied nations. The League of Nations was ever a toothless tiger, caught up as it was in nation-state and ideological disputes, such as the decision in 1920 by the United States not to be a member, its lukewarm reception by the Soviet Union which did not join until 1934, the withdrawal of Germany, Italy and Japan in response to this to form a separate anti-Soviet group, and the expulsion of the Soviet Union in 1939. Aside from the 1926 Slavery Convention, which effectively abolished the slave trade before there was any such thing as meaningful international law, the achievements of the League of Nations are hard to recall. The United Nations was designed not only to replace the League of Nations, but also to provide a far more effective structure for transnational governance, to move beyond the shortcomings of its predecessor. Born, as was the League of Nations, out of the noble and understandable desire to achieve peace, sustainability and prosperity after a time of total war and destruction, the UN was designed to tackle such issues as global poverty and unemployment, to provide strategies for conflict resolution and to oversee global social development and world economic policies.

The structure of the United Nations is quite complex, because it has many agencies attached to it which operate semi-autonomously in the pursuit of specific goals, but which are in principal accountable to the UN's central machinery. The chief decision-making forum of the UN is called the General Assembly. This is comprised of representatives from each member state, each possessing one vote regardless of relative size or economic power. The General Assembly votes on resolutions which are not legally binding, which are carried either by a two-thirds or a simple majority. The General Assembly also oversees the work of certain specialist agencies, such as the United Nations High Commissioner for Refugees (UNHCR), the United Nations Children's Fund (UNICEF) and the United Nations Conference on Trade and Development (UNCTAD). But despite being the chief decision-making body of the UN, the General Assembly is not responsible for making the most important decisions. Those are left to the Security Council, a sub-group of 15 members which decides whether the UN should intervene in conflict situations, involve itself in peacekeeping operations or impose sanctions against states. Although comprised of 15 members, at present only ten of these are elected on a rotational basis, usually for two years. The other five seats on the Security Council are held by the permanent members, namely China (formerly the Republic of China, or Taiwan), France, Russia (formerly the Soviet Union), the United Kingdom and the United States. Why these five? It is clearly not because they are the largest economic or military powers – the exclusion of Germany and Japan is noticeable. What unites them, of course, is a share in the spoils as the five most prominent members of the victorious allied forces at the end of the Second World War. But their permanent status is far more than honorary – each of these five members has the right to exercise the power of veto, meaning that even if all 14 other members of the Security Council vote to pursue a particular course of action, it only takes one of these to exercise its power of veto for the decision to be overturned.

In addition to the General Assembly and the Security Council, there are three other components of the UN system. The largest of these is the Economic and Social Council, comprised of 54 elected members whose role is to oversee the economic, social and humanitarian work of the UN, which is largely achieved through certain specialist agencies such as the World Health Organization (WHO), the International Monetary Fund (IMF), the International Labour Organization (ILO), the World Bank and the United Nations Educational, Scientific and Cultural Organization (UNESCO). The Secretariat is the administrative arm of the UN, while the International Court of Justice, based in The Hague, deals with disputes between states. A sixth component, the Trusteeship Council, is largely inactive as it was designed to oversee the transition of newly independent states into full self-government.

Maurice Bertrand's (1994) system for dividing the history of the UN into certain phases remains one of the most effective schemes through which to understand the 'ups' and 'downs' of the UN. Bertrand begins by identifying a two-year period between 1945 and 1946 of enthusiasm for the potential of the UN, especially in the US and the West. However, between 1946 and 1953 this enthusiasm gave way to the reality of Cold War politics as the US succeeded in using the UN to support its intervention in Korea. Then, during a period of East–West stalemate, between 1953 and 1960, the UN turned its attentions towards peacekeeping operations following crises in the Middle East and Congo. Between 1960 and 1975, during a period of decolonization, the UN focused its efforts on liberation struggles and the constitutional concerns of the newly independent states. But between 1975 and 1985 the UN system underwent a period of crisis, as two significant proposals – one made by a number of developing countries and supported by the Soviet Union for the UN to take a more active role in global wealth redistribution, the other made by various Arab nations wanting action taken against the state of Israel for its activities in Palestine – were both met by the US with the threat of withdrawal, which would have resulted in severe financial problems for an organization funded by its member states in proportion to their economic status. However, according to Bertrand, the fall of the Berlin Wall and the end of the Cold War, the end of apartheid in South Africa and the generally supported allied campaign against Iraq in the 1991 Gulf War, contributed to a period of renewed optimism from 1986. O'Byrne (2003: 81) suggests that this period came to an end around 1993 and was succeeded by a period of uncertainty, pessimism and loss of faith, caused in part by the perceived impotence of the UN to do anything about the genocides in Rwanda and the former Yugoslavia, plus growing concern about transnational corporate power, the rise of the anti-global capitalism movement (see Chapter 3) and concerns over national sovereignty and democratic accountability.

Whatever the weaknesses might be in respect of the United Nations and similar institutions, their very existence must count as a significant characteristic of any model of global society. One of the most prominent commentators on this is the international relations scholar James Rosenau (1980, 1989, 1990), who for many is one of the pioneers of the study of global change, certainly within his particular discipline. For him, technological developments have led to unprecedented turbulence in the international political arena. Rosenau states quite clearly the challenge this transformation has for the traditional study of world politics:

> The very notion of 'international relations' seems obsolete in the face of an apparent trend in which more and more of the interactions that sustain world politics unfold without the direct involvement of nations or states. So a new term is needed, one that denotes the presence of new structures and processes...A suitable label would be *postinternational politics*. (Rosenau 1990: 6)

Following this, Rosenau develops a model of contemporary world politics which views its subject matter in terms of 'two worlds' (Rosenau coins the useful phrase, the 'bifurcated world'): a 'traditional' state-centric world and a multicentric world of disparate actors, including transnational corporations (and probably classes). The same actors inhabit these two worlds but their trajectories are quite different. Post-international – or what we would call transnational – politics is thus a complex arena in which nation-states and other core actors exploit a variety of methods to secure self-interest, in contrast to the more orthodox 'realist' (state-centric) or 'liberal' (internationalist) agendas (see Chapter 8 and Chapter 2 respectively for more on these).

Biography Box 20:   James Rosenau

James Rosenau (1924–) is an American international political theorist and former President of the International Studies Association. He is currently University Professor of International Affairs at the Elliott School of International Affairs at the George Washington University. His publications on political interdependence, conflict and turbulence in the 1980s are considered to be among the earliest engagements with contemporary global theory within his discipline.

Some of the most important developments in transnational governance have been the attempts by the UN to strengthen international law, including international humanitarian law (the Geneva and Hague Conventions) and international human rights law (the International Bill of Rights comprised of the non-binding UN Declaration of Human Rights 1948 and the 1966 Covenants on Civil and Political Rights and Economic, Social and Cultural Rights, plus specific, binding Conventions abolishing torture, genocide, slavery and protecting the rights of children, women, refugees, migrants and so on). Despite the efforts of campaigners, adherence to international law has historically been treated *de facto* as non-binding by member states, unwilling to surrender the sovereignty of their own legal systems. This was largely down to the absence of any means of actually policing it. In 1998 in Rome, the UN formally, finally, agreed upon the establishment of a permanent International Criminal Court (ICC) empowered to try cases of genocide, crimes against humanity or war crimes under international law. Welcomed by many as a positive step towards the eradication of the perceived authority of the nation-state to commit acts of 'legalized' violence, the ICC has nonetheless been plagued by disagreements over its reach and renewed disputes over the proclaimed superior authority of international law over nation-state law.

It is precisely in respect of such concerns that scholars such as Ulrich Beck, Richard Falk, Jürgen Habermas and David Held have developed what has become known as the 'cosmopolitan' theory of transnational relations. For such commentators, the process of transnationalization – defined, as throughout this chapter, as being the 'lifting' of institutions, practices and powers to a level above that of the nation-state – provides the opportunity to build a more peaceful and sustainable world, by denying the nation-state its excesses.

However, such optimism is guarded, given the reality of the situation, and demands are made, and schemes devised, for the greater empowerment of international law and the transnational institutions which regulate it. Beck defines this clearly when he calls for a politics of global interdependence that possesses a political legitimacy that transcends and overrides the will and self-interest of individual nation-states, and is thus equipped to deal with the ecological, economic, terrorist and moral risks and challenges facing the world. For Beck (Beck and Sznaider 2006: 11), as for Bauman (2002), the acceptance and application of a cosmopolitan vision is the only meaningful way of addressing these risks and challenges, but the vision itself needs to be institutionalized. In other words, transnational institutions are only half the solution – they are meaningless without the simultaneous transnationalization of a cosmopolitan will (Beck and Sznaider 2006: 13). The current absence of any such synergy is well illustrated in Kate Nash's account of the relative success *and* failures of the 2005 'Make Poverty History' campaign (Nash 2008).

7.7   Reflexive modernization

If Harvey presents us with an attempt to theorize the transition from early to late capitalism within a broader critique of postmodernism, more general theories of global change which help us make sense of the process of transnationalization have been presented by Anthony Giddens and Ulrich Beck. Independently of one another (although they subsequently came together) these major figures have developed complex accounts of the global condition based on the radicalization of modernity and the impact of reflexivity and risk.

Giddens's work grew out of his earlier development of the theory of structuration, an attempt to bridge the historical divide in sociological theory between structure-based and agency-based theories of the constitution of society. In developing his theory of global change (what he refers to as 'globalization') Giddens clearly distances himself from contemporaries such as Roland Robertson, for whom globalization is a long-term historical process pre-dating and indeed driving forward modernization. Giddens, by contrast, emphasizes the extent to which this globalization is a relatively recent phenomenon, and one which brings about a rupture in the logic of modernity. That is to say, globalization occurs as a moment *within* modernity, in which the constitutive forces of modernity become radicalized, extended beyond the confines of the nation-state. Significantly, though, Giddens does not present the case that globalization brings about the *end* of modernity, or of the modern age (as does another of his contemporaries, Martin Albrow); rather, the forces remain the same, different in scope rather than content, meaning the transformation is a shift within modernity. The resultant 'age' is not 'global' nor 'postmodern', but rather *late* modern, or, to be more precise, an era of *reflexive modernity*. As he writes: 'rather than entering a period of postmodernity, we are moving into one in which the consequences of modernity are more radicalized and universalized than before' (Giddens 1990: 3).

In developing his theory, Giddens draws on a variety of influences to come up with an acceptable definition of *modernity*. It is characterized, he claims, by four principal forces: a nation-state system, a world capitalist economy, an international division of labour and a world military order. The growth of information and communications technology and the rise of planetary consciousness have contributed to the radicalization of these forces, but ultimately, for Giddens, modernity is itself inherently globalizing. Modernity has ever been about *progress*, about the drive *forwards*. In Giddens's words, it is akin to a relentless juggernaut. But 'progress' carries with it its own setbacks; it takes on a life of its own, becomes its own justification, the juggernaut speeds out of control with nobody at the wheel and, in the pursuit of progress, science creates dangers: think of nuclear technology used to build weapons, chemical technology damaging the earth's natural environment. We live in an age of what Ulrich Beck calls 'manufactured risk'. For Giddens, our awareness of this risk is tied to our changing 'ontological security', we lose faith in the capabilities of 'expert systems'. This results in a heightened sense of *reflexivity*, of our role in the world. The growth and spread of knowledge breeds self-awareness and reflexive thinking among individuals – as a result, modernity has itself 'matured' from its industrial stage, and is now 'coming to understanding itself' (*ibid.*: 48)

For Giddens, reflexivity and reflexive thinking is 'characteristic of all human action', because 'to be a human being is to know ... both what one is doing and why one is doing it' (Giddens 1991: 35). This marks a significant step away from premodernity and industrial modernity, for as we saw in the last chapter, the 'reflexive monitoring of the self' has been stifled by tradition. In contrast, the present social context social practices can now be 'constantly examined and reformed in the light of incoming information about these very practices' (*ibid.*: 38). As a result, through the exchange and flows of information across the globe 'traditional' culture and behaviour becomes newly contextualized, allowing it to be compared and evaluated in relation to other, potentially more attractive lifestyle choices. This could include secularism in place of religion, consumer identity in favour of a class identity, or mobility instead of fixity. All of this is relevant to the broader debates around the emergence of late, consumerist capitalism, or late modernity.

Giddens suggests that globalization, which we prefer to call transnationalization, is characterized by two main processes: 'disembedding' and 'time–space distanciation'. We have come across 'disembedding' already in this volume. It refers to the process by which corporations, people, cultures, symbols and so on become lifted out of their association with specific *places*, and can be relocated anywhere in the world. Disembedding is central to the post-Fordist production systems of late capitalism. It signifies the decreasing significance of place in the contemporary world, and our changing relationship with *space*. 'Time–space distanciation' is the process through which the *logics* of time and space become detached. Technological innovations render 'space' insignificant as much of the world is accessible almost immediately. This is similar to what Harvey calls 'time–space compression', the *annihilation of space through time* (Harvey 1989: 240–1):

> The history of capitalism has been characterized by speed-up in the pace of life…that the world sometimes seems to collapse inwards upon us…As space appears to shrink to a 'global village'…and as time horizons shorten to the point where the present is all there is…we have to learn to cope with an overwhelming sense of compression of our spatial and temporal worlds. (*Ibid*.: 240)

Biography Box 21:   Anthony Giddens

Anthony Giddens (1938–) is now Baron Giddens of Southgate. He did his undergraduate degree at the University of Hull and his MA at the London School of Economics before moving to Leicester to work with the great German sociologist Norbert Elias. He went to King's College, Cambridge, where he completed his PhD and became lecturer in sociology in 1969; he was promoted to Professor of Sociology in 1987. He left in 1997 to become Director of the London School of Economics, a position he retired from in 2003, although he remains attached to the institution as an Emeritus Professor. In the 1970s he was best known for his writings on classical sociological theory, but in the 1980s he began to develop his theory of structuration, which propelled him to international recognition. He then turned his attention to the newly emerging field of the sociology of globalization in his short but important book *The Consequences of Modernity* (1990). More recently he has been a key advisor to former British Prime Minister Tony Blair, and is credited with inventing the concept of the 'Third Way'.

Harvey presents his theoretical account within the framework of capitalism. Like Giddens, Ulrich Beck attempts to conceptualize global change within the discourse of modernity. Starting from similar foundations (in what he prefers to term a 'second' modernity), Beck has sought to conceptualize the social, political, economic and environmental transformations across the globe by establishing their essential (and essentially new) properties. In short, Beck argues that the common bond for these changes is the concept of risk, and that we are living in a world 'risk society' (1992, 1999).

Beck's theory of risk society can be separated into two distinct categories (Turner and Rojek 2001: 187): 'type one risks' which deal with environment and scientific knowledge and 'type two risks' which concern social change in work, politics and identity. Beck argues that the unity of risk society – risk being defined as the anticipation of catastrophe (Beck 2006a) – derives from the development of instrumental rational control, which the process of modernization promotes in all spheres – from individual risk of accidents and illnesses to collective risks of environmental hazards and war (Elliott 2002: 295). The unity of risk society is advanced by Beck's assertion that these risks are developing *simultaneously*. As a result, he believes that contemporary society has become increasingly occupied with 'debating, preventing and managing risks that it has itself produced' (Beck 2006a: 4).

Like Giddens, Beck argues that the risk society places new demands on the individual. In the new modernity, Beck argues, traditional and institutional forms of coping with fear and insecurity – class, tradition, family, religion and the state – are in decline. These forms all relate to the regeneration of capital from its 'classical industrial design', to a reflexive, dynamic and global model, the 'disorganization' of capitalism in the 1980s identified by Lash and Urry (1987). What results is the emergence of new, 'life politics' divorced from nation-state and class, and a process Beck refers to as the 'individualization' of society (Beck 1992: 88). The politics of self-identity and cultural consumption take on increasing significance. Individuals have, in effect, become the 'experts' in respect of the issues that impact upon them.

All in all, it argued that transnationalization has radicalized the dimensions of modernity through the greater mobility demands of the labour market and the proliferation of knowledge beyond states and cultural elites. This radicalization of modernity opens up a new paradigm – the transnational. Whereas Wallerstein's world systems theory tended to focus on the structural interplay between (clearly demarcated) national and international spheres, transnationalization advances this image by seeing the national and international as merging into one (Beck and Sznaider 2006: 16–17). As a result, global change is no longer something that takes place 'out there' – it is actively absorbed and internalized into our daily lives. Transnationalization is thus taking place *from below, within* nation-states. Nobody describes this better than Doreen Massey, whose work *Space, Place and Gender* (1994) is a quiet classic within global studies and social science in general. In this book Massey describes what she refers to as 'power geometry', that is, the way individuals *relate* to the processes of time–space compression so well defined by Harvey (albeit, for Massey, in an overly economistic way).

The contributions of these writers have revolutionized social science. Concepts such as 'risk' and 'reflexivity' are now considered essential teaching in any university course on contemporary social theory. For Beck, as for Sklair, the 'old ways' of doing social science, bound up as they are in biases either towards the nation-state or – in Wallerstein's work – to a state-centric view of the world-system are ill equipped to understand this complex transformation.

Biography Box 22:   Ulrich Beck

Ulrich Beck (1944–) is Professor of Sociology at the University of Munich and is Centennial Professor in the Department of Sociology at the London School of Economics. Since the publication of *Risk Society* (1986 in German, 1992 in an English translation) he has served as a policy advisor as well as theorist on environmental risk. He is widely considered to be one of the world's leading theorists of cosmopolitanism (Beck 2006b).

7.8   Conclusion

The transnational perspective has attracted considerable support within the emerging field of global studies. No doubt this is in part because it seems to overcome some of the perceived deficiencies of the other frameworks without *necessarily* negating them. If globalization seems to present an optimistic development of McLuhan's global village and an over-emphasis on the recognition of 'one world', transnationalization acknowledges the relative decline of the nation-state in respect of capitalist production and political and legal sovereignty without appealing directly to the still-abstract concept of 'the globe'. As Beck explains, it is the rootedness of transnationalization that distinguishes it from the theory of globalization (and, indeed, liberalization):

> It means having roots and wings at the same time. It means not being a global player; it is not the perspective for those privileged to inhabit frequent traveller lounges. It is rooted, rather, in the sensitivities and solidarities that organize most people's sense of identity and location in the world; it is redefining the local in a translocal perspective. This means combining local, national and global perspectives in special conceptual frames of references. (Beck in Gane 2004: 148)

Yet it sides with the globalization framework in readily accepting that some kind of transformation *has* taken place in respect of such matters, and takes issue with both the Americanization paradigm and some contributions to the polarization one which seem rooted on old-fashioned nation-statism. Yet it is not entirely incompatible with the polarization model – Sklair and Harvey both emphasize the increasing polarization brought about by the new capitalism – and for those drawing on liberal rather than Marxist theory it is not incompatible with liberalization either. Nor is it incompatible with creolization – to some extent there is a unity between the two paradigms, exemplified by the shared connection to the New Times movement of the late 1980s. There is even some overlap with the McDonaldization tradition, although the two appear to be discussing quite different structures and processes. Finally, it seems eminently plausible to suggest that the 'balkanization' framework discussed in the following chapter has emerged as a response to the failures of transnationalization.

Even so, the paradigm has its critics. For one thing, while neo-Marxian commentators identify issues of power inequality in the new capitalism, those advocates of a cosmopolitan outlook who put their faith for a better world can be accused of underplaying the role of those who *drive* this cosmopolitanism forward. Linked to this, radical opponents of global capitalism have preferred to put their faith in civil society movements than in an improved system of transnational governance. In addition to such criticisms from the Left, cosmopolitans are under fire from political realists such as Danilo Zolo for putting their faith in the impossible concept of 'humanity' (Zolo's trenchant critique of the cosmopolitan vision of the likes of Habermas will be discussed in the next chapter). How have the transnationalist and cosmopolitan theorists responded? There is no clear answer to this. Anthony Giddens famously went on to develop a new politics of the 'Third Way', beyond capitalism and socialism, which inspired the UK Labour government under Tony Blair.

For others, such as Richard Falk and, especially, Leslie Sklair, the solution remains rooted in the process of transnationalization itself: human rights. Drawing on Antonio Gramsci's famous claim that to combat the hegemonic culture-ideology of capitalism, one needs a counter-hegemony, Sklair, who identifies the culture-ideology of global capitalism as consumerism, posits human rights as its counter-hegemony, the ideology of an alternative, socialist globalization. Not only is this a welcome alternative to the usual, rather reactionary, assumption that the ideology of human rights is born out of Western liberalism and thus part of the same project as capitalism, it is a clear articulation of the basic solution to global problems shared by transnationalist writers, whether Marxist or liberal: that a cosmopolitan transnationalism is needed to override the deficiencies of economic and political transnationalism, and moreover, that this is possible.

Balkanization: A Clash of Civilizations

8

8.1 Introduction

The 'balkanization' framework focuses on the extent to which, in the post-1989 world, a new international order (or more aptly disorder) is in place, in which nation-state rivalries exist simultaneously with resurgent tribal nationalisms. It serves as an important counterpoint to much of the literature in global studies which analyzes global change in terms of some degree of convergence, for good or ill. Rather than seeing the world as somehow coming together or engaging in new practices, this model suggests that it remains rooted in ideological and political conflict. Building on the earlier realist approaches to world politics, the balkanization model begins with Huntington's famous claim that, in contemporary conditions, old conflicts between nation-states have been replaced by new ones between cultural and ideological blocs, on the basis of values, religions and traditions rather than orthodox geopolitics. The contemporary, 'global' world is thus a world of deep division, conflict and anarchy, resulting largely from the end of the Cold War and the absence of any single threat capable of uniting competing power blocs. For some, in such a world, the United States, as the only remaining superpower, should ensure political and economic stability by operating as a 'benign liberal hegemony' (Gilpin 1987); indeed, global anarchy may be inevitable without this hegemony (Mearscheimer 1990; Kaplan 1994).

Advocates of this position tend to be sceptical at best about the claims made by those who favour the 'liberalization' or 'globalization' models. Claims that the world is becoming increasingly interdependent, and that this represents the 'end of history' and the triumph of liberal democracy, are dismissed as naive, in the light of experience. In the absence of any single world authority, there can be only disorder. As has been suggested, some advocates of this framework maintain that conflict between nation-states remains the dominant global dynamic, while others turn instead to new forms of intercultural conflict. In either case, 'global society' is by no means a potentially harmonious world of economic interdependence and moral and cultural unity, but rather a deeply divided arena riddled with civilizational conflicts (Gilpin 1981; Huntington 1997; Barber 2003). In such a world, the significance of the nation-state has not been eroded – rather, its role has been fundamentally altered so as to take account of the 'post-realist' political conditions (Gilpin 1981). Perhaps understandably, this model has been looked upon favourably by neo-conservative commentators, particularly in the United States, who advocate strong, hawkish foreign policies to defend American political, economic and cultural interests against the perceived threat imposed by other 'civilizations'.

However, the implications derived from this framework for US foreign policy are by no means homogeneous. On the one hand, the balkanization framework presents a warning against undue intervention, in so far as any such intervention fuelled by ignorance is damaging to national interests (Huntington 1997). Contrary to this, in the hands of neo-conservative policy advisors, this warning serves to justify the need for intervention as a means of protecting US political interests and cultural values (Frum and Perle 2003/4). Necessarily, then, this chapter will examine the naissance of neo-conservative thinking, and its growing influence on US foreign policy, developed from its origins in welfare and cultural policies, and trace the uneasy relationship between neo-conservative and neo-realist strands which both employ this framework but which emphasize, respectively, cultural values and political interests – evidence that, as with the remainder of models discussed in this volume, there is no singular ideological position attributable to this framework.

8.2   The legacy of political realism

The pre-history of the balkanization framework, though, is found in the realist school of international relations. Essentially, realism begins with the assertion by the Enlightenment English political philosopher Thomas Hobbes that humans are, by their very nature, sinful, violent and committed to self-preservation (Morgenthau 1946, 1948, 1951; Kennan 1993). Thus, the 'state of nature', the world where there is no form of social control, is a state of anarchy. Order is maintained because of the presence of a strong state and the rule of law. However, while this applies to the realm of domestic politics, in the field of international relations, where the natural condition is anarchy between states, there is no central authority, no world government, to create such order. Furthermore, because states are actors who always act in their own best interests, the very idea of such a world government or some similar overarching power structure is not feasible, and because war and violence have always been central to international politics, the idea of perpetual peace, as advocated by cosmopolitan liberals such as Immanuel Kant, is naive. Conflict between states is seen as natural and inevitable – the international arena is a battlefield between states seeking to achieve power over the others in order to protect their own interests. There is in realism an implicit recognition of the 'survival of the fittest' as the basis of power politics, of the legitimate authority of the militarily strong states in world affairs, the theory of *realpolitik*. Such a position, influenced by a long line of major theorists from Thucyides via Macchiavelli to Weber, was held by the two most important figures in realist theory, Hans Morgenthau (1946, 1948, 1951) and the socialist E. H. Carr (1946), as well as by the celebrated American statesman Henry Kissinger (1969).

However, lest one think that the core message of realism is to promote violence and conflict, it should be stated that the chief priority of any country's foreign policy should be to protect its national interests. Embarking on wars or international crusades of any other type for any reason other than this would be deemed to contradict this chief priority. Realists would much rather the state remains at home, and only engages with the rest of the world when it is a matter of protecting the national interest. For sure, realists have soundly condemned the policies of 'liberal internationalism', and American foreign policy during much of the Cold War, for being moralistic and ideological rather than geopolitical (Kennan 1951; Kissinger 1969; Morgenthau 1951). Generally, realists prefer policies of détente and containment to direct intervention.

As a theory of international relations, realism always had much in common with the sociological approach known as 'conflict theory'. This approach, derived without coincidence from Weber, treats societies largely as marketplaces in which rival interest groups compete for scarce resources. However, an inherent problem with realism, from Hobbes onwards, was always that it was largely premised on the intrinsically violent nature of humankind. Such a premise does not explain peaceful situations, and realists sought out more sophisticated bases for their theory. Sociological conflict theorists of the Weberian school have historically distanced themselves from the more individualistic rational choice theorists by focusing on how the logic of conflict operates at the societal level and, in similar fashion, 'neo-realists' such as Kenneth Waltz (1979) have drawn on Rousseau's version of the 'social contract' to argue that the 'natural state' of any individual actor is irrelevant, because the conditions which breed violence and war are properties of the social structure. In other words, war is a structural condition of the international political arena, and conflicts erupt even if states engage in benign interaction with one another. Neo-realists thus focus on states as rational actors within the international order, rather than merely as manifestations of the national interest, particularly as what is deemed rational at one level might be considered irrational at the other (Krasner 1978).

So, within international relations, realists and neo-realists have between them exerted considerable influence on understanding the world in terms of conflict. With their more structural approach, neo-realists have been more sensitive to historical change, to considering how the hegemonic powers within the world order undergo periods of rise and decline, engaged as they are in a quasi-Darwinian struggle for survival against emerging powers (Gilpin 1981), and between competing interests and ideologies (Krasner 1985). The balkanization framework clearly derives from such an approach to the world, and contemporary neo-realists, seeking to understand the dynamics of contemporary global change, belong in this camp.

Nowhere is this approach more significantly articulated than in the work of Robert Gilpin. Gilpin makes it absolutely clear that any form of global transformation is entirely dependent upon the ability (and will) of the most powerful states to impose and maintain an appropriate form of open and interdependent world order, what he calls 'benign hegemony' (Gilpin 1987). That which others call 'globalization' or 'liberalization' or even 'transnationalization', and suggest may represent some new phase in history, some break with the past, is for Gilpin only possible because of the specific configurations of power politics in the twentieth century, specifically, those which served to facilitate American hegemony. Gilpin's argument is clearly a case *for* Americanization and a warning that the perceived stability of the current global condition is, indeed, *conditional* upon it:

> Since the end of the Second World War, American global hegemony, the anti-Soviet alliance, and a Keynesian welfare state ideology...cemented together economic relations among the three principal centres of industrial power outside the Soviet block – the United States, Japan and Western Europe...It was on the basis of this conceptualization of the relationship between international economics and politics that...[there was scepticism] of the argument of the more extreme exponents of interdependence theory...It neglected the political base on which this interdependent world economy rests and, more importantly, the political forces that were eroding these political foundations. (Gilpin 1986: 311–12; summarized in McGrew 1992: 85)

Gilpin's work is essential in the development of global studies within the existing field of international relations. Given that he presents the case for interdependence and global cooperation as being contingent on American 'benign hegemony', the clearly the relative decline of America as the world's great hegemonic power brings with it the associated problem of a return to statist self-interest and power politics. Tony McGrew provides an excellent statement of Gilpin's theory in this respect:

> This is a very timely argument, since the relative decline of the US, the absence of a global ideological threat to unite the most powerful capitalist states, and the resurgence everywhere of nationalist and protectionist political forces suggest the end of the 'golden era' of globalization. Accordingly, for 'realists', globalization does not prefigure the emergence of a 'world

society'. On the contrary, the world is still best described (and understood) as a 'society of states'. (McGrew 1992: 85)

It is worthwhile reading this quote again. While it gives a clear statement of Gilpin's theory and of the potential dangers faced by the end of American hegemony, it does make one presumption (as indeed does Gilpin) which makes it seem outdated. That is, it states that the absence of a 'shared enemy' has led to a decline in American hegemony, and by this it means the global condition in the post-Cold War era. This is not a mistake made by Samuel Huntington, for whom the demise of the Soviet Union represents the end (perhaps only temporarily) of one major cleavage in the world today. It would, however, be naive to equate the end of the Cold War with the end of world conflict, and this is why Huntington, whose work does not actually originate in the realist tradition at all, but whose 'clash of civilizations' thesis mixes civilizational theory, cultural relativism and historical sociology with a spicy dosage of neo-realist conflict theory, is arguably the most important writer within the 'balkanization' framework.

Biography Box 23: Robert Gilpin

Robert Gilpin (1930–) is Eisenhower Professor of Public and International Affairs, Emeritus, at Princeton University. One of the most significant contemporary theorists within the realist tradition of international relations, he has contributed to our understanding of international political economy as well as American foreign policy.

8.3 The 'clash of civilizations' debate: Huntington and his critics

Huntington's position – often misunderstood – is outlined in detail in his book *The Clash of Civilizations and the Remaking of World Order* (1997). His premise is simple, and undeniable, enough – *culture matters*. The Cold War had been defined as a clash of political ideologies – America and its Western allies against the artificial political machine that was the Soviet Union and its various satellites. In the post-Cold War era, such political machineries have given way to cultural allegiances. 'In the post-Cold War world flags count and so do other symbols of cultural identity, including crosses, crescents, and even head coverings,' Huntington points out, 'because culture counts, and cultural identity is what is most meaningful to most people. People are discovering new but often old identities and marching under new but often old flags which lead to wars with new but often old enemies' (Huntington 1997: 20). Or, to put it another way: 'The question, "Which side are you on?" has been replaced by the much more fundamental one, "Who are you?"' (1997: 125).

For Huntington, the world today is defined in terms of distinctions not so much between nations or political blocs as between *civilizations*. He contrasts this with four other paradigms. The first is the view, associated with Fukuyama and endorsed by other liberals; that the post-1989 world is unifying under the banner of a triumphant liberal democracy – a view we have already covered in this volume. The second is the view that the world is divided between 'the West and the rest', a wholly misleading view that lumps everywhere not defined as 'the West' together in some meaningless amorphous category. The third is the realist view that the world remains an arena of conflict and competition in which nation-states are the key actors. The fourth is the view that increasingly unpredictable developments at sub-national, supra-national and transnational levels have led to a world of 'sheer chaos'. Each of these paradigms is dismissed as inadequate when trying to make sense of contemporary global conditions. Instead, he proposes a paradigm focusing on relations between eight main civilizations, which can be crudely placed in tabular form alongside their (approximate) geographical locations (see Table 8.1).

Huntington makes it clear that the world he is describing is historically distinct. Earlier forms of modernization – already discussed in previous chapters – were easily equitable with Westernization. Indeed, in his earlier work, Huntington himself was a major contributor to the theories of modernization and convergence which largely presumed synonymy with 'progress' along Western lines. That is no longer the case. The economic, political and military developments of non-Western societies have been with a view to preserving and enhancing, rather than eroding, their cultural traditions. The spread of Western consumer culture around the world does not at all result in the spread of Western values and thus of

Table 8.1 World civilizations

African	Sub-Saharan Africa
Hindu	Indian subcontinent, dating back at least as far as 1500 BC
Islamic	Middle East, North Africa, parts of South and South-east Asia, dating back to 600–700 AD
Japanese	Japan, emerging during the period 100–400 AD
Latin American	South and Central America
Orthodox	Russia and parts of South-east Europe
Sinic	China and parts of East and South-east Asia, dating back at least to 1500 BC
Western	Western Europe, North America, Australasia, emerging 700–800 AD

Source: Adapted from Huntington (1997: 45–7).

'Westernization' broadly conceived (Huntington 1997: 58). Nor is it right to presume that Western (or more specifically American) military, economic, political and cultural imperialism has resulted in a world dependent upon the last great superpower. Rather, civilizational blocs have been formed because countries have tended to enter into strategic alliances with those with whom they share cultural beliefs and values, and, as a result, Western hegemony has been in decline (*ibid.*: 20). Paralleling this Western decline has been the significant challenge to its hegemony posed by other civilizations, notably the main Asian ones, the Sinic and Japanese civilizations, due to their increased economic power, and the Islamic civilization, due in no small part to its dramatic population expansion (*ibid.*: 102–21). And with the re-emergence of culture as a source of identity and solidarity comes a resurgence of religion as the bedrock for such cultures – if earlier forms of modernization presumed the inevitability of secularization, the view from the turn of the millennium tells us how unfounded such presumptions were (*ibid.*: 95–101). In particular, the Islamic civilization is inseparable from its religious base, but the religious resurgence is prevalent in other civilizations as well – Christianity of varying denominations has enjoyed a revival as a source of shared identity in the Western and Latin American civilizations. Huntington also points out how, towards the end of the twentieth century, in a curious reversal of Max Weber's famous assessment at the beginning of the century, Chinese political leaders were attributing much of the country's progress to its shared cultural base in Confucianism (*ibid.*: 106).

Huntington makes it clear that the emergence of a world dominated by civilizations does not render the nation-state obsolete. Rather, each civilization tends to cluster around a dominant power, its 'core state'. In the West, it is largely undeniable that the United States exerts the greatest influence and is the most powerful state economically, politically and militarily. In so far, though, as the battleground for intra-civilizational supremacy is cultural, American cultural imperialism, as discussed in Chapter 4, may – if we follow Huntington's line – prove to be more significant as a means of ensuring and sustaining core status within Western civilization than as a strategy for expanding the boundaries of American empire beyond the West. Elsewhere, China and Russia exercise implicit imperial powers as the core states in the Sinic and Orthodox civilizations. India dominates the Hindu world. Of the major civilizations, the Islamic one remains the most de-centred. Of the possible contenders for the title of core state in the Islamic world, Indonesia, while massive in population, remains peripheral and too 'Asian'; Turkey and Iran both have a historical cases to make but the former is identified as what Huntington calls a 'torn country', with a history of trying to assimilate to another civilization, namely the West, and is too secular, while the latter too Shi'ite to appeal to the Sunni majority; Egypt is too poor and too dependent upon the West; Pakistan is too poor and suffers from its ongoing hostilities with India; Saudi Arabia is probably the strongest contender but again, remains closely allied to the West (*ibid.*: 177–9).

Huntington's thesis moves beyond a benign description of the world as merely 'multi-civilizational' into a disturbing depiction of a world in which conflict between cultures is inevitable, and in some cases the implications of such conflict global. Cultural identity as a source of solidarity is, after all, only meaningfully defined in relation to an *Other* (*ibid.*: 129) and, while political and ideological distinctions are negotiable, cultural and religious distinctions are usually entrenched in dogma. In many respects, his analysis begins at a point not dissimilar to that which has been of central importance to sociological conflict theorists in the tradition of Weber – conflict within nation-states between ethnic groups, understood as *interest groups*, competing for scarce resources, is the basic dynamic of all societies. However, Huntington is right to draw a distinction between conflicting ethnic groups *within* civilizations, and conflicting *civilizational groups* within nation-states. In the latter scenario, the implications of such conflict beyond the borders of the particular nation-state are more evident:

> The bloody clash of clans in Somalia poses no threat of broader conflict. The bloody clash of tribes in Rwanda has consequences for Uganda, Zaire, and Burundi but not much further. The bloody clashes of civilizations in Bosnia, the Caucasus, Central Asia, or Kashmir could become bigger wars. In the Yugoslav conflicts, Russia provided diplomatic support to the Serbs, and Saudi Arabia, Turkey, Iran, and Libya provided funds and arms to the Bosnians, not for reasons of ideology or power politics or economic interest but because of cultural kinship. (*Ibid.*: 28)

The world described by Huntington is characterized by such conflicts between civilizations. Consider the following examples, some mentioned by Huntington and others apparent since the publication of his book. The Balkans proved to be the crossroads at which the Islamic, Orthodox and Western civilizations met, and fought the bloodiest of inter-civilizational wars. The Orthodox–Islamic conflict continued on the battlefields of Chechnya. The Hindu and Islamic civilizations continue to face off against each other with steely resolve at the India–Pakistan border. In the Sudan, the Islamic and African civilizations battle for power under banners proclaiming authenticity. Once political allies back in the age of ideology, Russia and China, the core states of the Orthodox and Sinic civilizations, co-exist in the most tenuous of relationships, to say the least, and so, for that matter, do China and Japan. On the Mexican border, 'Western' Americans react angrily against immigration from the Latin American civilization. But for Huntington, the chief concern is with the relationships – conflictual or otherwise – between the three dominant civilizations in world politics – the Western, Islamic and Sinic civilizations. On behalf of the Sinic civilization, Huntington suggests, China has made steady progress in forming alliances with the Islamic world, united as they appear to be against a common enemy. And clearly – more evident to the lay observer since the events of 11 September 2001 but by no means originating on that fateful day – the greatest cleavage in the world is between the Western and Islamic civilizations.

How, then, are we to react in a world riddled with such inter-civilizational disputes? How is peace to be maintained? This, perhaps, is the *coup de grace* of Huntington's argument. He describes a futuristic scenario in which the world finds itself totally at war (*ibid.*: 313–16). The scenario seems implausible, but what its author wants us to consider is its cause – the intervention of a country from one civilization (the United States, in his imaginary scenario) in a conflict between two states from another (hypothetically, China and Vietnam). The only way of avoiding this nightmare is for civilizations to learn to cooperate with one another, to develop mutual respect and, above all, to resist the temptation to intervene – whether through the imposition of moral or cultural values or through military force – in the affairs of each other.

How are we to receive Huntington's claims and proposals? Clearly, much depends on the extent to which we accept his central premise – that the most significant collective units in global politics today are civilizations, defined by culture. One cause for concern in his argument is the extent to which these civilizations are truly 'united'. There are numerous internal disputes within each of these civilizations, whether in the form of cultural sub-distinctions, such as between Shi'ites and Sunnis in the Islamic world, Protestants and Catholics within Western Christianity and so on, or in the form of states refusing to accept the hegemony of the core state within their civilization – think of France's famous and persistent resistance to Americanization. At the same time, perhaps because of a history of colonialism or perhaps because of trade relations, certain countries from different civilizations have a great deal culturally in common with one another. So, how useful are these civilizations as analytical tools, if it is not even clear that they actually exist? In his 2003 'Afterword' to his 1978 text *Orientalism*, Edward Said attacks Huntington for presenting these civilizations as fixed, rigid entities, thus grounding 'culture' in some essentialist foundations, instead of recognizing its fluency and adaptability. In any sense, while one's identity certainly derives in part from one's identification with culture and heritage, it is not wholly reducible to it. So, Huntington can be criticized for presenting an overly simplistic, at best, or inaccurate, at worst, mapping of the world, and an overly essentialist theory of culture.

Biography Box 24:   Samuel Huntington

Samuel Huntington (1927–2008) sparked off one of the most controversial debates in contemporary social science and in foreign affairs when he published his most famous work, *The Clash of Civilizations and the Remaking of World Order* (1997). He was Albert J. Weatherhead III University Professor at Harvard University, and also a long-standing advisor to the US State Department, National Security Council and the Central Intelligence Agency.

Note that Huntington makes quite clear that he believes the only possible and desirable action on the part of states is to accept that we live in a multi-civilizational world, and to try and understand but by no means intervene in or impose values on other civilizations. It is a gross misunderstanding of his analysis to suggest that he goes from describing a world of civilizational clashes to endorsing aggressive foreign policies aimed at securing power for one civilization over another.

8.4   The neo-conservative agenda

When Huntington's *Clash of Civilizations* was published, it sparked a considerable controversy. Its basic premise was certainly well received by the neo-conservatives in the United States government at the time. Neo-conservatives should not be confused with the neo-liberals who basically endorse the liberalization model of global society, although both are often lumped together under the 'New Right' banner. To be sure, the *social* theory of both groups derives from the suggestion that welfare provision serves to undermine the work ethic which is crucial for the stability of capitalism and democracy. Both, then, favour the 'rolling back' of the state from people's lives. For the neo-liberal, though, this is justified along standard liberal lines: the sovereignty of the possessive individual over the state, albeit repackaged in quasi-Darwinian terms. For the neo-conservative, it is largely a cultural concern, that is to say that the *culture* of contemporary (American) society is under threat from competing and contradictory *value* systems (over-reliance on welfare, culture of dependency and so on) (for more on the differences between neo-conservative and neo-liberal approaches, see O'Byrne 2004).

That neo-conservatism, with its roots in social policy, came to be seen as such a prominent position in respect of international relations and particularly US foreign policy, is precisely because of its emphasis on promoting and protecting a particular morality and culture, a way of life, from its challenges. Huntington's description of the new divided world speaks directly to the anxiety of those who fear that their culture is under threat, not just from the so-called 'underclass', but also from fast-emerging cultures and civilizations around the world. All it takes is the perception, never mind the reality, of a terrorist threat against the United States from an Islamic group for this concern with difference to be recast in the language, previously used by the realists, of national security. For such neo-conservatives, while the realist concern with the national interest in pure geopolitical terms might be outmoded, threats to a way of life seem very real and cannot be reduced to nation-states. Put another way, if a traditional realist position would have been to advocate military action to stave off a direct attack on the national interest (but not simply for the purpose of political, cultural or moral evangelizing), then a neo-conservative position would support a war against an entire way of life if that way of life could be construed as being threatening to the existing way of life. Therein lies the justification for fighting a moralistic war, articulated as a war of civilizations. The West must do whatever it needs to do in order to protect and extend its values in such an arena of conflict, through the advocacy of a programme of what Kristol and Kagan (1996) tellingly refer to as 'benevolent hegemony'.

Not that the direction taken by America after the 11 September attacks was entirely out of the blue, as Robert Kagan (2003) points out. Even before the Bush administration came to power commitments were made to increase military spending and promote strategic military activity in Iraq and across the Middle East (*ibid.*: 92). While the United States has for a long time seen the world through Hobbesian eyes, focusing on conflict and disorder, it had nonetheless abandoned its ideology of realism and narrow nationalism. As Kagan says, 'America did not change on September 11. It only became more itself' (*ibid.*: 85): this is a reference to what Kagan believes is America's "special kind of nationalism...with its sense of a universal mission and belief in the righteousness of its own power' (Kagan 2008: 49). Its core ideology in the post-Cold War era had become one of what we might call 'globalist nationalism', a recognition that 'a new configuration is reshaping the international order' (*ibid.*: 12), and that 'nationalism and the nation

---

Biography Box 25:   Robert Kagan

Robert Kagan (1958–) is one of the leading figures in the American neo-conservative movement and was co-founder (with William Kristol) of the Project for a New American Century. He is a regular contributor to public as well as scholarly journals and has held various policy advisory positions in the US State Department. His *The Return of History and the End of Dreams* (2008) deliberately takes issue with Francis Fukuyama's famous claim about the triumph of liberal democracy.

itself, far from being weakened by globalization, have now returned with a vengeance' (*ibid.*), the return of what Kagan calls 'great power national-isms'. The United States vies for power in this new world disorder alongside the emerging or re-emerging powers of Russia, China, India, Japan, Iran and Europe.

8.5   Islamism and balkanization

Following the collapse of the Soviet Union in 1991, the United States found itself in the unfamiliar position of the world's lone, uncontested super-power. This presented something of a conundrum for US foreign policy: although there remained plenty of 'enemy states' across the world, none were capable of matching America for military power, economic wealth and resource access. Would this represent an 'end of history', the triumph of the West, as Fukuyama proclaimed, or as Gilpin argued the end of globalization through benign hegemony? Political realists would argue against the existence of such finalities, as no powerful agent can expect to have won the battle indefinitely. However, America's response to this conundrum, abetted by the seismic shock of 9/11, has not only transformed pre-existing political cleavages, but has also raised fundamental questions about the possibilities for any degree of consensus-led global governance in the world today.

In recalling Huntington's depiction of competing civilizations, the Islamic world might not initially appear to represent a prime candidate to rival America's benign hegemony. The absence of a core state is partially a reflec-tion of its own internal conflicts between Islam's different denominations, suggesting that Said's criticisms of Huntington's model were valid. Yet in many ways, both were right: the Islamic world is indeed internally divided, but has nevertheless been identified by the United States as its major con-temporary rival in the clash of civilizations. While this conflict undoubtedly represents a crude construction of Islam as a united front in anti-American extremism, its extremist factions nevertheless propound a holistic religious ideology that directly challenges the values of the American hegemony (Castells 2004). Moreover, it has been argued that the terrorist attacks carried out in mainland United States were historically unprecedented in scale and symbolism (Kepel 2006: 1). And while the nature of these attacks did not conform to the traditional conventions of civilizations at war, America's neo-conservative emphasis on preventive action in foreign policy arguably sought to construct it as such, thus reinforcing a binary view of balkanization which Barber (2003) famously characterized as 'Jihad versus McWorld'.

The concept of a united Islamic civilization – known as the caliphate – has existed for over 1,000 years and until the dissolution of the Ottoman Empire in 1924, was borne out in varying degrees as a practical reality. The slow decline of the final caliphate in the nineteenth and early twentieth centuries ran parallel to the rise of the Western modernization through industry, empire and capitalism. As a result, many of the Ottoman Empire's territories were taken over by European powers, leading to the growing influence of Western ideas and values in Islamic states and regions. For a number of radical scholars across the Middle East, the failure of the caliphate stemmed from a stagnation of learning and knowledge among Muslim scholars and the creeping in of Western 'excesses' in everyday social life. What was needed, the radicals argued, was an Islamic response to this growing Western cultural and political hegemony, a return to a 'true' Islam purged of pagan and Western influences, but one that was also in tune with the needs of modern society (Hussein 2010: 2).

Over the first half of the twentieth century, a number of radical parties and organizations were formed across the Middle East with varying degrees of success. Hassan al-Banna's influential Muslim Brotherhood was a radical network organization based in Egypt, and would provide an important training ground for a number of key extremist figureheads. The political party Hizb ut-Tahrir was founded in 1953 and proposed the idea of an Arab supernation state, but was unsuccessful in gaining popular support for its ideas having failed in coup attempts in Syria, Jordan and Iraq. The political party Jamaat-i-Islami, under Syed Abul ala Mawdudi, became an influential pressure group within Pakistani politics, albeit again without significant popular support in elections. More significant, however, were the works and ideas produced by these groups and parties, which would provide the blueprint for Islamism as a global ideology. Ala Mawdudi's words are a clear illustration of this world-view.

> Islam wishes to destroy all states and governments anywhere on the face of the earth, which are opposed to the ideology and programme of Islam regardless of the country or the nation which rules it. The purpose of Islam is to set up a state on the basis of its own ideology and programme... Islam requires the earth – not just a portion, but the whole planet. (Ala Mawdudi 1927: 6)

Ala Mawdudi writes of a need to engage in violent conflicts with the non-Islamic world in order to create a universal Islam, representing a deliberate response to what radical Muslims saw as a social, political and economic Westernization taking place across the world. In Egypt in particular, radical Muslims objected strongly to a succession of pro-Western governments throughout the 1950s that had violently repressed members of the Muslim Brotherhood. Among those tortured was the intellectual Syed Qutb who articulated the growing anti-secularism and anti-Americanism in Islamic fundamentalism, complaining about the 'free mixing of the sexes, materialism, individual freedoms and the lack of emphasis on moral and spiritual values'.

His portrayal of Islam's conflict with the West arguably depicted balkanization from an Islamist perspective:

> There is only one place on earth which can be called the home of Islam...and it is that place where the Islamic state is established and the Shari'ah is the authority and God's limits are observed...The rest of the world is the home of hostility...A Muslim can have only two possible relations with [the rest of the world]: peace with a contractual agreement, or war: A country with which there is a treaty will not be considered the home of Islam. (Syed Qutb 2007: 118)

Qtub's ideas were predicated on the belief that all leaders in Muslim societies were illegitimate because their accepting of certain aspects of Westernization represented a reversion to pre-Islamic ignorance. He also rejected nationalism within Islamic states on the grounds that it glorifies the power of the state and its leaders above Allah, and through democratic processes perpetuates denominational divisions among believers. Therefore to regenerate humanity, Islamism must proceed through jihad – *struggle* on behalf of Islam – first against those who have helped secularize Muslim societies, and then the whole world. Following Qtub's death in 1966 his works became popular among Islamic scholars in the universities of Saudi Arabia, gaining followers in Abdullah Azzam and Osama bin Laden. There, Qtub's Islamism would come into contact with Wahabism, a particularly conservative brand of Islam from the eighteenth century. A fusion of the two would provide the inspiration for contemporary Islamic fundamentalism, including Osama bin Laden's al-Qaeda network.

Transforming Islamic fundamentalism from an intellectual, clerical movement to a populist movement remained a struggle for much of the twentieth century. From the 1970s onwards, however, the growing difficulties experienced in adapting Middle Eastern economies to the new conditions of a liberalized global economy began to generate greater political unrest as its states became more and more dependent on the West. According to Kepel (2006), this had the effect of uniting a new generation of educated middle-classes together with the new urban poor in its opposition to Westernized, state-centric Islam and a favouring of a new fundamentalist identity. For Castells (2004), this identity was a curiously globalized one: although derived ideologically from a premodern conception of Islamic faith, it nevertheless operated as a post-material identity construction, one that is post-traditional in the sense that it represents a reflexive response to modernization and a *conscious attempt to re-embed* with traditional values. And, as we saw in Chapter 4, such reflexivity was apparent in the Iranian revolution of 1979 where the Ayatollah Khomeini's radical regime galvanized the masses and mobilized the deprived against the immoralities of Westernization.

Yet by the end of the twentieth century Iran would remain the only Islamic revolution that had managed to seize state power. Palestine and Iraq remained states preoccupied by nationalism, whereas countries such as Egypt and Saudi Arabia retained – at least at a diplomatic level – loyalties to America and the West. Even in Iran, the power of the ayatollahs would become marginalized through state-directed processes of modernization and democratization. But as Castells is keen to point out, to cite these cases as an illustration of Islamism's failure is to employ a very narrow means of measuring its power and influence today. The battle for minds, as opposed to the fight over state institutions would arguably provide a more accurate portrayal of the cult of Islamism, expressed especially through the network organization al-Qaeda led by Osama bin Laden.

In many ways, al-Qaeda represents the strongest expression of Islamic balkanization yet, as it prioritizes the defence of the holy sites of Islam, Mecca, Medina, Jerusalem, occupied by the Christians and the Jews. This infers a call to arms against opposing forces, where al-Qaeda funds and organizes training camps for extremists to engage in terrorist attacks against Islamic states and America's benign global hegemony on an unprecedented scale. However, when considering the mobile, subterranean networks through which it operates, al-Qaeda is also a quintessentially global phenomena. As Castells argues:

> Al-Qaeda and Osama bin Laden ... form only one component of the movement, but they are the symbol, the role models, and the main nodes of a vast, diversified network of terrorist groups, some of which are rooted in Islamist movements, but many of which are largely autonomous cells, or country-specific Islamic organizations. They are all inspired by a common hatred of the adversary, and a common belief in the goodness of the martyrdom on behalf of Islam, as freely interpreted by each of the components of the movement. (Castells 2004: 110)

To be both united by a common cause yet largely trans-territorial is to highlight al-Qaeda's key strength, one that arguably takes its lead from Westernization through liberalization and Americanization. They are pragmatic militants in the sense that the process is more important than the ultimate outcome as they know their immediate task is to engage in conflict against a powerful, multifaceted enemy (*ibid.*: 113). So the response is to fight Western Imperialism with its own brand of Islamist imperialism: by spreading its ideas through media technologies and its strength through seemingly random yet expertly coordinated terrorist attacks, bin Laden has become a mythical hero for thousands of disaffected young Muslims, an outlaw fighting on behalf of Islam against the forces of Western imperialism. As we saw in Chapter 1, the terrorist attacks of 11 September 2001 were not only an act of bloody mass-murder, they were also a carefully orchestrated 'global event' designed as both an inspiration and a call to arms for Muslims worldwide.

The subterranean nature of al-Qaeda also makes it very difficult for the United States to know exactly who it is declaring war against: its ideas are freely available and exchanged across global communications networks and using the fluid networks of neo-liberal capitalism, funds can be exchanged via complex connections of indirect benefactors. The cult of al-Qaeda can be seen in the case of Saudi Arabia: although its government is allied with the United States, the country has nevertheless become a principal source of funding for Islamist terrorism. These fluidities have also allowed the armed struggle to be taken on by anyone convinced by the ideals of al-Qaeda, resulting in 9/11 being followed by a series of violent and highly effective spin-off attacks in Bali, Madrid and London.

In this sense, Islamic fundamentalism barely equates to an image of balkanization at all: it is a declaration of war from an invisible opponent, situated nowhere in particular. With little political representation inside Islamic states, which are often the subject of terrorist attacks themselves, Huntington's image of an Islamic civilization fighting against its adversaries appears grossly misrepresentative. Yet as we shall now see, the post-9/11 War on Terror has oscillated uncertainly between accepting the realities of a trans-territorial conflict and imposing its own image of a balkanized clash of civilizations.

8.6   Balkanizing Islam: the neo-conservative response

For all of the scale and symbolism of the atrocities committed in the 9/11 terrorist attacks, the origins of America's neo-conservative foreign policy in the 2000s preceded the rise of Islamist terrorism. If anything, the use of terrorism above more orthodox channels of political activism provides palpable illustration of the lengths that America's adversaries have had to go to in order to inflict significant damage, though the nature of this resistance arguably makes America's commitment to a territorialized, state-defined balkanized response more difficult to sustain.

American preparation for a post-Cold War clash of civilizations began only shortly after the fall of the Soviet Union when, in 1992, the Defense Department under George Bush Senior produced a blueprint for maintaining its position of global pre-eminence. Reflecting on America's advantageous position its authors recommended shaping global security so that it would remain in line with American principles and interests so as to preclude the rise of a great power rival. Secretary Dick Cheney argued that the US 'can either sustain the [armed] forces we require and remain in a position to help shape things for the better, or we can throw that advantage away. [But] that would only hasten the day when we face greater threats, at higher costs and further risk to American lives' (Kagan *et al.* 2000: ii). Once published, however, the proposals were mostly dismissed as an example of a defence department overstating threats to security and, by the time the Democrats under Bill Clinton came to power later that year, the proposals were largely forgotten. Clinton's Democrats would preside over an era of foreign policy diplomacy rather than neo-conservative military intervention, a switch symbolized by their reduction of US military spending to as low as 3 per cent of its GDP – less than at any time since before the Second World War. Declining US intervention would coincide with the rise in the role of transnational governance in foreign affairs, reflected in the building of specific institutions to manage transnational issues and interests. Although the US would play a significant diplomatic role over affairs in Ireland and the Balkans, it nevertheless retained a mostly unilateral attitude towards hopes for a transnational polity, rejecting a number of proposals including the Kyoto protocol, the International Criminal Court and a treaty banning personnel mines.

If the Democrats justified US foreign policy through pragmatism, the neo-conservatives of the previous administration saw America's position of bartering shared governance with its own unilateralism as an impossible contradiction. The Republicans' victory in the 2000 elections would precipitate a significant shift back towards a more active unilateralism in foreign policy. This would be exemplified by the controversial report produced in September 2000 by the neo-conservative think-tank Project for the New American Century (PNAC) led by Robert Kagan, which recommended that America 'should seek to preserve and extend its position of global leadership by maintaining the pre-eminence of US military forces' (Kagan, Schmitt and Donnelly 2000: iv). Americanization had been successful at least via the spread of democracy, the neo-liberal market and consumerism across the globe, but it was not enough to secure American *political* supremacy in the long term. On the contrary, they warned that 'no moment in international politics can be frozen in time' and 'even a global *pax Americana* will not preserve itself' (*ibid.*: 1). Taking this into account, it was argued that since the demise of the Soviet Union the United States had wasted an 'unprecedented strategic opportunity' to enhance its interests and ideals worldwide.

This highlighted a significant shift in US military strategy, one in which foreign policy is determined not by military defence against a powerful opposing state but rather instead by military defence against a known adversary that *might* be capable of posing a threat to US security. This would be illustrated in the emphasis the report placed on deterring the rise of 'great-power competitors' (see Table 8.2), with China identified as a potential candidate. More substantive threats, however, were found to be in Iran, Iraq and North Korea, all of which were claimed to be 'rushing to develop ballistic missiles and nuclear weapons as a deterrent to American intervention in regions they seek to dominate' (*ibid.*: 4). As a result, the US military

Table 8.2   Cold War and post-Cold War US foreign policy strategies

	Cold War	21st century
Security system	Bipolar	Unipolar
Strategic goal	Contain Soviet Union	Preserve *Pax Americana*
Main military mission(s)	Deter Soviet expansionism	Secure and expand zones of democratic peace; deter rise of new great-power competitor; defend key regions; exploit transformation of war
Main military threat(s)	Potential global war across many theatres	Potential theatre wars spread across globe
Focus of strategic competition	Europe	East Asia

Source: Kagan, Schmitt and Donnelly (2000).

would need to monitor technological and weapons proliferation in enemy states and retain sufficient forces in preparation for 'multiple simultaneous large-scale wars' – in other words, be prepared for any conflict of any scale, at any time, anywhere.

While a multitude of states represented varying degrees of antagonism towards US interests, arguably none represented a 'great power rival' capable of providing a genuine threat to national security, leaving the claims made by the PNAC report appearing somewhat inflated. 11 September 2001 would change this. Not only were the simultaneous acts of terrorism committed on US mainland, causing the death of thousands of civilians, they, further, represented a carefully orchestrated symbolic attack on US hegemony, with its hijacked planes striking America's major economic and political centres.

For the still-new Republican administration, the 9/11 attacks provided every justification that could ever be needed for implementing a preventive foreign policy strategy as recommended by the PNAC. The role of Islamism as the central ideological thrust of the attacks was said to provide ample evidence that the US had maintained a line that was too deferential towards Muslim states. Neo-conservative thinkers Frum and Perle (2003/4) argued that the lack of unequivocal condemnations of the 9/11 attacks by 'Islamic authorities' (Frum and Perle 2003/4: 152) suggested that the Islamic world had generally sided with the terrorists above America. President George W. Bush's stance on this was clear, announcing only a week after 9/11 that 'every nation, in every region, now has a decision to make. Either you are with us or you are with the terrorists'.

Bush's words arguably symbolized more than a realization of a new global enemy, they set the agenda for a balkanized approach to foreign policy. In the days and weeks after 9/11, the attacks were transformed into an abstract conflict. The government would start to repeat the argument that 'war had been declared on America', though as we noted earlier it was not entirely clear *who* the declarers of war actually were, beyond the 19 terrorists responsible for the attacks. Al-Qaeda was based mostly in Afghanistan but the terrorists themselves originated from a number of different countries, and had been living in America for up to a year before 9/11. Nevertheless, in the immediate aftermath Republican strategist Paul Wolfowitz advocated not just the pursuit of al-Qaeda but a 'broad and sustained campaign' that would involve 'removing' and 'ending states' (Halper and Clarke 2004: 204). Yet unlike previous conflicts there appeared to be no 'gathering storm' of states in support of terrorism befitting Wolfowitz's rhetoric. As Boyle (2008) argues, 'the vast majority of states in the international system... do not support terrorist groups as a strategy of opposition to the United States' and that 'even in the Middle East, where the problem of this new transnational terrorism is primarily (though not exclusively) located, most governments support an anti-terror agenda and were quick to line up behind US efforts to construct a global anti-terror regime' (Boyle 2008: 195).

Despite problems in imposing a state framework on Islamism and the perpetrators of 9/11, the Bush administration continued to construct America's opponents in such terms in its self-defined 'War on Terror'. In January 2002 President Bush claimed the existence of an 'axis of evil', consisting of three 'terror' states associated by a common hatred against the United States. The three states in question – Iran, Iraq and North Korea – were familiar foes to the US, though none appeared to have had any direct association each other, or with the 9/11 attacks. Yet as states with mutually oppositional interests to the United States, they were now implicated as part of a network of states that could, potentially, form alliances. Neo-conservatives also identified several further states that were permissive towards acts of terrorism and therefore potential associates of the War on Terror, including Syria, Yemen, Cuba and Libya.

America's War on Terror began in earnest with the invasion of Afghanistan in October 2001, as its Taliban regime had been harbouring al-Qaeda training camps since the late 1990s. Once defeated, however, it soon became clear that the US was planning an invasion of Iraq. This was unusual in the sense that there was no strong evidence to suggest that Iraq had any association with 9/11 or al-Qaeda, indeed Klare (2003) notes that Iraqi leader Saddam Hussein was a life-long enemy of militant Islamists such as bin Laden who saw nationalist states as not representing true Islam. Nevertheless, as hypothetical allies in their opposition to the US, al-Qaeda and Saddam Hussein were morphed into a common enemy. Neo-conservatives were keen to point out the potential for cross-pollination between the two, Kagan and Kristol (2002) laying out 'indisputable' evidence that Iraq was in possession of enough precursor chemicals for 200 tons of poison, and that there 'may have been' some interaction between Saddam Hussein and Osama bin Laden. The evidence for Iraq's procurement of chemical weapons was shaky in 2002–3, and ultimately described as 'false or uncorroborated' by 2004 (Halper and Clarke 2004: 217), but what mattered more was the *potential* threat that Iraq under Saddam Hussein posed. Frum and Perle are blunt in their defence of preventive action:

> Opponents of the Bush administration in Congress and the press sometimes suggest that it was overcautious and unnecessary to worry today about Saddam's weapons of tomorrow. The threat, they say, wasn't 'imminent'. It was never quite clear how 'imminent' would have been imminent enough to suit these critics. Should we have waited one month before Saddam got a nuclear bomb or a weaponized smallpox? One week? Until the stuff actually rolled out of the lab?...American intelligence is not the all-knowing, all-seeing spy service of the movies: 'No need to strike yet, Mr President, our agents tell us we have ninety-seven days and thirteen hours before Iraq's new superviruses become available.' (Frum and Perle 2003/4: 33–4)

Taken in this way, the conservative logic posits that any state that may oppose US interests could, by proxy, harbour terrorist activity, or stockpile chemical weapons for use against the America and its allies. In this sense, Iraq was a less pressing candidate for invasion than some of the other enemy states that had stronger al-Qaeda links, but the US arguably saw Iraq as an opportunity to finish off an old personal enemy, and one rich in oil resources. Furthermore, Kagan and Kristol saw the deposition of Saddam Hussein and the installation of a democratic government would have 'a seismic impact on the Arab world – for the better', possibly leading to smaller powers jumping on the bandwagon (Kagan and Kristol 2002).

The arbitrary construction of an 'enemy empire' out of Islamic states opposed to US interests; states which might have a permissive view of terrorist networks, and even states that might *potentially* sell weapons to US enemies, arguably represents a conscious desire to reassert nation-state dynamics ahead of global flows and present a fully balkanized view of the globe. As Mary Kaldor (2007) argues, globalization has fundamentally undermined the power and authority of states, particularly in their capacity to mobilize citizens in pursuit of narrowly defined national interests. Following 9/11, however, US neo-conservatives were able to push hard for an image of foreign relations in which individuals and states could be separated as being simply 'for' or 'against' the terrorists. Of course, one can argue that this binary model has ignored the more complex relationships that exist between states, cultures and ethnicities and, in contrast to the general thrust of ideas presented in this book, can be seen to resemble a stubborn attempt to fight against the tide of global transformations. Nevertheless, balkanization in its neo-conservative form has nevertheless generated a genuine challenge to global or transnational models of governance. First, balkanization has entailed a symbolic marginalization of transnational governing institutions, particularly the United Nations. The cosmopolitan idealism of the UN and the unilateral realism of American neo-conservatism were always predisposed to clash: the UN is predicated on the notion of transnationalization as a legitimate process, whereas neo-conservatives Frum and Perle dismiss the romanticized notion that a vast international bureaucracy could sustain and enforce the 'pretence' that all countries are of equal worth (Frum and Perle 2003/4: 120). They argue that this admission to democratic fairness is self-defeating, rendering most of its peacekeeping operations toothless, as key states have been known to use their power of veto (such as Russia during the Yugoslav war) to protect the interests of their allies. The UN inspection mission to Iraq in 2002–3 was initially set up to appease some of America's more sceptical European allies, but when they found insufficient evidence to suggest Iraq held weapons of mass destruction, the US chose to ignore their findings and invade anyway.

Second, the rejection of the UN as a legitimate institution of global governance implies a superiority of the values and intentions behind America's action. Balkanization holds the view that the most powerful state is best equipped to manage global affairs on the basis that the more powerful a state becomes, the greater number of political 'interests' it has in other countries' affairs. By contrast, smaller, less powerful nations are only capable of acting in the interests of an unrepresentative minority. For America, however, its position as the world's most powerful nation means that *its own interests are everybody's interests*, and that it should therefore 'assume its responsibility and leadership without hesitation' (Castells 2004: 348). The role of the US as the supreme power is thus held accountable for its moral behaviour. Frum and Perle again:

What some Europeans decry as 'unilateralism' many Americans regard as *leadership*. The concept of leadership implies a willingness to act in a good cause, even – indeed especially – when others are reluctant to do so … Our claims to world leadership rest not just on our power and wealth but on our moral authority. If we say one thing and do another, if we appear to uphold our principles only when they serve our immediate interests, then our actions give credibility to our enemies when they call us a rogue nation, an imperial state, and a threat to the world order. (Frum and Perle 2003/4: 243, 268)

Inferring a moral accountability to American behaviour while at the same time accepting that its interests are also the world's interests arguably employs a performative contradiction, as any resistance to the American agenda can be itself discredited simply for coming from a 'biased' and 'partial' smaller power. As already noted, one of many motives for the invasion of Iraq and toppling of Saddam Hussein was to tighten control over Iraq's much sought-after oil and gas resources, and the US, of course, is the principal actor in managing this financially lucrative process. This opens up questions over how the United States prioritizes its interventions, bearing in mind at least its inability to occupy every country deserving of regime change. Kaplan and Kristol (2003) argue that 'national security strategy commits the United States to champion the cause of human dignity ... by creating a balance of power that favors human freedom' (2003: 95–9), yet the US has been accused of taking a permissive view of human rights abuses in its own 'client states', including Uzbekistan, Kyrgyzstan and Turkmenistan, while condemning comparable behaviour in countries such as Iran and Iraq (Halper and Clarke 2004: 219). Moreover, some of the practices used in the War on Terror have been roundly condemned for effectively normalizing forms of torture, contravening the Universal Declaration of Human Rights. Neo-conservatives have defended the application of extraordinary rendition measures as being symptomatic of the new realities of terrorism and the irrepressible will of fundamentalists, which render traditional interrogation methods increasingly obsolete. Yet the revelations from Abu Ghraib and Guantanamo Bay suggest that America's advocacy of preventive methods such as withdrawing human rights in the short term to protect human rights in the long term no longer hold sway with the public.

8.7 Conclusion

The balkanization model presents an entirely different globe to that of the liberal 'globalists' whose ideas dominate the globalization and liberalization traditions. This could not be put any plainer than it is by Robert Kagan, whose 2008 monograph, *The Return of History and the End of Dreams*, is an explicit negation of Fukuyama's neo-liberal tome *The End of History* (1991). Equally, it has little in common with the social democrats who advocate the transnationalization model or the postmodernists who emphasize creolization. With its focus on conflict and power politics, the politics of self-interest (national security), this model actually has more in common with the frameworks favoured by the neo-Marxists and critical theorists – Americanization and polarization, if not so much McDonaldization. The neo-conservative Right and the neo-Marxist Left, though diametrically opposed to one another on normative grounds, stand united, as it were, against the perceived naivety of the liberal centre.

One writer quick to point out this naivety, in respect of the transnationalization model, is Danilo Zolo (1997, 2002). Zolo has presented one of the most theoretically sophisticated condemnations of the assumption made by transnationalist scholars such as Richard Falk and David Held that 'cosmopolis' is achievable through this institutional route (Zolo 1997). Applying his cynicism towards this approach to the failings of the NATO 'humanitarian intervention' in the Balkans in 1999, Zolo recruits cultural relativism and Carl Schmitt simultaneously into his cause, inspired as he is by the long-standing cultural relativist critique of universal human rights in favour of a more detached appreciation for local cultural and ethical differences, and also by Schmitt's maxim: 'Whoever invokes humanity is trying to cheat.' For Zolo, writing in the immediate aftermath of the NATO bombings, 'military force not only has failed to protect human rights, but has violated them as well. NATO's ambition to act as the champion of universal values, with little concern for legal norms and political legitimacy, has proved equally incongruous' (Zolo 2002: 168). Such universalizing projects as democracy, human rights, liberal markets, driven as they are by Western interests, will always be met with resistance. The balkanized world is a world of irreconcilable differences.

Zolo is a sophisticated social and political theorist, as is Huntington, but the problem with such post-realist accounts of the global condition is that they leave themselves wide open to abuse from the political right wing, get distorted and become populist in their appeal. Edward Said notes that 'Huntington, and behind him all the theorists and apologists of an exultant Western tradition, like Francis Fukuyama ... (have) retained a good deal of their hold on the public consciousness' (2003: 349), and draws the reader's attention to a *New York Times Magazine* article by polemicist Paul Johnson in April 1993, in which the author calls for the 'civilized nations' to 're-colonize Third World countries' which are perceived of as being *un*civilized, noting that, as with European colonialism in the nineteenth century, imposing order in this way is beneficial to Western trade interests (*ibid.*).

Given this lack of certainty, then, we should take care to question whether balkanization in US foreign policy is an empirical or normative construct. As Castells (2004) observes, the unilateralism of America as the world's leading nation-state either underplays or outright ignores significant global processes of interdependence that transcend the will of any particular nation-state: indeed, most of the chapters in this book point to one type of global integration that falls outside of the balkanization model. America, like any nation-state, is opened up to the unifying opportunities and vagaries of the global stage, is subject to the fluctuations of the neo-liberal global marketplace, has its cultural values and practices repackaged and reinterpreted and has its labour market subjected to the homogenizing (or creolizing) forces of transnational corporations. In short, to impose a nation-state model on a world increasingly characterized by global flows is to limit a theory's explanative power: even al-Qaeda, with its reflexive re-engagement with Islamic fundamentalism, is a reflection of globalized resistance, one that is largely transnational and subterranean in its movements. Yet Castells also warns that the normative foundations of balkanization may yet become self-fulfilling in practice. Not only has it compromised transnational models of governance, it has also balkanized Islamism as a single unit of conflict against US interests. Noting how both North Korea and Iran increased their nuclear programmes as a consequence of the invasion of Iraq, Castells concludes his analysis by speculating on whether the United States's advocacy of preventive strikes will soon be countered by pre-emptive preventive strikes from one of its adversaries (Castells 2004: 354).

Today, however, the future of balkanization is unclear. The election of Barack Obama's Democrats in 2008 signalled at least the end to a decade of neo-conservative foreign policy in the United States government. Yet the world that Obama has inherited from Bush reflects deep-seated policy directives that are not easily overturned, making for a more constrained reality than his supporters may have initially hoped for (Sangar 2009: 448). During his presidential campaign, Obama said of his hopes for foreign policy that he wished to 'rebuild the alliances, partnerships and institutions necessary to confront common threats and enhance common security', but claimed that this would not be achieved by 'bullying other countries to ratify changes we hatch in isolation. It will come when we convince other governments and peoples that they, too, have a stake in effective partnerships' (quoted in Renshon 2010: 2). If such rhetoric pointed to an American renewal with the institutions of transnational governance, his practices so far retain certain tenets of the Republicans' balkanization model. Although he immediately set a time frame for the closing of the controversial Guantanamo Naval Base upon reaching office, he has also chosen to retain the controversial policy of 'extraordinary rendition', albeit on a short-term basis. Obama's attitude towards preventative strikes is also ambiguous, to say the least, claiming at one point that 'no president should ever hesitate to use force – unilaterally, if necessary – to protect ourselves and our vital interests when we are attacked or immediately threatened' (*ibid.*: 6), a pledge that somewhat stands against his earlier promise for 'effective partnerships'. Ascertaining exactly what constitutes the 'immediate threat' of US interests will arguably determine the fate for balkanization in the next decade.

To follow the balkanization model seems, then, to undertake a journey in global studies which denies the globalizing processes which give life not only to the other models discussed in this volume, but also to global studies itself as a field of enquiry. But as the contributors to at least one recent volume show, this need not be the case (Berger and Huntington 2002). The sheer diversity of the modern world, which is *cultural* diversity, may in fact give rise to *many* globalizations (hence the title of the book) and to multiple sub-globalizations. A world of difference is a world of complexity. No single, overarching theory of change can really capture it. Or at least, not yet.

Conclusion

9

In this volume we have presented eight different models of global change. Table 9.1 provides a convenient summary. We do not claim that this list is exhaustive of all possible such models, nor do we claim that the models we have selected should be treated as anything more than 'ideal types'. We have not set ourselves the task of comparing or contrasting models in terms of our perception of their reality or accuracy. They are discussed because in each case a significant enough body of scholars has seen fit to describe the world principally in respect of them. Readers are at liberty to agree or disagree with, approve or disapprove of, any as they see fit (just as we are). At no point have we suggested that these models stand in any sort of exclusive relationship to one another. In fact, quite the opposite – empirically, they don't, and we have made every effort to emphasize that.

Table 9.1   Summary of the eight models

Model	Image of world society
Globalization	Orientation to 'one world'
Liberalization	Erosion of barriers between nation-states
Polarization	World divided into rich and poor
Americanization	American empire sustained through hard and soft power
McDonaldization	Standardization of practices across the world
Creolization	Ongoing local transformations through regional flows
Transnationalization	Emergence of level of governance above the nation-state
Balkanization	Division of world into distinct and conflicting cultural blocs

This book serves the purpose of helping to structure and define a growing academic discourse which is being called 'global studies'. It is not intended to serve as a polemic, presenting the case for any one framework for understanding and interpreting global change above all others. In any case, if anything, the *reality* of the situation is that *all* of these models are 'real' and 'happening', and, probably, at the same time, *none* of them are. The contemporary global condition can best be described as a complex social formation driven by forces which are at the same time globalizing, liberalizing, polarizing, Americanizing, McDonaldizing, creolizing, transnationalizing and balkanizing.

Even so, some of the models selected for inclusion here engage more explicitly in a debate with others. Polarization, for example, is presented primarily as the outcome of global economic processes the supporters of which claim lead instead to liberalization. Many of those who present the case for the global condition to be understood primarily in terms of the polarization of north and south (or within nation-states) tend to accept, with the neo-liberal advocates of liberalization, an economic model of global change. What separates them (quite emphatically) is more than how they interpret the 'evidence', but rather a moral condemnation or acceptance of the consequences of a global capitalist economy.

Similarly, one can put Americanization, transnationalization and balkanization into a convenient narrative. Transnationalization and Americanization present alternative accounts of the dynamics of power (political and economic) in the world. Balkanization may be what results from the perceived failures of transnationalization emerging as a response to the perceived reality of Americanization. It is the emphasis which is different.

Creolization, meanwhile, is not necessarily incompatible with globalization: many of the theorists of cultural globalization see its lived reality at the local level very much in terms of a creolized, hybridized culture. Neither is it incompatible with transnationalization: one might say that creolization is the cultural manifestation of these transnationalizing forces. However, where creolization is most effectively articulated as a transformative process in its own right is as a critique of the perceived homogeneity of culture contained within the alternative McDonaldization and Americanization frameworks.

In so far as such dialogues can be identified within the structure of this volume, they are so within the relatively conventional distinction between the economic, political and cultural spheres of action. Liberalization and polarization are competing theories of the global economy. Transnationalization and balkanization are competing theories of the global political system (the former even when it addresses the dynamics of late capitalism, because its focus remains on the distribution of *power* within capitalism – that is, in the hands of transnational classes and corporations, rather than the actual dynamics of economic flows which are otherwise dealt with under liberalization and polarization). McDonaldization and creolization are competing theories of global culture. Globalization and Americanization sit somewhat outside this orthodoxy. Globalization is a more generic model, while Americanization lends itself to all three spheres and thus enters each of the debates.

In this conclusion, we want to bring these models together and ask what they might tell us about the core questions of the day. We are going to divide the remainder of this conclusion up into three important questions, and use these as a basis for evaluating the usefulness of the eight paradigms. These questions are:

1. What are the perceived advantages and disadvantages of the eight models as paradigms for the global system?
2. What does each of the eight models tell us about the future role of the nation-state?
3. What implications can we deduce from each of the eight models about the problem of human rights?

Let us begin by comparing the relative pros and cons of the eight models. Of course, we acknowledge that this seems like a pointless, albeit interesting, little exercise, as clearly any discussion of advantages and disadvantages is dependent on the prior question: advantageous or

Table 9.2   Advantages and disadvantages of the eight models

Model	Advantages	Disadvantages
Globalization	Emergence of egalitarian global consciousness	High degree of abstraction
Liberalization	Freedom to trade and of movement	Economic instability
Polarization	Economic prosperity for some	Poverty for many
Americanization	Peace and stability achieved through benign hegemony	Unequal global power dynamics
McDonaldization	Modernization brings existential familiarity and harmony	Erosion of local cultures
Creolization	Cultural diversity and enrichment	Uncertainty due to loss of tradition
Transnationalization	International law and regulative power	Absence of legitimacy and accountability
Balkanization	Re-empowerment of cultural identity	Inevitability of conflict

disadvantageous for whom? The polarization model presents the most direct response to this question: the wealthy 'core' countries benefit at the expense of the poorer 'peripheral' ones. Of course, the liberalization approach would negate this, emphasizing the benefits of free trade and freedom of movement despite the dangers of economic instability. Other models do not so easily lend themselves to subjective ethical comparisons. Table 9.2 provides a summary of the possible advantages and disadvantages.

The Americanization and McDonaldization models are usually presented by those who take an explicit ethical stance in opposition to these paradigms, which overpower local cultures and reproduce hierarchies of domination, and yet one can imagine a defensive response, along the lines of 'West is best', similar perhaps to Gilpin's benign hegemony thesis discussed in Chapter 8, and perhaps even pointing out that sometimes, a little standardization might be a good thing, as too much difference can be existentially challenging. Of course, these pros and cons are turned on their sides by the creolization paradigm – in that cultural diversity and enrichment is the advantage, while a perceived loss of tradition and national identity would be for some a drawback. Transnationalization is welcomed by those who see it as the means of empowering international law to protect human rights, and denying nation-states the indulgence to behave beyond reproach, but it brings with it genuine concerns over the legitimacy and accountability of transnational institutions. The balkanization framework suggests an immediate problem – the apparent inevitability of conflict, but at the same time suggests a strong re-empowerment of cultural identity among the competing 'civilizations' or nation-states. Globalization offers the promise of an emergent global citizenship, a potentially egalitarian sense of global consciousness, but as its critics are quick to point out, this remains on the whole a heavily abstract ideal, and for many an unrealizable and perhaps even undesirable one.

Many of these 'pros' and 'cons' are grounded in the future each model carves out for the nation-state: is it being eroded, weakened, or sustained? This is interesting in part because it is commonly assumed that global transformations threaten the continued existence of the nation-state. In fact, not all of the models discussed in this volume suggest that. Table 9.3 provides a rough summary.

Of the eight, the globalization model poses the biggest challenge to the nation-state. The emergence of a global consciousness and of the globe as the central unit of analysis necessitates a decline in the nation-state's defining role. Other models do suggest a weakening of the state's centrality, a significant shift from its current role. The liberalization framework is prefaced on the assumption that nation-state *borders* are eroded and the autonomy of nation-state economies is undermined – however, this does not mean the actual *end* of the nation-state, despite this being the

Table 9.3 Role of the nation-state in each of the eight models

Model	Role of nation-state
Globalization	Eroded
Liberalization	Weakened
Polarization	Sustained
Americanization	Weakened
McDonaldization	Sustained but altered
Creolization	Weakened
Transnationalization	Weakened
Balkanization	Sustained or weakened

title of a book by one of the major advocates of this model, Kenichi Ohmae. Americanization weakens the autonomy of the nation-state, reducing it to the status of an outpost dependent on the imperial capital. Transnationalization also weakens the nation-state's autonomy, and certainly its sovereignty, through the transfer of political power to the structures and institutions of global governance and of economic power to transnational corporations. Creolization weakens the nation-state in a different way, by detaching cultural from political identity, nation from state, and thus challenging the nation-state's claims of tradition and presumptions of authenticity. McDonaldization does not presuppose the end of the nation-state at all, rather it continues in full flow but is transformed into a standardized model, its distinctiveness eroded. Balkanization can be interpreted as suggesting the end of the nation-state through Huntington's claim that interstate conflicts have given way to inter-civilizational ones, but the model itself does not necessarily presume this, and many neo-realist models of global change remain wholly state-centric. The role of the nation-state in the polarization model is less well defined, and there is no obvious challenge to its autonomy suggested, rather, the distinction between economically rich and poor nation-states is highlighted.

What, then, does each model imply for the pursuit of human rights? Again, a crude summary of responses is presented in Table 9.4. Three of the models are broadly housed within a 'Westernization' framework, so it is unsurprising that for these three – liberalization, Americanization and McDonaldization – there is a limited advocacy of human rights – 'limited' because the Western liberal tradition historically treats human rights as synonymous with civil and political rights, freedoms of the individual from state interference. Thus, the rights of the human are inseparable from the rights of the consumer, or the citizen.

Table 9.4 Implications of the eight models for human rights

Model	Implications for human rights
Globalization	Universalization of human rights problematizing nation-state citizenship claims
Liberalization	Proliferation of Western liberal tradition emphasizing civil and political rights
Polarization	Civil and political rights set in opposition to demands for economic and social rights
Americanization	Western liberal tradition of civil and political rights used as 'swords of empire'
McDonaldization	Rights language institutionalized in standardized political structures, but superficially
Creolization	Universalist-relativist dilemma; 'clash of liberalisms'
Transnationalization	Role of international law contested and defined in transnational arena
Balkanization	Cultural relativization emphasized; 'clash of civlizations'

Such a concept of human rights is grounded in the same Western model of individualism from which come the ideas of democracy and capitalism. In the liberalization model, all of these ideas are exported through free trade and take root around the world as nation-state borders are relaxed. Fukuyama would hail the successful achievement of this as the 'end of history', the final triumph of the West. For Robert Nozick (1974) the triumph of these values is inherently morally defensible: liberals uphold a belief that all is fair that stems from equality of opportunity. Americanization presumes something similar but in a less triumphant or sympathetic way. Western, particularly American, values, including civil and political rights, are imposed on the world as 'swords of empire' (Bartholomew and Breakspear 2003). The McDonaldization framework would view these values and practices, including the establishment of democratic political structures (Diamond 1993), as part of the standardizing process. However, this rights-language becomes what Costas Douzinas (2000) calls a 'free-floating signifier', emptied out of actual content and meaning. Both the polarization and balkanization models accept the basic premise of the Americanization model but place more emphasis on the clash of alternative rights-claims and demands. Accordingly, in the polarization model, the promotion of civil and political rights is championed by the richer north but the economic and social rights demanded by the global south are ignored, removed from the general discourse on human rights. Thus, the very language of human rights becomes a contested space.

This conflict of rights-claims is presented in a very different fashion in the balkanization paradigm. Herein, civilizations are defined by their contrasting values. The balkanization model adheres to the theory of cultural relativism, that values are socially and culturally embedded and have to be understood in their contexts. Western values such as civil and political rights are therefore counterpoised against other sets of cultural values (consider, for example, the discussion of 'Asian values' within the human rights literature), and the entire 'clash' of rights-claims is housed within a broader debate on cultural rights. This same debate fuels the creolization paradigm, wherein the emphasis is on cultural heterogeneity within as well as beyond nation-states. In increasingly creolized societies, the perceived conflict between a commitment to the values of universal egalitarianism and the values of ethnic and cultural diversity becomes politicized within what we can call a 'clash of liberalisms' (as exemplified by the responses of the French and Belgian governments to the demand by members of the Muslim community for recognition of their cultural rights, specifically, veil-wearing among women and girls). Such problems are also addressed within the globalization paradigm. Roland Robertson (1992: 27) specifically addresses this issue, pointing out that while Western societies have for centuries articulated rights-claims within an individual-society problematic, the addition of a third level, that of humankind, complicates matters by relativizing the problem of self-identity among individuals and the problem of citizenship among states through demands for *human* rights. Such demands cause tensions between nation-states within the world-system of states due to the apparent crisis of nation-state sovereignty in world society. The transnationalization paradigm explicitly takes up this challenge. Indeed, it has more to say about the promotion of human rights than the other models, which is understandable given its cosmopolitan advocacy of a strengthened role for transnational political and legal institutions in protecting human rights. For proponents of this model, though, these rights need not be synonymous with Western liberal rights – indeed, for the neo-Marxist Sklair, an ideology of human rights is potentially oppositional to the ideology of consumerism.

These three questions are presented to the reader in order to better make sense of the relationship between the eight models. They contain no answers per se, but the task of theorizing global studies is far from complete, and such questions serve as useful guides on the journey. What of the future? There is no reason to suggest that other, equally striking paradigms will not emerge. At present, Islamicization and sinoization are best understood either as counter-arguments to Americanization or as evidence of balkanization, but they may require more dedicated attention in the near future. Another problem in desperate need of attention is the gender bias in the global studies literature. With certain notable exceptions, most of the major contributors, from whichever disciplinary background, have been men, and while there have certainly been important feminist analyses of specific global problems, such as trafficking, 'honour killings' and the sexual division of labour, there is currently no systematic feminist theorization of global change per se. Should this volume require a second edition, we hope that this omission has been addressed.

Readers will no doubt have spotted other omissions and flaws. We do not claim that this volume is entirely comprehensive, although in attempting to bring in literature from a variety of disciplines we have tried to be as comprehensive as possible given that space is not unlimited. If anything, we hope to have shown that global studies is a potentially vast field of study, but also that, at the same time, it has a core, an internal coherence, and demands closer inspection beyond the confines of existing disciplinary boundaries.

Bibliography

Aalbers, M. (2009) 'Geographies of the Financial Crisis', in *Area* 41,1, 34–42,

Adams, J. T. (1931) *The Epic of America*, Boston, MA: Little, Brown.

Adiga, A. (2006) 'The Spice of Life', www.time.com/time/magazine/article/0,9171,1174750,00.html

Adonis, A. and Pollard, S. (1997) *A Class Act: The Myth of Britain's Classless Society*, London: Penguin.

Adorno, T. (2001) *The Culture Industry: Selected Essays in Mass Culture*, London: Routledge.

Ala Mawdudi, Syed Abul (1927) *Jihad in Islam*, Beirut: The Holy Koran Publishing House.

Albrow, M. (1990) 'Introduction', in M. Albrow and E. King (eds), *Globalization, Knowledge and Society: Readings from International Sociology*, London: Sage.

Albrow, M. (1996) *The Global Age: State and Society beyond Modernity*, Cambridge: Polity Press.

Albrow, M. and O'Byrne, D. (2000) 'Rethinking State and Citizenship under Globalised Conditions', in H. Goverde (ed.), *Global and European Polity?*, Aldershot: Ashgate.

Amin, S. (2001) 'Imperialism and Globalization', *Monthly Review*, 53, 2, 6–14.

Amin, S., Arrighi, G., Frank, A. G. and Wallerstein, I. (eds) (1982) *Dynamics of Global Crisis*, New York, NY: Monthly Review Press.

Appadurai, A. (1990) 'Disjuncture and Difference in the Global Cultural Economy', in M. Featherstone (ed.), *Global Culture: Nationalism, Globalization and Modernity*, London: Sage.

Appadurai, A. (1996) *Modernity at Large: Cultural Dimensions of Globalization*, London: University of Minnesota Press.

Appadurai, A. (2008) 'How to Make a National Cuisine: Cookbooks in Contemporary India', in C. Counihan and P. Van Esterik (eds), *Food and Culture*, 2nd edn, London: Routledge.

Aronowitz, S. and Cutler, J. (eds) (1998) *Post-Work*, London: Routledge.

Arrighi, G. (1994) *The Long Twentieth Century: Money, Power and the Origins of Our Times*, London: Verso.

Ash, T. G. (2005) 'What Will Be Left?', *Guardian*, 6 January.

Baran, P. (1957) *The Political Economy of Growth*, New York, NY: Monthly Review Press.

Barber, B. R. (2003) *Jihad vs McWorld*, 2nd edn, London: Corgi.

Barnet, R. J. and Muller, R. E. (1974) *Global Reach*, New York, NY: Simon & Schuster.

Bartholomew, A. and Breakspear, J. (2003) 'Human Rights as Swords of Empire', in L. Panitch and C. Leys (eds), *The New Imperial Challenge: Socialist Register 2004*, London: Merlin Press.

Bartlett, C. A. and Goshall, S. (1989) *Managing Across Borders: The Transitional Corporation*, Boston, MA: Harvard Business School Press.

Baudrillard, J. (1983) *Simulations*, New York: Semiotext(e).

Baudrillard, J. (1988a) *America*, London: Verso.

Baudrillard, J. (1988b) *Selected Writings*, ed. M. Poster, Berkeley, CA: California University Press.

Baudrillard, J. (1995) *The Gulf War Did Not Take Place*, Sydney: Power.

Baudrillard, J. (2002) *The Spirit of Terrorism*, London: Verso.

Bauman, Z. (1989) *Modernity and the Holocaust*, Cambridge: Polity Press.

Bauman, Z. (1991) *Modernity and Ambivalence*, Cambridge: Polity Press.

Bauman, Z. (1992) *Intimations of Postmodernity*, London: Routledge.

Bauman, Z. (1998) *Globalization: The Human Consequences*, Cambridge: Polity Press.

Bauman, Z. (2000) *Liquid Modernity*, Cambridge: Polity Press.

Bauman, Z. (2001) *The Individualized Society*, Cambridge: Polity Press.

Bauman, Z. (2002) *Society Under Siege*, Cambridge: Polity Press.

Bauman, Z. and Tester, K. (2001) *Conversations with Zygmunt Bauman*, Cambridge: Polity Press.

Beck, U. (1992) *Risk Society: Towards a New Modernity*. London: Sage.

Beck, U. (1999) *World Risk Society*, London: Sage.

Beck, U. (2006a) 'Living in a World Risk Society', Hobhouse Memorial Public Lecture, London School of Economics, 15 February.

Beck, U. (2006b) *The Cosmopolitan Vision*, Cambridge: Polity Press.

Beck, U. (2007) 'Beyond Class and Nation: Reframing Social Inequalities in a Globalizing World', *British Journal of Sociology*, 58, 4, 679–705.

Beck, U. and Beck-Gernsheim E. (2002) *Individualization*, London: Sage.

Beck, U. and Sznaider, N. (2006) 'Unpacking Cosmopolitanism for the Social Sciences: A Research Agenda', *British Journal of Sociology*, 57, 1, 1–23.

Beck, U., Giddens, A. and Lash, S. (1994) *Reflexive Modernization: Politics, Tradition and Aesthetics in the Modern Social Order*, Cambridge: Polity Press.

Bell, D. (1973) *The Coming of Post-Industrial Society*, New York, NY: Basic.

Bello, W. (2004) *Deglobalization: Ideas for a New World Economy*, London: Zed.

Bello, W. (2009) *The Food Wars*, London: Verso.

Bennett, A. and Kahn-Harris, K. (eds) (2004) *After Subculture: Critical Studies in Contemporary Youth Culture*, Basingstoke: Palgrave Macmillan.

Berger, P. and Huntington, S. (eds) (2002) *Many Globalizations: Cultural Diversity in the Contemporary World*, New York: Oxford University Press.

Bertrand, M. (1994) 'The Role of the United Nations in the Context of the Changing World Order', in Y. Sakamoto (ed.), *Global Transformation: Challenges to the State System*, New York, NY: United Nations University Press.

Bhabha, H. K. (ed.) (1990) *Narrating the Nation*, London: Routledge.

Bhabha, H. K. (1994) *The Location of Culture*, London: Routledge.

Bhagwati, J. (2004) *In Defense of Globalization*, Oxford: Oxford University Press.

Bhagwati, J. (2008) 'Does the Free Market Corrode Moral Character? To the Contrary', at www.templeton.org/market/pdf/bhagwati.pdf.

Bircham, E. and Charlton, J. (eds) (2001) *Anti-Capitalism: A Guide to the Movement*, London: Bookmarks.

Blair, T. (2005) 'Europe is Falling Behind', *Newsweek*, November.

Blauner, R. (1964) *Alienation and Freedom*, Chicago: University of Chicago Press.

Boli, J. and Thomas, G. M. (1997) 'World Culture in the World Polity: A Century of International Non-Governmental Organization', *American Sociological Review*, April.

Bourdieu, P. (1984) *Distinction: A Social Critique of the Judgement of Taste*, London: Routledge.

Bourdieu, P. and Wacquant, L. (1999) 'On the Cunning of Imperialist Reason', *Theory, Culture, Society*, 16, 1, 41–58.

Bourguignon, F. and Morrisson, C. (2002) 'Inequality Among World Citizens, 1820–1992', *American Economic Review*, 4, September, 727–44.

Boyle, M. J. (2008) 'The War on Terror in American Grand Strategy', *International Affairs*, 84, 2, 191–209.

Bramble, B. and Porter, G. (1992) 'Non-Governmental Organizations and the Making of US International Environmental Policy', in A. Hurrell and B. Kingsbury (eds), *The International Politics of the Environment: Actors, Interests, and Institutions*, Oxford: Clarendon Press.

Brecher, J and Costello, T. (1998) *Global Village or Global Pillage: Economic Reconstruction from the Bottom Up*, Cambridge, MA: South End Press.

Brecher, J., Brown Childs, J. and Cutler, J. (eds) (1993) *Global Visions: Beyond the New World Order*, Boston, MA: South End Press.

Buira, A. (2004) 'The Governance of the IMF in a Global Economy', G24 Research Paper, at http://g24.org/buiragva.pdf

Burton, J. (1972) *World Society*, Cambridge: Cambridge University Press.

Bushrui, S., Ayman, I. and Laszlo, E. (eds) (1993) *Transition to a Global Society*, Oxford: OneWorld.

Butler, D. (2005) 'Agencies Fear Global Crises Will Lose Out to Tsunami Donations', *Nature*, 433, 94.

Caldwell, M. L. (2004) 'Domesticating the French Fry: McDonald's and Consumerism in Moscow', in J.X. Inda and R. Rosaldo (eds), *The Anthropology of Globalization*, 2nd edn, Oxford: Blackwell.

Caplan, P. (1997) 'Approaches to the Study of Food, Health and Identity', in P. Caplan (ed.), *Food, Health and Identity*, London: Routledge.

Cardoso, F. (1977) 'The Consumption of Dependency Theory in the United States', *Latin American Research Review*, XII.

Carr, E. H. (1946) *The Twenty Years Crisis, 1919–1939*, 2nd edn, London: Macmillan.

Castells, M. (1989) *The Informational City*, Oxford: Blackwell.

Castells, M. (1999) *The Rise of the Network Society*, 2nd edn, Oxford: Blackwell.

Castells, M. (2000) *The End of Millennium*, 2nd edn, Oxford: Blackwell.

Castells, M. (2004) *The Power of Identity*, 2nd edn, Oxford: Blackwell.

Chang, H.-J. (2007) *Bad Samaritans: Rich Nations, Poor Policies, and the Threat to the Developing World*, London: Random House.

Chase-Dunn, C. (1989) *Global Formation: Structures of the World-Economy*, Cambridge, MA: Basil Blackwell.

Chase-Dunn, C. (1999) 'Globalization: A World-Systems Perspective', *Journal of World-Systems Research*, 5, 2, 187–216.

Chomsky, N. (2003) *Hegemony or Survival: America's Quest For Global Dominance*, London: Hamish Hamilton.

Chomsky, N. (2005) *Imperial Ambitions: Conversations on the Post-9/11 World*, New York, NY: Metropolitan.

Chouliaraki, L. (2008) 'The Mediation of Suffering and the Vision of a Cosmopolitan Public', *Television New Media*, 9, 5, 371–91.

Cioffi, J. (2000) 'Governing Globalization?: The State, Law and Structural Change in Corporate Governance', *Journal of Law and Society*, 27, 4, 572–600.

Cleveland, J. W. (2003) 'Does the New Middle Class Lead Today's Social Movements?', *Critical Sociology*, 29, 2, 163–88.

Cohen, P. (1972) 'Sub-Cultural Conflict and Working-Class Community', *Working Papers in Cultural Studies*, 2, Birmingham: CCCS.

Collingham, L. (2005) *Curry: A Tale of Cooks and Conquerors*, London: Vintage.

Corner, J. and Pels, D. (2003) 'Introduction: The Restyling of Politics', in J. Corner and D. Pels (eds), *Media and the Restyling of Politics: Consumerism, Celebrity and Cynicism*, London: Sage.

Coupland, D. (1991) *Generation X: Tales for an Accelerated Culture*, New York, NY: St Martin's Press.

Dallmayr, F. E. (2002) 'Globalization and Inequality: A Plea for Global Justice', *International Studies Review*, 4, 137–56.

Dasgupta, S. and Kiely, R. (eds) (2006) *Globalization and After*, New Delhi: Sage.

De Grazia, V. (2005) *Irresistible Empire: America's Advance through Twentieth-Century Europe*, Cambridge, MA: Belknap Press.

De Tocqueville, A. (1968) *Democracy in America*, London: Collins.

Derrida, J. (1994) *Specters of Marx: State of the Debt, the Work of Mourning and the New International*, London: Routledge.

Diamond, L. (1993) 'The Globalization of Democracy', in R. O. Slater, B. Schultz and S. R. Dorr (eds), *Global Transformation and the Third World*, Boulder, CO: Rienner.

Dicken, P. (2003) *Global Shift: Mapping the Changing Contours of the World Economy*, 4th edn, London: Sage.

Dollar, D. (2005) 'Globalization, Poverty, and Inequality', in M. M. Weinstein, *Globalization: What's New*, New York: Columbia University Press.

Douzinas, C. (2000) *The End of Human Rights: Critical Legal Thought at the Turn of the Century*, Oxford: Hart.

Doyle, M. W. (1983) 'Kant, Liberal Legacies and Foreign Affairs', *Philosophy and Public Affairs*, 12, 3, 205–35.

Driver, S. and Martell, L. (1998) *New Labour: Politics after Thatcherism*, Cambridge: Polity Press.

Duffield, M. (2007) *Development, Security and Unending War: Governing the World of Peoples*, Cambridge: Polity.

Eade, J. (1997) 'Identity, Nation and Religion: Educated Young Bangladeshis in London's East End', in J. Eade (ed.) *Living the Global City*, London: Routledge.

Elliott, A. (2002) 'Beck's Sociology of Risk: A Critical Assessment', *Sociology*, 36, 2, 293–315.

Evans, E. J. (1997) *Thatcher and Thatcherism*, London: Routledge.

Falk, R. (1993) 'The Making of Global Citizenship', in J. Brecher, J. Brown Childs and J. Cutler (eds), *Global Visions: Beyond the New World Order*, Boston, MA: South End Press.

Featherstone, M. (1991) *Consumer Culture and Postmodernism*, London: Sage.

Fieldhouse, D. K. (1986) 'The Multinational Corporation: Critique of a Concept', in A. Teichova, M. Levy-Leboyer and H. Nussbaum (eds), *Multinational Enterprise in Historical Perspective*, Cambridge: Cambridge University Press.

Fiske, J. (1987) *Television Culture*, London: Routledge.

Fiske, J. (1989a) *Reading the Popular*, London: Unwin Hyman.

Fiske, J. (1989b) *Understanding Popular Culture*, London: Unwin Hyman.

Foreign Policy (2008) *The 2008 Global Cities Index*.

Ford, H. (1922) *My Life and Work*, New York, NY: Garden City.

Frank, A. G. (1967) *Capitalism and Underdevelopment in Latin America*, New York: Monthly Review Press.

Frank, A. G. (1972) *Lumpenbourgeoisie-Lumpendevelopment*, New York, NY: Monthly Review Press.

Frank, A. G. (1975) *On Capitalist Underdevelopment*, Oxford: Oxford University Press.

Frank, A. G. and Gills, B. K. (1993) *The World System: Five Hundred Years or Five Thousand?*, London: Routledge.

Friedman, J. (1994) *Cultural Identity and Global Process*, London: Sage.

Friedman, T. L. (1999) *The Lexus and the Olive Tree*, New York, NY: Farrar, Strauss & Giroux.

Frith, S. (1987) 'Towards an Aesthetic of Popular Music', in R. Leppert and S. McClary (eds), *Music and Society: The Politics of Composition, Performance and Reception*, Cambridge: Cambridge University Press.

Frobel, F., Heinrichs, J. and Krey, O. (1980) *The New International Division of Labour*, Cambridge: Cambridge University Press.

Frum, D. and Perle, R. (2003/4) *An End to Evil: How to Win the War on Terror*, New York: Random House.

Fukuyama, F. (1989) 'The End of History?', *The National Interest*, 16, Summer, 3–18.

Fukuyama, F. (1991) *The End of History and the Last Man*, New York, NY: Free Press.

Furtado, C. (1964) *Development and Underdevelopment*, Berkeley, CA: University of California Press.

Furtado, C. (1969) *Economic Development in Latin America*, Cambridge: Cambridge University Press.

Gaiman, N. (2005) 'Keeping it (un)real', *Wired Magazine*, Issue 13.7 at www.wired.com/archive/13.07/gorilla (accessed January 2010).

Gamble, A. (2009) *The Spectre at the Feast: Capitalist Crisis and the Politics of Recession*, Basingstoke: Palgrave Macmillan.

Gane, N. (2004) *The Future of Social Theory*, New York: Continuum.

Giddens, A. (1990) *The Consequences of Modernity*, Cambridge: Polity Press.

Giddens, A. (1991) *Modernity and Self-Identity: Self and Society in the Late Modern Age*, Cambridge: Polity Press.

Giddens, A. (1994) *Beyond Left and Right: The Future of Radical Politics*, Cambridge: Polity Press.

Gilpin, R. (1981) *War and Change in World Politics*, Cambridge: Cambridge University Press.

Gilpin, R. (1986) 'The Richness of the Tradition of Political Realism', in R. Keohane (ed.), *Neo-Realism and Its Critics*, New York, NY: Columbia University Press.

Gilpin, R. (1987) *The Political Economy of International Relations*, Princeton, NJ: Princeton University Press.

Gilpin, R. (2000) *The Challenge of Global Capitalism: The World Economy in the 21st Century*, Princeton, NJ: Princeton University Press.

Gilpin, R. (2001) *Global Political Economy: Understanding the International Economic Order*, Princeton, NJ: Princeton University Press.

Gilroy, P. (1993) *The Black Atlantic: Modernity and Double Consciousness*, London: Verso.

Goldman, P. and Van Houten, D. R. (1980) 'Bureaucracy and Domination: Managerial Strategy in Turn-of-the-century American Industry', in D. Dunkerley and G. Salaman (eds), *The International Yearbook of Organizational Studies*, London: Routledge.

Gorz, A. (1982) *Farewell to the Working Class: An Essay on Post-Industrial Socialism*, London: Pluto Press.

Gowan, P. (1999) *The Global Gamble: Washington's Bid for World Dominance*, London: Verso.

Gowan, P. (2002) 'The American Campaign for Global Sovereignty', in L. Panitch and C. Leys (eds), *Fighting Identities: Race, Religion and Ethno-Nationalism: Socialist Register 2003*, London: Merlin Press.

Gowan, P., Panitch, L. and Shaw, M. (2001) 'The State, Globalization and the New Imperialism: A Round Table Discussion', *Historical Materialism*, 9, 4–38.

Grewal, I. and Kaplan, C. (1994) *Scattered Hegemonies: Postmodernity and Transnational Feminist Practices*, Minneapolis, MI: University of Minnesota Press.

Grint, K. (2005) *The Sociology of Work*, 3rd edn, Cambridge: Polity Press.

Habermas, J. (1976) *Legitimation Crisis*, London: Heinemann.

Halal, W. E. (1986) *The New Capitalism*, New York, NY: Wiley.

Hall, S. (1991a) 'The Local and the Global: Globalization and Ethnicity', in A. D. King (ed.), *Culture, Globalization and the World-System*, Basingstoke: Macmillan.

Hall, S. (1991b) 'Old and New Identities, Old and New Ethnicities', in A. D. King (ed.), *Culture, Globalization and the World-System*, Basingstoke: Macmillan.

Hall, S. (1992a) 'New Ethnicities', in J. Donald and A. Rattansi (eds), *Culture and Difference*, London: Sage/Open University Press.

Hall, S. (1992b) 'The Question of Cultural Identity', in S. Hall, D. Held and T. McGrew (eds), *Modernity and Its Futures*, Cambridge: Polity Press/ Open University Press.

Hall, S. and Jacques, M. (eds) (1989) *New Times: The Changing Face of Politics in the 1990s*, London: Lawrence & Wishart.

Hall, S. and Jefferson, T. (eds) (1976) *Resistance through Rituals: Youth Sub-Cultures in Post-War Britain*, London: Routledge.

Hall, S., Critcher, C., Jefferson, T., Clarke, J. and Roberts, B. (1978) *Policing the Crisis*, Basingstoke: Macmillan.

Halper, S. and Clarke, J. (2004) *America Alone: The Neo-Conservatives and the Global Order*, Cambridge: Cambridge University Press.

Hannerz, U. (1990) 'Cosmopolitans and Locals in World Culture', in M. Featherstone (ed.), *Global Culture: Nationalism, Globalization and Modernity*, London: Sage.

Hannerz, U. (1996) *Transnational Connections: Culture, People, Places*, London: Routledge.

Hardt, M. and Negri, A. (2000) *Empire*, Cambridge, MA: Harvard University Press.

Hardt, M. and Negri, A. (2005) *Multitude: War and Democracy in the Age of Empire*, London: Penguin.

Harvey, D. (1989) *The Condition of Postmodernity*, Oxford: Blackwell.

Harvey, D. (2003) *The New Imperialism*, Oxford: Oxford University Press.

Hebdige, D. (1979) *Subculture: The Meaning of Style*, London: Routledge.

Heater, D. (1996) *World Citizenship and Government: Cosmopolitan Ideas in the History of Western Political Thought*, London: Macmillan.

Heckscher, C. (1994) 'Defining the Post-Bureaucratic Type', in C. Heckscher and A. Donnellon (eds), *The Post Bureaucratic Organization: New Perspectives on Organizational Change*, London: Sage.

Held, D. and McGrew, T. (2007) *Globalization/Anti-Globalization*, Cambridge: Polity Press.

Held, D., McGrew, T., Goldblatt, D. and Perraton, J. (1999) *Global Transformations: Politics, Economics and Culture*, Cambridge: Polity Press.

Hirst, P. and Thompson, G. (1999) *Globalization in Question: The International Economy and the Possibilities of Governance*, 2nd edn, Cambridge: Polity Press.

Hirst, P. and Thompson, G. (2002) 'The Future of Globalization', *Cooperation and Conflict*, 37, 3, 247–65.

Hixson, W. (2008) *The Myth of American Diplomacy: National Identity and US Foreign Policy*, New Haven, CT: Yale University Press.

Hodgson, D. E. (2004) 'Project Work: The Legacy of Bureaucratic Control in the Post-Bureaucratic Organization', *Organization*, 11, 1, 81–100.

Hoffman, D. E. (2002) *The Oligarchs: Wealth and Power in the New Russia*, Oxford: Public Affairs.

Hogan, M. J. and Paterson, T. G. (1991) *Explaining the History of American Foreign Relations*, Cambridge: Cambridge University Press.

Hoggart, R. (1958) *The Uses of Literacy*, Harmondsworth: Penguin.

Hopkins, T. K. and Wallerstein, I. (1982) *World-Systems Analysis: Theory and Methodology*, London: Sage.

Houlihan, B. (1994) 'Homogenization, Americanization and Creolization of Sport: Varieties of Globalization', *Sociology of Sport Journal*, 356–75.

Howes, D. (ed.) (1996) *Cross-Cultural Consumption: Global Markets, Local Realities*, London: Routledge.

Hudson, M. (2003) *Super-Imperialism: The Origin and Foundations of US World Dominance*, London: Pluto.

Hughes, T. P. (2004) *American Genesis: A Century of Invention and Technological Enthusiasm 1870–1970*, 2nd edn, Chicago, IL: University of Chicago Press.

Hunt, M. H. (2009) *Ideology and US Foreign Policy*, New Haven, CT: Yale University Press.

Huntington, S. (1976) 'The Change to Change: Modernization, Development and Politics', in C. E. Black (ed.), *Comparative Modernization*, New York, NY: Free Press.

Huntington, S. (1997) *The Clash of Civilizations and the Remaking of World Order*, New York, NY: Simon & Schuster.

Hussein, G. (2010) 'A Brief History of Islam. Quilliam Foundation', at www.quilliamfoundation.org/images/briefhistoryofislamism.pdf.

Immergluck, D. (2009) *Foreclosed: High Risk Lending, Deregulation, and the Undermining of America's Mortgage Market*, Ithaca, NY: Cornell University Press.

Jameson, F. (1991) *Postmodernism, Or, the Cultural Logic of Late Capitalism*, London: Verso.

James, A. (1997) 'How British is British Food?', in P. Caplan (ed.), *Food, Health and Identity*, London: Routledge.

Jenkins, P. (2003) *A History of the United States*, Basingstoke: Palgrave Macmillan.

Jenkins, R. (1987) *Transnational Corporations and Uneven Development*, London: Macmillan.

Johnson, C. (1991) *The Economy under Thatcher 1979–1990*, London: Penguin.

Johnson, R. D. (2004) 'Global Studies, Universal Bias', *FrontPageMagazine.com*, 6 August, at www.frontpagemagazine.com/Articles/ReadArticle/asp?ID=14537.

Jones, M. A. (1995) *The Limits of Liberty: American History, 1607—1992*, Oxford: Oxford University Press.

Jones, N. (1995) *Soundbites and Spin Doctors*, London: Cassell.

Kacowicz, A. M. (2007) 'Globalization, Poverty, and the North–South Divide', *International Studies Review*, 9, 565–80.

Kagan, R. (2003) *Of Paradise and Power: America and Europe in the New World Order*, New York, NY: Alfred Knopf.

Kagan, R. (2008) *The Return of History and the End of Dreams*, London: Atlantic Books.

Kagan, R. and Kristol, W. (2002) 'What to Do about Iraq', *Weekly Standard*, 21 January.

Kagan, R., Schmitt, G. and Donnelly, T. (2000) 'Rebuilding America's Defenses: Strategy, Forces and Resources: Project For a New American Century', at www.newamericancentury.org/RebuildingAmericasDefenses.pdf.

Kaldor, M. (2007) *Human Security: Reflections on Globalization and Intervention Policy*, London: Polity.

Kaplan, R. (1994) 'The Coming Anarchy', *The Atlantic Monthly*, February.

Kaplan, L. and Kristol, W. (2003) *The War over Iraq: Saddam's Tyranny and America's Mission*, San Francisco, CA: Encounter.

Kennan, G. (1951) *American Diplomacy 1900–1950*, Chicago, IL: University of Chicago Press.

Kennan, G. (1993) *Around the Cragged Hill*, New York, NY: W. W. Norton.

Keohane, R. O. and Nye, J. S. (1989) *Power and Interdependence*, Reading, MA: Addison-Wesley.

Kepel, G. (2006) *Jihad: The Trail of Political Islam*, 4th edn, London: I.B. Tauris.

Kerr, C., Dunlop, J.T., Harbison, F.H. and Myers, C.A. (1960) *Industrialism and Industrial Man*, Cambridge, MA: Harvard University Press.

Kidd, B. (1991) 'How Do We Find Our Voices in the "New World Order"? A Commentary on Americanization', *Sociology of Sport Journal*, 8, 178–84.

Kissinger, H. (1969) *American Foreign Policy*, London: Weidenfeld & Nicolson.

Klare, M. (2003) 'Deciphering the Bush Administration's Motives', *Foreign Policy in Focus*, 16 January.

Klein, A. M. (1991) 'Sport and Culture as Contested Terrain: Americanisation in the Caribbean', *Sociology of Sport Journal*, 8, 79–85.

Klein, N. (2000) *No Logo*, London: Flamingo.

Krasner, S. (1978) *Defending the National Interest*, Princeton, NJ: Princeton University Press.

Krasner, S. (1985) *Structural Conflict*, Berkeley, CA: University of California Press.

Kristol, W. and Kagan, R. (1996) 'Toward a Neo-Reaganite Foreign Policy', *Foreign Affairs*, July/August.

Lash, S. (1999) *Another Modernity, A Different Rationality*, Oxford: Blackwell.

Lash, S. and Urry, J. (1987) *The End of Organized Capitalism*, Cambridge: Polity Press.

Lash, S. and Urry, J. (1994) *Economies of Signs and Space*, London: Sage.

Lee, C. H. (2003) 'Introduction: Issues and Findings', in C. H. Lee (ed.), *Financial Liberalization and the Economic Crisis in Asia*, London: Routledge.

Legrain, P. (2003) *Open World: The Truth about Globalisation*, London: Abacus.

Levy, A. and Scott-Clark, C. (2004) 'He Won, Russia Lost', *Guardian*, 8 May.

Love, J.F. (1986) *McDonald's: Behind the Arches*, New York, NY: Bantam.

Luhmann, N. (1990) 'The World Society as a Social System', in *Essays on Self-Reference*, New York, NY: Columbia University Press.

Lyotard, J.-F. (1984) *The Postmodern Condition: A Report on Knowledge*, trans. G. Bennington and B. Massumi, Manchester: Manchester University Press.

Maccartney, H. (2009) 'Disagreeing to Agree: Financial Crisis Management within the "Logic of No Alternative" ', *Politics*, 29, 2, 111–20.

MacDonald, I. (1994) *Revolution in the Head: The Beatles' Records and the Sixties*, London: Pimlico.

Maguire, J. (1999) *Global Sport: Identities, Societies and Civilizations*, Cambridge: Polity Press.

Marcuse, H. (1964) *One-Dimensional Man: Studies in the Ideology of Advanced Capitalist Society*, Boston, MA: Beacon Press.

Massey, D. (1994) *Space, Place and Gender*, Cambridge: Polity Press.

Masuyama, S. (1999) 'Introduction: The Evolution of Financial Systems in East Asia and Their Responses to Financial and Economic Crisis', in S. Masuyama, D. Vandenbrink and C. S. Yue (eds), *East Asia's Financial Systems: Evolution and Crisis*, Tokyo: Nomura Research Institute.

McCormick, T. J. (1989) *America's Half-Century: United States Foreign Policy in the Cold War*, Baltimore, MD: Johns Hopkins University Press.

McGreal, C. (2010) 'Detroit Homes Sell for $1 amid Mortgage and Car Industry Crisis', *Guardian*, 2 March.

McGrew, T. (1992) 'A Global Society?', in S. Hall, D. Held and T. McGrew (eds), *Modernity and Its Futures*, Cambridge: Polity Press.

McGuigan, J. (1999) *Modernity and Postmodern Culture*, Buckingham: Open University Press.

McKay, J. and Miller, T. (1991) 'From Old Boys to Men and Women of the Corporation: The Americanization and Commodification of Australian Sport', *Sociology of Sport Journal*, 8, 86–94.

McLuhan, M. (1962) *The Gutenberg Galaxy: The Making of Typographic Man*, London: Routledge.

McLuhan, M. (1964) *Understanding Media*, New York, NY: Mentor

McMahon, R. J. (1991) 'The Study of American Foreign Relations: National History or International History?', in M. J. Hogan and T. G. Paterson (eds), *Explaining the History of American Foreign Relations*, Cambridge: Cambridge University Press.

McRobbie, A. (1991) *Feminism and Youth Culture*, Basingstoke: Macmillan.

Mearscheimer, J. (1990) 'Back to the Future: Instability after the Cold War', *International Society*, 15, 1, 5–56.

Mehdi, A. (2006) 'Globalization: Whose Benefit Anyway?', in S. Dasgupta and R. Kiely (eds), *Globalization and After*, New Delhi: Sage.

Metcalfe, B. (1997) 'Project Management System Design: A Social and Organisational Analysis', *International Journal of Production Economics*, 52, 3, 305–16.

Meyer, J. (1980) 'The World Polity and the Authority of the Nation-State', in A. Bergeson (ed.), *Studies of the Modern World System*, New York, NY: Academic Press.

Meyer, J. and Hannan, M. T. (eds) (1979) *National Development and the World System: Educational, Economic and Political Change, 1950–1970*, Chicago, IL: University of Chicago Press.

Meyer, J., Boli, J., Thomas, G. M. and Ramirez, F. (1979) 'World Society and the Nation-State', *American Journal of Sociology*, 103, 144–81.

Milanovic, B. (2005) *Worlds Apart: Measuring International and Global Inequality*, Princeton, NJ: Princeton University Press.

Mills, C. Wright (1956) *The Power Elite*, Oxford: Oxford University Press.

Mintz, S. (1984) 'Meals Without Grace', *Boston Review*, December.

Modelski, G. (1972) *The Principles of World Politics*, New York, NY: Free Press.

Moore, A. F. (2000) 'The Brilliant Career of Sgt Pepper', in A. Aldgate, J. Chapman and A. Marwick (eds), *Windows on the Sixties*, London: I.B. Tauris.

Morgenthau, H. (1946) *Scientific Man versus Power Politics*, Chicago, IL: Chicago University Press.

Morgenthau, H. (1948) *Politics Among Nations*, New York, NY: Alfred Knopf.

Morgenthau, H. (1951) *In Defence of the National Interest*, New York, NY: Alfred Knopf.

Mueller, J. (1990) *Retreat from Doomsday: Obsolescence of Major War*, New York, NY: Basic.

Nash, K. (2008) 'Global Citizenship as Show Business: the Cultural Politics of Make Poverty History', *Media, Culture and Society*, 30, 2, 167–81.

Nederveen Pieterse, J. (1995) 'Globalization as Hybridization', in M. Featherstone, S. Lash and R. Robertson (eds), *Global Modernities*, London: Sage.

Nederveen Pieterse, J. (2001) 'Hybridity, So What?: The Anti-Hybridity Backlash and the Riddles of Recognition' in *Theory Culture and Society*, 18, 2–3, 219–45.

Nelson, D. (1974) 'Scientific Management, Systematic Management and Labor, 1880–1915', *Business History Review*, 28, 479–500.

Notes from Nowhere (eds) (2003) *We Are Everywhere: The Irresistible Rise of Global Anti-Capitalism*, London: Verso.

Nozick, R. (1974) *Anarchy, State and Utopia*, Oxford: Blackwell.

O'Byrne, D. (1997) 'Working Class Culture: Local Community and Global Conditions', in J. Eade (ed.), *Living the Global City: Globalization as Local Process*, London: Routledge.

O'Byrne, D. (2002) *Human Rights: An Introduction*, London: Prentice-Hall.

O'Byrne, D. (2003) *The Dimensions of Global Citizenship: Political Identity beyond the Nation-State?*, London: Frank Cass.

O'Byrne, D. (2004) 'The Discourse of Human Rights and the Neo-Conservative Discourse of War', *Mediactive*, 3, 13–22.

O'Byrne, D. (2005) 'Towards a Critical Theory of Globalization', in R. Appelbaum and W. I. Robinson (eds), *Critical Globalization Studies*, New York, NY: Routledge.

Offe, C. (1985) *Disorganized Capitalism*, Cambridge: Polity Press.

Ohmae, K. (1990) *The Borderless World: Power and Strategy in the Interlinked Economy*, London: Collins.

Ohmae, K. (1994) *The End of the Nation-State*, New York, NY: Free Press.

Ohmae, K. (2005) *The Next Global Stage: The Challenges and Opportunities in Our Borderless World*, Pittsburgh, PA: Wharton School.

Ozanne, R. (1979) 'United States Labor-Management Relations 1860–1930', in N. Nakagawa (ed.), *Labor and Management*, Tokyo: University of Tokyo Press.

Pahl, R. (ed.) (1988) *On Work: Historical, Comparative and Theoretical Approaches*, Oxford: Blackwell.

Pakulski J. and Waters M. (1996) *The Death of Class*, London: Sage.

Panitch, L. (2000) 'The New Imperial State', *New Left Review*, 2000, 2.

Panitch, L. and Gindin, S. (2003) 'Global Capitalism and American Empire', in L. Panitch and C. Leys (eds), *The New Imperial Challenge: Socialist Register 2004*, London: Merlin Press.

Panitch, L. and Leys, C. (eds) (2003) *The New Imperial Challenge: Socialist Register 2004*, London: Merlin Press.

Panitch, L. and Miliband, R. (1991) 'The New World Order and the Socialist Agenda', in R. Miliband and L. Panitch (eds), *New World Order?: Socialist Register 1992*, London: Merlin Press.

Parker, M. and Jary, D. (1995) 'The McUniversity: Organization, Management and Academic Subjectivity', *Organization*, 2, 1–20.

Pearson, R. (1986) 'Female Workers in the First and Third Worlds: The Greening of Women's Labour', in K. Purcell *et al.* (eds), *The Changing Experience of Employment*, Basingstoke: Macmillan.

Perlmutter, H. (1991) 'On the Rocky Road to the First Global Civilization', *Human Relations*, 44, 9, 897–1010.

Petras, J. and Veltmeyer, H. (2001) *Globalization Unmasked: Imperialism in the 21st Century*, London: Zed.

Pilger, J. (1992) *Distant Voices*, London: Vintage.

Polanyi, K. (2001) *The Great Transformation: The Political and Economic Origins of Our Time*, Boston, MA: Beacon Press.

Prebisch, R. (1949) 'The Economic Development of Latin America and Its Principal Problems', *Economic Review of Latin America*, 7.

Prebisch, R. (1950) *The Economic Development of Latin America and Its Principal Problems*, New York, NY: United Nations.

Prebisch, R. (1959) 'Commercial Policy in Underdeveloped Countries', in *American Economic Review*, 49.

Qutb, S. (2007) *Milestones*, New Delhi: Islamic Book Service.

Räisänen, C. and Linde, A. (2004) 'Technologizing Discourse to Standardize Projects in Multi-Project Organizations: Hegemony by Consensus?', *Organization*, 11, 1, 101–21.

Rauchway, E. (2006) *Blessed Among Nations: How The World Made America*, New York, NY: Hill & Wang.

Reddy, S. G. and Pogge, T. W. (2003) 'How Not to Count the Poor', at www.socialanalysis.org (accessed January 2010).

Redwood, J. (1994) *The Global Marketplace*, London: HarperCollins.

Renshon, S. A. (2010) *National Security in the Obama Administration: Reassessing the Bush Doctrine*, London: Routledge.

Ritzer, G. (1993) *The McDonaldization of Society*, Newbury Park, PA: Pine Forge Press.

Ritzer, G. (1996) 'McUniversity in the Postmodern Consumer Society', Plenary address presented to the conference on 'Dilemmas of Mass Higher Education', Staffordshire University, England, April.

Ritzer, G. (2004) *The Globalization of Nothing*, London: Sage.

Ritzer, G. (2008) *The McDonaldization of Society*, 5th edn, London: Pine Forge Press.

Robertson, R. (1990) 'Mapping the Global Condition: Globalization as the Central Concept', *Theory, Culture and Society*, 7, 15–30.

Robertson, R. (1992) *Globalization: Social Theory and Global Culture*, London: Sage.

Robertson, R. (1995) 'Glocalization: Time-Space and Homogeneity-Heterogeneity', in M. Featherstone, S. Lash and R. Robertson (eds), *Global Modernities*, London: Sage.

Robertson, R. and Chirico, J. (1985) 'Humanity, Globalization, and Worldwide Religious Resurgence', *Sociological Analysis*, Autumn.

Robertson, R. and Lechner, F. (1985) 'Modernization, Globalization and the Problem of Culture in World Systems Theory', *Theory, Culture and Society*, 2, 3, 103–19.

Robertson, R. T. (2003) *The Three Waves of Globalization: A History of a Developing Global Consciousness*, London: Zed.

Robins, K. (1991) 'Tradition and Translation: National Culture in Its Global Context', in J. Corner and S. Harvey (eds), *Enterprise and Heritage: Crosscurrents of National Culture*, London: Routledge.

Robinson, W. I. (2004) *A Theory of Global Capitalism: Transnational Production, Transnational Capitalists, and the Transnational State*, Baltimore, MD: Johns Hopkins University Press.

Robinson, W. I. and Harris, J. (2000) 'Towards a Global Ruling Class?: Globalization and the Transnational Capitalist Class', *Science & Society*, 64, 1, 11–5411.

Rolet, X. (2009) 'The Way Forward: Building a Sustainable Recovery and Driving Growth', at www.2.lse.ac.uk/publicEvents/pdf/20091028_XavierRolet.pdf.

Rosenau, J. (1980) *The Study of Global Interdependence*, London: Frances Pinter.

Rosenau, J. (1989) *Interdependence and Conflict in World Politics*, Lexington, TX: D.C. Heath.

Rosenau, J. (1990) *Turbulence in World Politics*, Brighton: Harvester Wheatsheaf.

Rosie, M. and Gorringe, H. (2009) 'What Difference a Death Makes: Protest, Policing and the Press at the G20', *Sociological Research Online*, 14, 5, at www.socresonline.org.uk/14/5/4.html (accessed March 2010).

Said, E. (1993) *Culture and Imperialism*, London: Vintage.

Said, E. (2003) *Orientalism*, 3rd edn, Harmondsworth: Penguin.

Sala-i-Martin, X. (2005) 'The World Distribution of Income. Draft Paper', at www.columbia.edu/~xs23/papers/pdfs/World_Income_Distribution_QJE.pdf

Sandbrook, D. (2005) *Never Had It So Good: A History of Britain from Suez to the Beatles*, London: Little, Brown.

Sangar, D. E. (2009) *The Inheritance: The World Obama Confronts and the Challenges to American Power*, New York, NY: Harmony Press.

Santos, B. S. (2006) 'Globalizations', *Theory, Culture and Society*, 23, 2–3, 393–9.

Santos, B. S. (2008) 'The World Social Forum and the Global Left', *Politics and Society*, 36, 2, 247–70.

Sardar, Z. (1998) *Postmodernism and the Other: The New Imperialism of Western Culture*, London: Pluto Press.

Sassen, S. (1991) *The Global City*, Princeton, NJ: Princeton University Press.

Sassen, S. (1998) *Globalization and Its Discontents*, New York, NY: New Press.

Schiller, H. (1992) *Mass Communications and American Empire*, 2nd edn, Oxford: Westview Press.

Schloss, J. G. (2004) *Making Beats: The Art of Sample-Based Hip Hop*, Middletown, PA: Wesleyan University Press.

Schouten, P. (2008) 'Theory Talk #13: Immanuel Wallerstein on World-Systems, the Imminent End of Capitalism and Unifying Social Science', at Theory Talks, at www.theory-talks.org/2008/08/theory-talk-13.html (accessed August 2008).

Sennett, R. (1998) *The Corrosion of Character*, London: W. W. Norton.

Shiva, V. (1993) 'The Greening of the Global Reach', in J. Brecher, J. Brown Childs and J. Cutler (eds), *Global Visions: Beyond the New World Order*, Boston, MA: South End Press.

Shiva, V. (2005) *Earth Democracy: Justice, Sustainability and Peace*, Cambridge, MA: South End Press.

Shiva, V. (2008) *Soil, Not Oil: Climate Change, Peak Oil and Food Insecurity*, London: Zed.

Silverman, B. and Yanowitch, M. (2000) *New Rich, New Poor, New Russia: Winners and Losers on the Russian Road to Capitalism*, Armonk, NY: M. E. Sharpe.

Sklair, L. (1991) *Sociology of the Global System*, Hemel Hempstead: Harvester Wheatsheaf.

Sklair, L. (2001) *The Transnational Capitalist Class*, Oxford: Blackwell.

Sklair, L. (2002) *Globalization: Capitalism and Its Alternatives*, Oxford: Oxford University Press.

Slater, D. (1997) *Consumer Culture and Modernity*, Cambridge: Polity Press.

Slater, D. and Tonkiss, F. (2001) *Market Society*, Cambridge: Polity.

Smith, A. (2008 (1776)) *An Enquiry into the Nature and Causes of the Wealth of Nations*, Oxford: Oxford University Press.

South Centre (1997) *Foreign Direct Investment, Development and the New Global Economic Policy*, Geneva: South Centre.

Spicker, P. (1999) 'Definitions of Poverty: Eleven Clusters of Meaning', in D. Gordon and P. Spicker (eds), *The International Glossary on Poverty*, London: Zed.

Spivak, G. C. (1999) *A Critique of Postcolonial Reason: Towards a History of the Vanishing Present*, Cambridge, MA: Harvard University Press.

Stephanson, A. (1995) *Manifest Destiny: American Expansionism and the Empire of Right*, New York, NY: Hill & Wang.

Stiglitz, J. (2000) 'Unravelling the Washington Consensus', *Multinational Monitor*, 21, 4.

Stiglitz, J. (2002) *Globalization and its Discontents*, London: Penguin.

Stopford, J. and Strange, S. (1991) *Rival States, Rival Firms: Competition for World Market Share*, Cambridge: Cambridge University Press.

Storey, J. (2003) *Inventing Popular Culture: From Folklore to Globalization*, Oxford: Blackwell.

Street, J. (2001) *Mass Media, Politics and Democracy*, Basingstoke: Palgrave Macmillan.

Strinati, D. (1995) *An Introduction to Theories of Popular Culture*, London: Routledge.

Swyngedouw, E. (1986) 'The Socio-Spatial Implications of Innovations in Industrial Organisation', Working Paper no. 20, Johns Hopkins European Center for Regional Planning and Research.

Sylvan, D. and Majeski, S. (2009) *US Foreign Policy in Perspective: Clients, Enemies and Empire*, London: Routledge.

Tabb, W. K. (2001) *The Amoral Elephant: Globalization and the Struggle for Social Justice in the Twenty-First Century*, New York, NY: Monthly Review Press.

Tan-Mullins, M., Rigg, J., Law, L. and Grundy-Warr, C. (2007) 'Re-mapping the Politics of Aid: The Changing Structures and Networks of Humanitarian Assistance in Post-Tsunami Thailand', *Progress in Development Studies*, 7, 4, 327–44.

Taylor, T. D. (1997) *Global Pop: World Music, World Market*, New York, NY: Routledge.

Thompson, J. B. (1995) *The Media and Modernity*, Cambridge: Polity Press.

Tomlinson, J. (1991) *Cultural Imperialism*, London: Pinter.

Tomlinson, J. (1999) *Globalization and Culture*, Cambridge: Polity Press.

Tomlinson, J. (2007) 'Globalization and Cultural Analysis', in D. Held and T. McGrew (eds), *Globalization Theory: Approaches and Controversies*, Cambridge: Polity Press.

Tunstall, J. (1994) *The Media are American: Anglo-American Media in the World*, 2nd edn, New York: Columbia University Press.

Tunstall, J. (2008) *The Media were American: US Mass Media in Decline*, New York, NY: Oxford University Press.

Turner, B. S. (1999) 'McCitizens: Risk, Coolness and Irony in Contemporary Politics', in B. Smart (ed.), *Resisting McDonaldization*, London: Sage.

Turner, B. S. and Rojek, C. (2001) *Society and Culture: Principles of Scarcity and Solidarity*, London: Sage.

UNCTAD (2001) *World Investment Report 2001*, Geneva: UN Conference on Trade Development.

UNCTAD (2006) *Trade and Development Report*, Geneva: UNCTAD.

Van der Pijl, K. (1984) *The Making of an Atlantic Ruling Class*, London: Verso.

Van der Pijl, K. (1998) *Transnational Classes and International Relations*, London: Routledge.

Villamil, J. J. (ed.) (1979) *Transnational Capitalism and National Development*, Hassocks: Harvester Wheatsheaf.

Wade, R. (2001) 'Inequality of World Incomes: What Should be Done?', at http://www.opendemocracy.net/node/257.

Wallerstein, I. (1974) *The Modern World-System* Volume 1: *Capitalist Agriculture and the Origins of the European World-Economy in the Sixteenth Century*, New York, NY: Academic Press.

Wallerstein, I. (1979) *The Capitalist World Economy*, Cambridge: Cambridge University Press.

Wallerstein, I. (1980) *The Modern World-System* Volume 2: *Mercantilism and the Consolidation of the European World-Economy 1600–1950*, New York, NY: Academic Press.

Wallerstein, I. (1983) *Historical Capitalism*, London: Verso.

Wallerstein, I. (1989) *The Modern World-System* Volume 3: *The Second Era of Great Expansion of the Capitalist World-Economy 1730–1840s*, Cambridge: Cambridge University Press.

Waltz, K. (1979) *The Theory of International Politics*, Reading, MA: Addison-Wesley.

Weber, M. (1978) *Economy and Society*, 2 vols, Berkeley, CA: University of California Press.

Weiß, A. (2005) 'The Transnationalisation of Social Inequality', *Current Sociology*, 53, 4, 707–28.

Wells, A. (1972) *Picture-Tube Imperialism: The Impact of US Television on Latin America*, Maryknoll, NY: Orbis.

Went, R. (2003) 'Globalization in the Perspective of Imperialism', *Science and Society*, 66, 4, 473–97.

White, J. (1986) *The Worst Street in North London*, London: Routledge & Kegan Paul.

Williamson, J. (1990) 'What Washington Means by Policy Reform', in J. Williamson (ed.), *Latin American Adjustment: How Much Has Happened?*, Washington, DC: Institute for International Economics.

Williamson, J. (1997) 'The Washington Consensus Reassessed', in L. Emmerij (ed.), *Economic and Social Development into the XXI Century*, Washington, DC: Inter-American Development Bank.

Willis, P., Jones, S., Canaan, J. and Hurd, G. (1990) *Common Culture: Symbolic Work at Play in the Everyday Cultures of the Young*, Milton Keynes: Open University Press.

Wolf, M. (2002a) 'Countries Still Rule the World', *Financial Times*, 6 February.

Wolf, M. (2002b) 'Is Globalization Causing World Poverty?', *Financial Times*, 25 February.

Wood, S. (1993) 'The Japanization of Fordism', *Economic and Industrial Democracy*, 14, 535–55.

World Bank (2001) *Poverty in the Age of Globalization*, Washington, DC: World Bank.

World Bank (2004) *World Development Indicators*, Washington, DC: World Bank, at www.worldbacnk.org/data.

Zolo, D. (1997) *Cosmopolis: Prospects for World Government*, Cambridge: Polity Press.

Zolo, D. (2002) *Invoking Humanity: War, Law and Global Order*, New York, NY: Continuum.

Index